HARLEY-DAVIDSON
DATA BOOK

Rick Conner

Motorbooks International
Publishers & Wholesalers ®

First published in 1996 by Motorbooks International Publishers & Wholesalers, 729 Prospect Avenue, PO Box 1, Osceola, WI 54020-0001 USA

Library of Congress Cataloging-in-Publication Data

ISBN 0-7603-0226-X

On the front cover: Flathead engines and tank shifters were the rule in 1934 as exemplified by this beautifully restored machine. *Jeff Hackett*

On the back cover: Top: Harley-Davidson's 1977 XLCR cafe racer has become a favorite among collectors. *Randy Leffingwell* Bottom: 1965 was the last year for the Panhead, and this FLH is certainly a prime example of the breed. *Greg Field*

Printed in the United States of America

ACKNOWLEDGMENTS

The road was long and the ride was hard but the journey is over.

Thanks to my parents, Fred and Donna; and to my brothers and sisters, Cathy, Jackie, Mike, Dave, Tom, and Steve, for putting up with me.

I owe special thanks to: Connie Martin who took the time and effort to assist me; Jack Bouziane, Larry and Pat Brotzman, Jeff Jinkins, Roger Oakleaf, Todd Quick, Phil Toler, Robin and Dave Turner, Dennis Vickerman, and all of my other friends too numerous to mention who gave their support and encouragement; to the many people I met through the Walneck's Classic Cycle Trader, some of whom were able to provide photos for this book; Randy Johnson for his help with paint color specifications; the people at Drag Specialties for allowing me to photograph their collection of motorcycles; Al Reichenbach of A.J.R. Accessories for his assistance; Greg Field for his expert knowledge of Harley-Davidson specifications and detail; and my editor, Zack Miller, for his help in making this book a reality.

PREFACE

Harley-Davidson exemplifies the phrase "survival of the fittest." From humble beginnings, the company has endured through wars, patent losses, the Depression, American and foreign competitors, automobile competition, and tariffs to become the business icon they are today.

My objective is to provide an accurate book of specifications that any Harley-Davidson enthusiast or restorer can turn to and rely on time and time again.

I hope this book provides a better understanding of the particulars of the many motorcycle models as they developed through the years.

CONTENTS

CHAPTER 1
1903-1909

Model Year 1903

Main Models

Model of 1903: 24.74ci (405.41cc) F-head single

Retail Prices

Model of 1903: $200

Production Totals

Model of 1903: 3

Options

None available

Paint Colors

Piano-finish Black with Gold double pinstriping

Model of 1903 F-Head Singles

First Year

Engine: 24.74ci (405.41cc) F-head single with automatic inlet valve and 3x3-1/2in bore and stroke

28in wheels

Wheelbase measures 51in

Weight is 185lb

Seat height is 21.5in

3-1/2in stroke

Two-ply, 1-1/4in-wide leather belt direct-drive to rear wheel hoop

Flat-topped bicycle-style saddle

Rigid-type front forks

Seven-piece-construction handlebars

Loop frame (curved front downtube on frame, midyear)

Fuel tank hung from crossbar

Coil-suspension saddle

Dual bicycle pedals

Chrome-nickel exhaust valves

Vacuum-operated inlet valves

Ball-bearing rear hub

Horizontal cooling fins on the cylinder head

Two-piece exhaust valve

Iron pistons

Step-joint piston rings

Exposed exhaust-valve springs

Plain-bearing connecting rod big end

Pedal-crank chain adjusted by moving rear wheel in frame

2in casing studs

Drip-feed and hand-pump motor lubrication as main lubrication

Starting by pedaling or running alongside

Bicycle-style wheel hubs and brakes

One-piece cylinder

Tapered pistons and straight cylinder bore

60deg seats on exhaust valves

0deg seats on automatic inlet valves

Eccentric piston rings

Clutchless single-speed transmission

Two-piece automotive-type connecting rods with bolt-on lower ends

Three-plate battery

Spoked flywheel with 7/8in diameter flywheel crankpin

Leather-belt-driven single-speed transmission

Filler caps with 1-3/8in diameter

28in tires standard

Fenders 3-3/4in wide

Hub internal brake

Frame with a horizontal top rail giving a bicycle look

Motor Company Minutes, 1903

Improvements are made to the 1902 prototype engine of 10.2ci (167cc) single with 2-1/8x2-7/8in bore and stroke and 5in flywheel.

Thrilling speeds up to 25mph.

First Harley-Davidson (H-D) motorcycle officially designed by William Harley, patterned by Arthur Davidson, and built by Walter Davidson.

First motorcycle customer, a Mr. Meyer.

In the fall, William Harley enrolls for classes in the Engineering Department at University of Wisconsin (UW), Madison.

Walter Davidson quits his position with the railroad in Kansas and finds employment with the railroad in Milwaukee.

H-D's stiffest transportation competitor begins production, Henry Ford's Model A.

The loop frame is William Harley's idea.

The FAM, Federation of American Motorcyclists, formed. Members of the Alpha Motorcycle Club join up with members of the New York Motorcycle Club.

The company lettering and double pinstriping was hand done by Aunt Janet Davidson.

Model Year 1904

Main Models
Model 0: 24.74ci (405.41cc) F-head single

Retail Prices
Model 0: $200

Production Totals
Model 0: 8

Options
None available

Paint Colors
Piano-finish Black with Gold double pinstriping

Series 0 F-Head Singles

First Year
Early method of model identification that matches year to model by subtracting four from the year
Crankcase baffle plates cast in

Motor Company Minutes, 1904
The first factory of the H-D Motor Company is built, a 10x15ft, one-story wooden shed built by William C. Davidson, the cabinetmaker father, in the Davidson's back yard located at 38th Street and Highland Avenue, housing a gas-powered lathe and drill press. The land is now owned by the Miller Brewing Company.
The first H-D dealership is founded by Mr. C. H. Lang of Chicago, Illinois. Mr. Lang sold all the motorcycles produced this year.
The factory then had four part-time employees.

Model Year 1905

Main Models
Model 1: 24.74ci (405.41cc) F-head single

Retail Prices
Model 1: $200

Production Totals
Model 1: 16

Options
None available

Paint Colors
Piano-finish Black with Gold double pinstriping

Series 1 F-Head Singles
No major changes or improvements for this model year

Motor Company Minutes, 1905
Factory addition, doubling size to a 10x30sq-ft single-story wooden structure.
Production of float-feed carburetors, boat motors, and reversible boat props to supplement income.
The first full-time employee is hired.

Racing Notes
On July 4 an H-D motorcycle sets a record time of 19:02 in a 15-mile race in Chicago.

Model Year 1906

Main Models
Model 2: 26.8ci (439.9cc) F-head single

Retail Prices
Model 2: $210

Production Totals
Model 2: 50

Options
26in wheels
Hand crank

Paint Colors
Piano-finish Black with Gold double pinstriping; available at extra cost is Renault Gray with Red double pinstriping

Series 2 F-Head Singles

First Year
Engine: 26.8ci (439.9cc) F-head single with automatic inlet valve and 3-1/8x3-1/2in bore and stroke
Hand crank designed into engine; optional
The nickname Silent Gray Fellow

Motor Company Minutes, 1906
Six full-time employees.
A factory is built at the Chestnut Street address, a wooden structure measuring 28x80ft. This street changed to Juneau Avenue years later.
After framework was constructed, railroad surveyors notified the company they were too close to the railroad tracks. Getting together 8 to 10 friends, they picked up the building and walked it over to its permanent site.
First business loan, acquired privately from maternal Uncle James McLay of Madison for purchase of land at 27th and Chestnut to build on. Uncle Jim, also a beekeeper, is respectfully called the "Honey Uncle."
H-D first advertises the Silent Gray Fellow.
Catalogs are published by the company for the public.

Model Year 1907

Main Models
Model 3: 26.8ci (439.9cc) F-head single

Specialty Models
Experimental V-twin featuring automatic suction inlet valves. Valve problems kept it from consistent running. No other details available.

Retail Prices
Model 3: $210

Production Totals
Model 3: 150

Options
26in wheels
Tank transfers with Red or Gold centers
Tank lettering Gold with Red outline or Red with Gold outline

Paint Colors
Renault Gray with Red double pinstriping; available at extra cost is Piano-finish Black

Series 3 F-Head Singles

First Year
Sager front fork
Oilers used for fork rocker plates
Engine hand crank standard

Motor Company Minutes, 1907
Eighteen employees.
William A. Davidson joins the company. He quit his job as Milwaukee Road Railroad tool foreman.
September 17, incorporation of the H-D Motor Company, stock split four ways between family members.
Walter Davidson is elected the company's first president.
William Harley is elected the company's first chief engineer and treasurer.
Arthur Davidson elected first secretary and general sales manager.
William Davidson is elected first vice president and works manager.
September 17, the first stockholders and board of directors meeting held.
The company totals $35,000 in capital stock.
Company shares are made available to employees for purchase.
A second floor is added to the factory, doubling the factory size.
Financing of the new building is done with stock sales.
The H-D Motor Company prints its first advertising brochure.
The company starts recruiting dealers, starting in New England.
An H-D V-twin is shown at a motorcycle show.
The initial stimulus for H-D's idea of putting together a V-twin engine came from seeing Rem Fowler win the first Isle of Man TT race this year, on a Norton with a Peugeot Twin engine.

Racing Notes
With a perfect score, Walter Davidson places in the top three in an endurance run covering 414 miles from Chicago to Kokomo, Indiana.

Model Year 1908

Main Models
Model 4: 26.8ci (439.9cc) F-head single

Specialty Models
Experimental V-twin using H-D single cylinders with a smaller-than-standard bore and mechanical inlet-valve action, activated by a tappet running off the timing pinion in engine case. No other details available.

Retail Prices
Model 4: $210

Production Totals
Model 4: 450

Options
26in wheels
Tank transfers with Red or Gold centers
Tank lettering Gold with Red outline or Red with Gold outline
Exhaust valve-stem cap in six different sizes

Paint Colors
Renault Gray with Red double pinstriping; available at extra cost is Piano-finish Black

Series 4 F-Head Singles

First Year
Exhaust-valve stem fitted with a steel cap for adjustment

Motor Company Minutes, 1908
Thirty-five employees.
Brick addition built on existing building, measuring 28x80ft.
A separate office processes production, sales, and purchasing.
Frederick Barr, an expert machinist, is hired to the production department.
George Nordberg, expert tool and die maker, hired as assistant to William A. Davidson in the production department.
William Harley graduates from UW Madison, coming back to the company full of new ideas.

Racing Notes
In the June 29 two-day FAM endurance run Walter Davidson rides a stock Silent Gray Fellow, tagged #35, and wins the Catskills-to-Brooklyn event with a perfect score of 1,000 points plus an extra five points and a diamond medal for consistency of rider and machine.
On July 3, Walter Davidson sets the FAM economy record at 188.234mpg. He used 1qt and 1oz of fuel
Harvey Bernard on 61ci flathead V-twin wins first place at hillclimb sponsored by Chicago Motor Club in Algonquin, Illinois

Model Year 1909

Main Models
Model 5: 30ci F-head single with 28in wheels and battery ignition
Model 5-A: 30ci F-head single with 28in wheels and magneto ignition
Model 5-B: 30ci F-head single with 26in wheels and battery ignition
Model 5-C: 30ci F-head single with 26in wheels and magneto ignition
Model 5-D: 50ci F-head V-twin with magneto ignition

Retail Prices
Model 5: $210
Model 5-A: $250
Model 5-B: $210
Model 5-C: $250
Model 5-D: $325

Production Totals
Model 5: 864
Model 5-A: 54
Model 5-B: 168
Model 5-C: 36
Model 5-D: 27

Options
Tank transfers with Red or Gold centers
Tank lettering Gold with Red outline or Red with Gold outline
Schebler Model H carburetor

Paint Colors
Renault Gray with Red double pinstriping; available at extra cost is Piano-finish Black

Series 5 F-Head Singles

First Year
Engine: 30ci F-head single with automatic inlet valves and 3-5/16x3-1/2in bore and stroke
Front fender mounted to the spring fork and moved with the fork
20-pint tank capacity
Bosch magneto on magneto-equipped models
Longer contour-styled tanks, formed in two halves, fitted around the frame and wedge-shaped to the rear
Wire-operated engine controls enclosed in handlebars

Series 5-D F-Head V-Twins

First Year

Engine: 50ci F-head V-twin with 3x3-1/2in bore and stroke and output of 7hp

V-twin engine design with one-piece cylinders
Iron pistons
Step-joint piston rings
7/8in-diameter flywheel crankpin
0.79mm inlet-valve opening
Automatic inlet valves
Tapered pistons and straight cylinder bores
Chrome-nickel two-piece exhaust valves
Eight-lug crankcase
Bicycle-style rear-wheel hub and brake
Wire-operated engine controls enclosed in handlebars
Oilers used on fork rocker plates
Sager front fork
Frame with a horizontal top rail giving a bicycle look
Twistgrip compression release
Handlebars of seven-piece construction
Coil-suspension saddle
Right tank for gas and left tank for oil only
Bosch brand magneto
Pedal-crank chain adjusted by moving rear wheel in frame
Horizontal cooling fins on cylinder head
Filler caps with 1-3/8in diameter
Fender 3-3/4in-wide
Dual bicycle pedal
Twenty-pint tank capacity
Exhaust-valve stem fitted with a steel cap for adjustment
Drip-feed motor lubrication
Exposed exhaust-valve springs
Three-plate battery
Contoured-style tanks, formed in two halves, fitted around the frame and wedge-shaped to the rear
Early method of model identification, matches year to model by subtracting four from the year
Mudguard 3-3/4in wide
Loop frame with curved front downtube
Front fender mounted to the spring fork and moved with the fork
Starting by pedaling or running alongside
Flat-topped bicycle-style saddle
28in wheels standard

Only Year

No belt-tightening system
Front-mounted magneto
1-1/4in-wide leather drive belt
Automatic inlet valves

Motor Company Minutes, 1909

Arthur Davidson attends the annual Rural Mail Carriers of America meeting. Bringing with him a demonstration motorcycle, he makes a big impression and even bigger sales.

The company has now opted for use of modern trucking, replacing the horse for delivery needs.

First motorcycle is sold for police duty and sent to the Pittsburgh police department.

Racing Notes

Walter Davidson, Robert Underhill, Crolius Lacey, and Frank Ollerman win team prize in Cleveland-to-Indianapolis endurance run.

CHAPTER 2

1910-1919

Model Year 1910

1910 G. *Doug Mitchel*

Main Models
Model 6: 30ci F-head single with 28in wheels and battery ignition
Model 6-A: 30ci F-head single with 28in wheels and magneto ignition
Model 6-B: 30ci F-head single with 26in wheels and battery ignition
Model 6-C: 30ci F-head single with 26in wheels and magneto ignition
Model 6-E Factory Stock Racer: 30ci F-head single

Retail Prices
Model 6: $210
Model 6-A: $250
Model 6-B: $210
Model 6-C: $250
Model 6-E: $275

Production Totals
Model 6: 2,302
Model 6-A: 334
Model 6-B: 443
Model 6-C: 88
Model 6-E: 1

Options
Tank transfers with Red or Gold centers
Tank lettering Gold with Red outline or Red with Gold outline
Schebler Model H carburetor
Acetylene lighting

Paint Colors
Renault Gray with Red double pinstriping; available at extra cost is Piano-finish Black

Series 6 F-Head Singles

First Year
Belt idler mechanism
1-3/4in leather drive belts
H-D bar-and-shield logo with word "Trademark"

Motor Company Minutes, 1910
149 employees.
The first concrete company structure is completed, giving a total of 9,250sq-ft.
Patent is applied for on a two-speed rear hub. Design never reaches production.

Racing Notes
Private H-D rider wins a perfect score at the Los Angeles Annual Endurance Contest
Private H-D rider wins perfect score at the New York Quarterly Trials
Private H-D rider wins perfect score at the Linden Endurance Contest
Private H-D riders win three-place sweep at the Oklahoma City Race meet
Private H-D rider wins first place at the Denver Stock Machine Race
Private H-D riders win five-place sweep at the South Bend Endurance Contest
Private H-D rider wins first place at the Minnesota Hill-Climb
Private H-D riders win first and second places at the Denver-Greeley Road Race

Model Year 1911

Main Models
7: 30ci F-head single with 28in wheels and battery ignition
7-A: 30ci F-head single with 28in wheels and magneto ignition
7-B: 30ci F-head single with 26in wheels and battery ignition
7-C: 30ci F-head single with 26in wheels and magneto ignition
7-D: 50ci F-head V-twin with 28in wheels and magneto ignition

Retail Prices
Model 7: $225
Model 7-A: $250
Model 7-B: $225
Model 7-C: $250
Model 7-D: $300

Production Totals
5,625 total; detailed figures not available

Options
Tank transfers with Red or Gold centers
Tank lettering Gold with Red outline or Red with Gold outline
Schebler Model H carburetor
Acetylene lighting

Paint Colors
Renault Gray with broad Red striping edged in Black with Gold center pinstripe; available at extra cost are broad Gray striping edged in Red with Gold center pinstripe, broad Dark Blue striping edged in Red with Gold center pinstripe, broad Dark Gray striping edged in Red with Gold center pinstripe, or broad Black striping edged in Red with Gold center pinstripe

Series 7 F-Head Singles

First Year
Vertical cooling fins on cylinder head
Straight-section front downtube on frame
One-piece steel exhaust valve

Series 7-D F-Head V-Twins

First Year
Mechanical inlet valves, cam-operated
Straight-section front downtube on frame
Full-baffle with three 3/8in holes in each side under front cylinder and half-baffle under rear cylinder
60deg seats on both intake and exhaust valves
One-piece steel exhaust valve
Vertical cooling fins on cylinder head
Tensioning system for drive belt

Motor Company Minutes, 1911
481 employees.
The company borrows from the Marshall and Ilsley (M&I) Bank to enlarge the factory.
Company enlarges again, now up to 80,000sq-ft.

Model Year 1912

1912 X-8-A. *Doug Mitchel*

Main Models
Model 8: 30ci F-head single with battery ignition
Model X-8: 30ci F-head single with battery ignition and rear-wheel clutch
Model 8-A: 30ci F-head single with magneto ignition
Model X-8-A: 30ci F-head single with magneto ignition and rear-wheel clutch
Model 8-D: 50ci F-head V-twin with magneto ignition
Model X-8-D: 50ci F-head V-twin with magneto ignition and rear-wheel clutch
Model X-8-E: 61ci F-head V-twin with chain final drive, magneto ignition, and rear-wheel clutch

Retail Prices
Model 8: $200
Model X-8: $210
Model 8-A: $225
Model X-8-A: $235
Model 8-D: $275
Model X-8-D: $285
Model X-8-E: $285

Production Totals
3,852; detailed figures not available

Options
Tank transfers with Red or Gold centers
Tank lettering Gold with Red outline or Red with Gold outline
Schebler Model H carburetor
Acetylene lighting

Paint Colors
Renault Gray with broad Red striping edged in Black with Gold center pinstripe; available at extra cost are broad Gray striping edged in Red with Gold center pinstripe, broad Dark Blue striping edged in Red with Gold center pinstripe, broad Dark Gray striping edged in Red with Gold center pinstripe, or broad Black striping edged in Red with Gold center pinstripe

Series 8 F-Head Singles

First Year
> New frame with a horizontal top frame rail sloping to the rear
> Pedal cranks mounted on a hub having eccentric end pieces holding hub into the frame
> Troxel saddle suspension system with Tru-form padded Ful-Floteing saddle and spring-adjustable center post
> Front-fender rear section designed with a slight valance
> Free-wheel clutch assembly in rear axle hub on models with "X" prefix; operated by handle on gas tank
> Redesigned tanks
> Oil tank under the seat

Series 8-D F-Head V-Twins

First Year
> New frame with the horizontal top frame rail sloping to the rear
> Troxel saddle suspension system with Tru-form padded Ful-Floteing saddle and spring adjustable center post
> Free-wheel clutch assembly in rear axle hub on X-8-D; operated by handle on gas tank
> Sprocket-shaft ball race
> Worm-actuated clutch
> Pedal cranks mounted on a hub having eccentric end pieces holding the hub into the frame
> Front fender rear section designed with slight valance
> Splined clutch hub
> Tank-mounted hand-operated oil pump as main lubrication

Series X-8-E F-Head Big Twins

First Year
> Engine: 61ci F-head V-twin with mechanical inlet valve and 3-5/16x3-1/2in bore and stroke
> Bosch magneto standard
> Roller chain drive
> Timed breather system using a slotted breather gear
> Tank-mounted hand-operated oil pump as main lubrication
> Connecting rods with roller-bearing big ends
> Twist-grip compression release
> Splined clutch hub
> Ball-bearing mainshaft with self-aligning bearings on sprocket side
> Vertical-radial pattern cooling fins on cylinder head
> Full baffle with three 3/8in holes in each side under the front cylinder and a half-baffle under rear cylinder
> Horizontal top frame rail sloping to the rear
> Pedal cranks mounted on a hub having eccentric end pieces holding hub into the frame
> Free-wheel clutch assembly
> Front-fender rear section designed with a slight valance

Only Year
> Iron pistons

Motor Company Minutes, 1912

1,076 employees (975 factory workers and 101 office personnel).

Construction of a five-story building begins that is to become the H-D headquarters. This addition now totals 187,750sq-ft.

A separate Parts and Accessories Department is formed.

This year automatic machinery is installed at the factory.

The free-wheel clutch assembly—rear wheel with multiplate clutch assembly working the same as an auto clutch—eliminated the need to run alongside or pedal to start the engine. Starting and stopping done by shifting a lever on the left side of the tank.

First export of H-D motorcycles to Japan. A small number of motorcycles, with no spare parts, ordered for the Japanese army.

Printing of new publication, *The Dealer*, giving tips and insights on selling techniques for dealers nationwide.

200-plus H-D Dealers nationwide.

Racing Notes

Frank Lightner wins third Annual Bakersfield Road Race in Bakersfield, California. Frank arrived one hour ahead of all other contestants on a factory stock Model X-8-E.

Ray Watkins and partner Ben Torres, Private Riders, win Sidecar San Jose Road Race, California, with record 49mph.

Eight private H-D riders win an Eight-Place Sweep in the Harrisburg to Philadelphia Race.

An H-D factory stock Model X-8-E wins San Jose Race.

Model Year 1913

Main Models
Model 9-A: 35ci F-head single with belt drive
Model 9-B: 35ci F-head single with chain drive
Model 9-E: 61ci F-head V-twin with chain drive
Model 9-F: 61ci F-head V-twin with chain drive
Model 9-G Forecar Delivery Van: 61ci F-head V-twin with front-mounted delivery box

Retail Prices
Model 9-A: $290
Model 9-B: $290
Model 9-E: $350
Model 9-F: N/A
Model 9-G: N/A

Production Totals
Model A: 1,510
Model B: 4,601
Model E: 6,732
Model C: 11
Model F: 49
Model G: 63

Options
26in wheels
Tank transfers with Red or Gold centers
Tank lettering Gold with Red outline or Red with Gold outline
Schebler Model H carburetor
Acetylene lighting
Troxel No. 1 saddle
Mesinger Super BA saddle
Mesinger Standard No. 4 saddle
Persons Model R saddle
U.S. Studded tread tires
Goodyear Studded tread tires
Empire Studded tread tires
Two-speed transmission for commercial/utility use

Paint Colors
Renault Gray with broad Red striping edged in Black with Gold center pinstripe; available at extra cost are broad Gray striping edged in Red with Gold center pinstripe, broad Dark Blue striping edged in Red with Gold center pinstripe, broad Dark Gray striping edged in Red with Gold center pinstripe, or broad Black striping edged in Red with Gold center pinstripe

Series 9 F-Head Singles

First Year
Engine: 35ci F-head single (called the "5-35" because it put out 5hp from its 35ci) with 3-5/16inx4in bore and stroke
Mechanical inlet valves
Iron-alloy pistons
Pistons, rods, and flywheels balanced as a unit
Magneto ignition standard

Only Year
Eccentric piston rings
Fender width 3-3/4in
Bicycle-style wheel hubs and brakes
Exposed exhaust valve springs
Starting by pedaling or running alongside
Plain-bearing connecting rod big ends

Series 9 F-Head Big Twins

First Year
Model G commercial delivery van model offered
Pistons, rods, and flywheels balanced as individual unit
Iron-alloy pistons

Motor Company Minutes, 1913
Annual sales of $12,904.

William Ottaway hired as assistant engineer to William Harley. He works as head of the new Racing Department. He previously worked at Thor Motorcycles.

In December, to the satisfaction of many a motorcycle rider, the first drive-in gas station was opened in Pittsburgh, Pennsylvania. Until now, gasoline was bought by riders at hardware stores, general stores, the local drugstore, and the blacksmith.

Only-year printing of *Los Entusiastas Latinos*, an owner's manual and catalog in Spanish.

H-D advertised their first motorcycle sold as having run over 100,000 miles with its original bearings.

Racing Notes
Private riders on H-D motorcycles win three-place sweep in 225-mile race from Harrisburg to Philadelphia and back.

Model Year 1914

Main Models
Model 10-A: 35ci F-head single with belt drive
Model 10-B: 35ci F-head single with chain drive
Model 10-C: 35ci F-head single with chain drive and two-speed rear hub
Model 10-E: 61ci F-head V-twin with chain drive
Model 10-F: 61ci F-head V-twin with chain drive and two-speed rear hub
Model 10-G Delivery Van: 61ci F-head V-twin with two-speed rear hub

Retail Prices
Model 10-A: $200
Model 10-B: $210
Model 10-C: $245
Model 10-E: $250
Model 10-F: $285
Model 10-G: N/A

Production Totals
Model 10-A: 316
Model 10-B: 2,034
Model 10-C: 877
Model 10-E: 5,055
Model 10-F: 7,956
Model 10-G: 171

Options
26in wheels
Tank transfers with Red or Gold centers
Tank lettering Gold with Red outline or Red with Gold outline
Acetylene lighting
Chain drive
Belt drive
Metal tube for speedometer gearing
Large gas canister for lighting. Mounts by rear wheel
Troxel No. 1 saddle
Troxel Truform saddle
U.S. Studded tread tires
Goodyear Studded tread tires

Paint Colors
Renault Gray with broad Red striping edged in Black with Gold center pinstripe; available at extra cost are broad Gray striping edged in Red with Gold center pinstripe, broad Dark Blue striping edged in Red with Gold center pinstripe, broad Dark Gray striping edged in Red with Gold center pinstripe, or broad Black striping edged in Red with Gold center pinstripe

Series 10 F-Head Singles

First Year
Step starter system
Tapered cylinder bores and straight pistons
Concentric piston rings
Carburetor choke
Padded chainguard
Clutch pedal
Brake pedal
H-D brand brakes, except on Model 10-A
H-D brand front and rear wheel hubs, except on Model 10-A
Tank-mounted hand-operated oil pump
Two-piece telescopic enclosure for exhaust valve
Roller bearings on the connecting rod big end
One-piece connecting rods, except on Model 10-A
Fender width 4-1/2in
Rectangular folding footboards
Internal-expanding rear brake bands

Series 10 F-Head Big Twins

First Year
Step starter system
Nine-lug crankcases—late year
Clutch pedal
Brake pedal
Padded chainguard
Fender width of 4-1/2in
Rectangular folding footboards
Concentric piston rings
Internal-expanding rear brake bands
H-D brand brakes
H-D brand front and rear wheel hubs
Two-piece telescopic enclosure for each exhaust-valve spring
Mechanically operated rotary relief valve
Tapered cylinder bores and straight pistons

Only Year
Two-speed rear hub transmission (used on Model 10-F)

Specialty Notes
"A" motor high-performance motor featuring 1in inlet manifolds optional
Racing motor I.D. numbers begin with letter "M"

Motor Company Minutes, 1914

Annual sales of $16,284.

The hand-operated clutch system is William Harley's design.

A sixth floor added to existing building, now over 297,110sq-ft.

Motorcyclists encounter the first traffic light in the United States. Built in Cleveland, Ohio, at the intersection of 105th Street and Euclid Avenue, it uses red and green lights and buzzers.

This year founding of the American Motorcycle Manufacturers Association, in the fall, with Arthur Davidson on the board. Becomes the American Motorcycle and Allied Trades Commission.

First H-D Dealership in San Francisco, California. Al Maggini and Dudley Perkins originally co-owned the dealership at 626 Market Street until Perkins buys Maggini out. The dealership remains in business in the 1990s.

H-D orders 2,500 sidecar units from the Rogers Company.

By now, 4,800 H-D motorcycles have been sold to and used by the United States Postal Service alone.

Racing Notes

H-D wins One Hour National Championship in Birmingham, Alabama.

Walter Cunningham places second in 300-Mile Dodge City Classic on Model 11-K. First race debut for Model 11-K in July.

Model Year 1915

Main Models

Model 11-B: 35ci F-head single

Model 11-C: 35ci F-head single with two-speed rear-hub transmission

Model 11-E: 61ci F-head V-twin with single-speed transmission

Model 11-F: 61ci F-head V-twin with three-speed transmission

Model 11-G Delivery Van: 61ci F-head V-twin with three-speed transmission

Model 11-H: 61ci F-head V-twin with single-speed transmission and electric lighting

Model 11-J: 61ci F-head V-twin with three-speed transmission and electric lighting

Model 11-K Stripped Stock: 61ci F-head V-twin with three-speed transmission

Specialty Models

11-K4 Track Racer: F-head single with magneto

11-K5 Roadster Racer: F-head single with magneto

11-K12: "Fast Motor" F-head V-twin with magneto

11-K12H: "Fast Motor" F-head V-twin with electrical system

11-KT Track Racer: F-head V-twin with magneto

11-KR Roadster Racer: F-head V-twin with magneto

11-KRH Roadster Racer: F-head V-twin with electrical system

11-KTH Track Racer: F-head V-twin with electric

Sidecars and Chassis

11-L: right-hand single-passenger sidecar

L-11-L: left-hand single-passenger sidecar

11-M: standard commercial sidecar

Retail Prices

Model 11-B: $200

Model 11-C: $230

Model 11-E: $240

Model 11-F: $275

Model 11-H: $275

Model 11-J: $310

Model 11-K: $250

Production Totals

Model B: 670

Model C: 545

Model E: 1,275

Model F: 9,855

Model G: 98

Model H: 140

Model J: 3,719

Model KR: 121

Model KT: 37

Model K-4: 30

Delivery Van: 3

Options

26in wheels
Tank transfers with Red or Gold centers
Tank lettering Gold with Red outline or Red with Gold outline
Foot clutch
Hand clutch
Magneto ignition
Acetylene lighting
Two-unit electrical system
Extra-large tanks for twin models
Detachable sidecar apron
Folding tops and side curtains on sidecars
Hand painting of company names, logos, and information
U.S. studded tread tires
Goodyear studded tread tires
Troxel suspension saddle
Troxel Truform saddle

Paint Colors

Renault Gray with broad Red striping edged in Black with Gold center pinstripe; available at extra cost are broad Gray striping edged in Red with Gold center pinstripe, broad Dark Blue striping edged in Red with Gold center pinstripe, broad Dark Gray striping edged in Red with Gold center pinstripe, or broad Black striping edged in Red with Gold center pinstripe

Series 11 F-Head Singles

First Year

Ball bearings installed on left side of two-speed transmission (Model 11-C)
45deg seats on intake and exhaust valves
Rear brake made double-acting with leverage applied to both ends of the expanding band
Motor-driven automatic oil pump with sight glass
Exhaust-lifter-pin screw for adjustments
Hand pump integrated with the oil tank and featuring a lock-down device
1in diameter flywheel crankpin
Two-piece construction pressed tubular steel handlebars
Grease cups on fork rocker plates
Tank-mounted hand-pump now emergency only

Series 11 F-Head Big Twins

First Year

Three-speed sliding-gear transmission with final and primary drive on the same side (Models 11-F and 11-J)
Vertical clutch arm in three-speed transmission (Models 11-F and 11-J)
Gear-clutch interlock in three-speed transmission (Models 11-F and 11-J)
All-steel muffler with foot-controlled cutout, larger expansion chamber, and tailpipe
Rear brake made double-acting with leverage applied to both ends of the expanding band
Shifter gate (Models 11-F and 11-J)
Oil pump and magneto-drive cover integrated
Motor-driven automatic oil pump with sight glass
Exhaust-valve lifter-pin screw for adjustments
Tie-boss added to the forked connecting rods
45deg seats on intake and exhaust valves
Connecting-rod wrist-pin bushing machined with a spiral groove and slotted at the top
Crankcase breather pipe designed at top of valve-action housing
Hand pump integrated with oil tank
Two-unit Remy Model 15 magneto-generator for electric light system (Models 11-H and 11-J)
Electrical system, with headlight, removable taillight, horn, and ignition (Models 11-H and 11-J)
Oil deflector designed into the left side of three-speed transmission (Models 11-F and 11-J)
Two-piece-construction pressed-tubular-steel handlebars
Oil tank a part of the gas tank assembly
Hand-pump lock-down mechanism
1in diameter crankpin
Four-row roller bearing, two rows on each connecting-rod big end
H-D brand roller bearings
Roller bearing width 1-3/4in-wide
Transmission mainshaft bushing
Grease cups on fork rocker plates

Only Year

Transmission countershaft supported by phosphor bronze bushings on three-speed models
Remy Model 15 magneto-generator with vacuum-operated battery cutout (Models 11-H and 11-J)

Motor Company Minutes, 1915

Annual sales of $16,645.

Model 11-K developed by Harry Ricardo, a leading English engine expert, and Bill Ottaway.

Model 11-K prototypes originally had problems with the chain breaking and spark plugs fouling.

Hand painting of company names, logos and information on side-vans begins at a cost of 10 cents per letter.

More than 5,000 H-D motorcycles have been sold to various mail carriers around the country.

First year of U.S. Postal Rural Free Delivery (RFD) system. H-D spends a large amount of money advertising motorcycles for RFD use.

5,000 sidecar units are ordered from the Rogers Company.

Racing Notes

Otto Walker places second at Tacoma Board Track, Washington.

Red Park wins the Sheepshead Bay Board Track, Washington, with record 89.01mph on July 25.

H-D wins Phoenix 200-Mile Race.

H-D Team Riders place second, third, fourth, and sixth at Sheepshead Bay Board Track on July 25.

Otto Walker wins 100-Mile Maywood Board Speedway Race in Chicago with record 89.11mph.

Irving Janke wins third Annual 300-Mile Dodge City Classic Race, with record 79.79mph on Model 11-K.

H-D wins Venice International Grand Prize.

Model Year 1916

1916 J. *Doug Mitchel*

Main Models

Model 16-B: 35ci F-head single

Model 16-C Solo: 35ci F-head single with three-speed transmission

Model 16-E: 61ci F-head V-twin with single-speed transmission

Model 16-F Stock Competition: 61ci F-head V-twin with three-speed transmission

Model 16-J: 61ci F-head V-twin with three-speed transmission and electrical system

Model 16-S Stripped Stock Racer: 35ci F-head single

Model 16-R Roadster Racer: 61ci F-head V-twin

Model 16-T Track Racer: 61ci F-head V-twin

Sidecars and Chassis

16-LC: single-passenger sidecar chassis-right-hand

16-XT: double-bar chassis with suit box and motorcycle

16-L: right-hand single-passenger sidecar

16-LCL: single-passenger sidecar chassis-left-hand

16-M: standard commercial sidecar

16-RFD: commercial sidecar with rural free delivery box

16-P: commercial sidecar with double-bar chassis and closed box

16-U: commercial sidecar with double-bar chassis and open box

16-V: commercial sidecar with double-bar chassis and double covered box

16-GC: gun car

16-AC: ammunition car

16-SC: sidecar chassis and stretcher, complete

Retail Prices

Model B: $200

Model C: $230

Model E: $240

Model F: $265

Model J: $295

Production Totals

Model B: 292

Model C: 862

Model E: 252

Model F: 9,496

Model J: 5,898

Model R: 82
Model S: 12
Model T: 23
Delivery Van: 7

Options

Sidecar motor
Sidecar ratchet brake lock
Sidecar auxiliary hand brake
Detachable sidecar apron
Flat front mudguard
26in wheels
Hand-painted company names, logos, and information
Full electric
Two-unit electrical system
Foot clutch
Hand clutch
Acetylene lighting
Magneto ignition
Tank transfers with Red or Gold centers
Tank lettering Gold with Red outline or Red with Gold outline
Extra-large tanks for twins
Forks, brakes, clutch, and handlebars (racing models)
Troxel Jumbo saddle
U.S. chain tread tires
U.S. corrugated tread tires
Goodyear Blue Streak tires
Firestone Non-Skid tires
Rear-stroke step starter
Forward-stroke step starter

Paint Colors

Renault Gray with broad Red striping edged in Black with Gold center pinstripe; available at extra cost are broad Gray striping edged in Red with Gold center pinstripe, broad Dark Blue striping edged in Red with Gold center pinstripe, broad Dark Gray striping edged in Red with Gold center pinstripe, or broad Black striping edged in Red with Gold center pinstripe

Series B and C Singles

First Year

Single-pedal, rear-stroke starter on Model C (Model B retained the bicycle-style forward-stroke starter)
Tanks with rounded edges
Wider front forks
Fender width of 5-1/4in
Stronger wheel rims
Improved front hub
Filler caps 1-1/2in diameter
Steering head bearing receives larger head cone and two more balls in bearing
Revised model identification system: engine number lists actual year of model as prefix
"Standardization policy": same frame, footboards, and brake rod used on all models
Small working parts heat-treated
22-pint tank capacity
Dual function left tank—both gas and oil compartments
Forward front fender brace
45deg seats on intake and exhaust valves
Shorter clutch hand lever
New drive gear for magneto or generator

Series E, F, and J Big Twins

First Year

Single-pedal, rear-stroke starter on Model C (Model B retained the bicycle-style forward-stroke starter)
Tanks with rounded edges
Wider front forks
Fender width of 5-1/4in
Stronger wheel rims
Improved front hub
Filler caps 1-1/2in diameter
Steering head bearing receives larger head cone and two more balls in bearing
Revised model identification system: engine number lists actual year of model as prefix
"Standardization policy": same frame, footboards, and brake rod used on all models
Small working parts heat-treated
22-pint tank capacity
Dual function left tank—both gas and oil compartments
Forward front fender brace
45deg seats on intake and exhaust valves
Shorter clutch hand lever
New drive gear for magneto or generator
Model 250 Remy generator with a mechanical switch
Roller bearings supporting transmission countershaft (three-speed models)
Self-aligning clutch thrust bearing outer ball race and housing (three-speed models)

Specialty Notes

First Year

Four-Valve overhead-valve (OHV) racing singles with four valves
Eight-Valve OHV racing twins with four valves per cylinder and four cam lobes

Only Year

Experimental Model 16-GC sidecar gun carriage for military use; the sidecar served as a platform for a Colt machine gun

Motor Company Minutes, 1916

Arthur Davidson announces his new system that is designed for better factory-to-dealer liaison.
Last year of competition racing, which is suspended in the fall until further notice.
First year H-D magazine *The Enthusiast*, at the price of a nickel. Sent to all dealers and registered H-D owners.
Last year publication of H-D's *The Dealer*. First year 1912.

Racing Notes

H-D wins first and second place at the 450-Mile Omaha, Nebraska, run.
H-D team sidecar riders win 24-hour Worcester, Massachusetts, run with 1,000-point score and receive Gold Medal.
H-D team sidecar riders win 24-hour Poughkeepsie run with 1,000-point score.
Leslie "Red" Parkhurst sets new 24-hour record at Sheepshead Bay, New York, with impressive 1,452 miles.
Floyd Clymer wins World Dirt Track Title.
Otto Walker and teammate Carl Lutgens set motorcycle sidecar record totaling 1,158 miles.
Irving Janke wins first place 300-Mile Dodge City Race.

1917 J. Doug Mitchel

Main Models

Model 17-B: 35ci F-head single
Model 17-C: 35ci F-head single with three-speed transmission
Model 17-E: 61ci F-head V-twin with single-speed transmission
Model 17-F: 61ci F-head V-twin with three-speed transmission
Model 17-J: 61ci F-head V-twin with three-speed transmission and electrical system
Model 17-S Stripped Stock Racer: 35ci F-head single cylinder
Model 17-R Roadster Racer: 61ci F-head V-twin
Model 17-T Stripped Stock Racer: 61ci F-head V-twin

Sidecars and Chassis

17-L: right-hand single-passenger sidecar
L-17-L: left-hand single-passenger sidecar
17-LC: right-hand single-passenger sidecar chassis
17-LCL: left-hand single-passenger sidecar chassis
17-M: standard commercial sidecar
17-N: commercial sidecar (rural free delivery)
17-P: commercial sidecar with double-bar chassis and closed box
17-U: commercial sidecar with double-bar chassis and open box
17-V: commercial sidecar with double-bar chassis and double covered box

Retail Prices

Model B: $215
Model C: $240
Model E: $255
Model F: $275
Model J: $310
Model R: $280
Model T: $280
Model S: $225

Production Totals

Model B: 124
Model C: 605
Model E: 68
Model F: 8,527
Model J: 9,180
Model R: 12
Model S: 5
Model T: 1

Options

Sidecar motor
"Fast motor"
Schebler Deluxe carburetor
Flat front mudguard
26in wheels
Hand painting of company names, logos, and information
Foot clutch
Hand clutch
Acetylene lighting
Tank transfers with Red or Gold centers
Tank lettering Gold with Red outline or Red with Gold outline
Goodyear Blue Streak tires
Firestone Non-Skid tires
United States tires
Troxel Jumbo saddle
Troxel Wizard saddle

Paint Colors

Olive Green with Pullman Coach Green broad striping edged in Gold pinstripes with a center Gold pinstripe (only year)

Series B and C Singles

First Year
Olive painted crankcases
Coach Green broad stripe down middle of front fender

Only Year
Dixie-brand magneto

Series E, F, and J Big Twins

First Year
Olive-painted crankcases
Coach Green broad stripe down middle of front fender
Four-lobe cam
Revised valve timing for more valve overlap
Valve roller arms (midyear)
Pushrod spring covers
Pistons grooved above the lower edge of the piston skirt
Holed pistons. Holes drilled around the skirt
Dixie-brand magnetos
Revised right and left crankcases
Revised inlet housing, inlet housing cap, inlet valve springs, inlet manifold, and inlet valves
Inlet valve pushrod springs enclosed
Pushrod spring covers
Crankpin double-row roller bearings
Revised transmission mainshaft roller bearing
Revised clutch hub shell ring and clutch key ring
Revised rear mudguard

Specialty Notes

First Year

Engine with "Fast Motors" classification. These are standard motors that are precision fit and set up with looser clearances; motor numbers 500 to 999.

"Fast Motors" receive new front and rear cylinders, front and rear inlet valve housings, inlet-valve caps, inlet-housing-cap clamp nuts, inlet valves, inlet-valve springs, inlet pushrods, pushrod springs exhaust valves (each with a key), and right and left crankcases.

Motor Company Minutes, 1917

July, first year H-D Service School started to teach motorcycle maintenance and repair to military personnel.

H-D starts supplying the Army with motorcycles and almost half of models manufactured go to the military to be used as message runners and for traffic duties.

H-D is given the official U.S. Government Classification of B-4, designating the industry and its products of essential need for the war effort.

Last year exportation of motorcycles to the Japanese army.

Racing Notes

Allen Bedel sets new record in 1,000-mile nonstop endurance run at Ascot Park, 21 hours, averaged 48.3mph.

Model Year 1918

Main Models

Model 18-B: 35ci F-head single with high-tension magneto ignition

Model 18-C Solo: 35ci F-head single cylinder with three-speed transmission and high-tension magneto ignition

Model 18-E: 61ci F-head V-twin with single-speed transmission and high-tension magneto ignition

Model 18-F Solo: 61ci F-head V-twin with three-speed transmission and high-tension magneto ignition

Model 18-J Solo: 61ci F-head V-twin with three-speed transmission and electrical system

Model 18-R Roadster Racer: 61ci F-head V-twin with three-speed transmission

Model 18-FUS Presto Lite Equipped Government Use only: 61ci F-head V-twin with three-speed transmission

Specialty Models

Model 18-FA: "A" motor F-head V-twin with three-speed transmission and magneto ignition

Model 18-JA: "A" motor F-head V-twin with three-speed transmission and electrical system

Model 18-FB: "B" motor F-head V-twin with three-speed transmission and magneto ignition

Model 18-JB: "B" motor F-head V-twin with three-speed transmission and electrical system

Model 18-FCA: "500 CA" motor F-head V-twin with three-speed transmission and magneto ignition, 3-1/2in stroke, and aluminum pistons

Model 18-FF: "500" motor F-head V-twin with three-speed transmission and magneto ignition

18-JF: "500" motor F-head V-twin with three-speed transmission and electrical system

18-FFA: "500 A" motor F-head V-twin with three-speed transmission, 3-1/2in stroke, aluminum pistons, and magneto ignition

18-FCAB: "500 CAB" motor F-head V-twin with 4in stroke, aluminum pistons, and magneto ignition

Sidecars and Chassis

18-L: right-hand single-passenger sidecar

L-18-L: left-hand single-passenger sidecar

18-LC: right-hand single-passenger sidecar chassis

18-LCL: left-hand single-passenger sidecar chassis

18-M: standard commercial sidecar

18-N: commercial sidecar, rural free delivery

18-Q: two-passenger sidecar chassis, 56in tread

18-QA: standard closed commercial van, 56in-tread chassis

18-QB: standard open commercial van, 56in-tread chassis

18-QD: two-compartment Parcel Car, 56in-tread chassis

18-QL: right-hand two-passenger sidecar

18-QC3: three-stake platform Parcel Car, 56in-tread seat chassis

18-QC4: four-stake platform Parcel Car, 56in-tread chassis

Retail Prices
Model B: $235
Model C: $260
Model E: $275
Model F: $290
Model J: $320

Production Totals
Model B: 19
Model C: 251
Model F: 11,764
Model J: 6,571
Model E: 5
Model R: 3
Model FUS: 8,095

Options
Sidecar motor
Fast Motor
Schebler Deluxe carburetor
Flat front mudguard
26in wheels
Hand painting of company names, logos, and information
Foot clutch
Hand clutch
Rear brake, hand-operated
Acetylene lighting
Tank transfers with Red or Gold centers
Tank lettering Gold with Red outline or Red with Gold outline
Firestone Non-Skid tires
Goodyear Blue Streak tires

Paint Colors
Olive Green with Pullman Coach Green broad striping edged in Pea Green pinstripes with a Black center pinstripe

Series B and C Singles

First Year
Oil-hole cover
Berling-brand magneto
Revised front chainguard
Relief-pipe clamp and screw
Series B and C single discontinued at the end of the model year

Series E, F, and J Big Twins

First Year
Model 235 Remy generator (early year)
Oil-hole cover
Revised relief-pipe clamp and screw
Revised front chain guard
Revised clutch bearings oiled by rider, through actuating plate
Revised upper exhaust-valve cover
Revised lower exhaust-valve cover
Revised magneto gear
Revised generator drive case
Revised generator intermediate gear
Revised generator drive gear
Revised generator gear stud
Revised generator stud collar
Revised generator control rod
Revised hand-brake handle
Revised clutch-hub shell and sprocket
Revised foot clutch-lever rod
Revised clutch driving hubs and nuts

Motor Company Minutes, 1918
Construction on new factory addition begins in the fall.
The company borrows $3,000,000 from M&I Bank for its construction project.
This year there are approximately 1,000 dealers nationwide.

Racing Notes
H-D wins 300-Mile Dodge City Race.

Model Year 1919

1919 W Sport Twin. *Randy Leffingwell*

Main Models

19-WF Solo: 35.64ci (584.03cc) horizontally opposed twin with three-speed transmission and magneto ignition

19-F Solo: 61ci F-head V-twin with three-speed transmission and magneto ignition

19-FS Sidecar Twin: 61ci F-head V-twin "sidecar motor" with three-speed transmission

19-J Solo: 61ci F-head V-twin with three-speed transmission

19-JS Sidecar Twin: 61ci F-head V-twin with three-speed transmission

Specialty Models

19-FCA: "500 CA" motor F-head V-twin with three-speed transmission, 3-1/2in stroke, and aluminum pistons

19-FF: "500" motor F-head V-twin with three-speed transmission and magneto ignition

19-FB: "B" motor F-head V-twin with three-speed transmission and magneto ignition

19-FFA: "500 A" motor F-head V-twin with three-speed transmission, 3-1/2in stroke, and aluminum pistons

19-FCAB: "500 CAB" motor F-head V-twin with three-speed transmission, 4in stroke, aluminum pistons, and magneto ignition

19-JA: "A" motor F-head V-twin with three-speed transmission and electrical system

19-JB: "B" motor F-head V-twin with three-speed transmission and electrical system

19-JF: "500" motor F-head V-twin with three-speed transmission and electrical system

19-FUS Presto Lite Equipped Government Use only: 61ci F-head V-twin with three-speed transmission

Sidecars and Chassis

19-L: right-hand single-passenger sidecar

19-LUS: right-hand single-passenger sidecar for U.S. Government

19-LC: right-hand single-passenger sidecar chassis

L-19-L: left-hand single-passenger sidecar

L-19-LC: left-hand single-passenger sidecar chassis

19-M: standard commercial sidecar

19-Q: two-passenger sidecar chassis, 56in tread

19-QA: standard closed commercial van, 56in-tread chassis

19-QB: standard open commercial van, 56in-tread chassis

19-QD: two-compartment Parcel Car, 56in-tread chassis

19-QL: right-hand two-passenger sidecar

19-QC3: three-stake platform Parcel Car, 56in-tread chassis

19-QC4: four-stake platform car, 56in-tread chassis

Retail Prices

Model WF: $335

Model F: $350

Model FS: $350

Model J: $370

Model JS: $370

Bicycles: $30-$45

Production Totals

Model F: 5,064

Model J: 9,941

Model W: 753

Model FUS: 7,521

Options

Fast motor

Schebler Deluxe carburetor

Flat front mudguard

Acetylene lighting

Rear brake, hand-operated

Foot clutch

Hand clutch

Magneto ignition

Paint Colors

Olive Green with Pullman Coach Green broad striping edged in Pea Green pinstripes with a Black center pinstripe

Series F and J Big Twins

First Year

Engine-casting clamp plates

Handlebars 2.5in wider and painted Olive Drab

Clutch pull rod

Cam-actuated clutch (late year)

Clutch-actuating-cam guard (late year)

Clutch connecting link and pin (late year)

Series W Sport Twins

First Year

The Sport Twin is an all-new model introduced in mid-1919
Engine: 35.64ci (584.03cc) horizontally opposed flathead twin with 2-3/4x3in bore and stroke and output of 6hp
Nondetachable cylinder heads
Compression ratio 3.75:1
Unit construction of both engine and transmission
Crankshaft turns on roller bearings
Roller bearings on connecting rod big ends
3/8in rollers for big end of crankshaft
Single camshaft directly transmits cam motion to both intake and exhaust valves
Inlet and exhaust manifold cast together
Engine prefix M for magneto model
Screw-in valve guides
Oil plunger pump
Crankcase unpainted
Pressed-steel cover over flywheel
Three-speed sliding-gear transmission
Keystone frame; engine is the main stress bearer of frame
Trailing-link forks
Front fender fully sprung
Totally enclosed rear chain drive
Flat-topped bicycle saddle
Primary drive transmits through three helical gears to the wet clutch
Two-piece-construction pressed-tubular-steel handlebars

Only Year

Starter crank cap screw
2-5/8in front motor-clamp plate studs

Specialty Notes

First Year

Two-Cam F-head racers; last year 1929
Two-Cam eight-valve racer; last year 1929
Two cam gears, each with two lobes (Two-Cam racer); last year 1929
Two cam valve-lifting mechanism (Two-Cam racer); last year 1929
Pivoted lifter arms (Two-Cam racer); last year 1923
Lifter blocks cast in (Two-Cam racer); last year 1923

Only Year

Banjo timing-case cover
Only year special-order J-type single-cylinder engines

Motor Company Minutes, 1919

Production totals 16,095 sidecars.
First position of publicity manager is filled. Julian C. "Hap" Scherer is hired. Julian was former sales manager for Firestone Tire Company.
Reactivation of the competition racing program, in the spring, under direction of William Ottaway.
The Sport Twin is not welcomed by home market but exported with great acceptance to England, Europe, Australia, and New Zealand.
Renewed export to Britain. Duncan Watson reopens his H-D dealership at 74 Newman St., London.
Exportation of 50 motorcycles to England, 15 of these are Sport Twin Model WJs.
The Enthusiast starts monthly publication.
The H-D riding Charlotte (North Carolina) Police Department is founded.

Racing Notes

Hap Scherer sets new record for 1012-Mile Run from New York to Chicago with record 31 hours and 24 minutes on August 27 on Model W Sport.
Ralph Hepburn wins 200-Mile Los Angeles Ascot Speedway Race, June 22.
Otto Walker wins Los Angeles Ascot Speedway Race, November 30.
H-D team riders place second and third, Los Angeles Ascot Speedway Race, November 30.

CHAPTER 3

1920-1929

Model Year 1920

1920 L20T. *Doug Mitchel*

Main Models

20-WF Sport Model Solo: 35.64ci (584.03cc) horizontally opposed twin with three-speed transmission

20-WJ Sport Model Solo: 35.64ci (584.03cc) horizontally opposed twin with three-speed transmission and electrical system

20-F Solo: 61ci F-head V-twin with three-speed transmission and magneto ignition

20-FS Sidecar Twin: 61ci F-head V-twin with three-speed transmission, magneto ignition, and sidecar gearing

20-J Solo: 61ci F-head V-twin with three-speed transmission and electrical system

20-JS Sidecar Twin: 61ci F-head V-twin with three-speed transmission, electrical system, and sidecar gearing

Specialty Models

20-FF: "500" motor F-head V-twin with three-speed transmission and magneto ignition

20-FFA: "500 A" motor F-head V-twin with 3-1/2in stroke, aluminum pistons, magneto ignition, and three-speed transmission

20-FCAB: "500 CAB" motor F-head V-twin with 4in stroke, aluminum pistons, magneto ignition, and three-speed transmission

20-FB: "B" motor F-head V-twin with three-speed transmission and magneto ignition

20-FE: "E" motor F-head V-twin with three-speed transmission and magneto ignition

20-FD: 74ci F-head V-twin with three-speed transmission and magneto ignition

20-FDS: 74ci F-head V-twin with three-speed transmission, magneto ignition, and sidecar gearing

20-FCA: "500 CA" motor F-head V-twin with 3-1/2in stroke, aluminum pistons and magneto ignition with three-speed transmission

20-JF: "500" motor F-head V-twin with three-speed transmission and electrical system

20-JB: "B" motor F-head V-twin with three-speed transmission and electrical system

20-JE: "E" motor F-head V-twin with three-speed transmission and electrical system

20-FA: "A" motor F-head V-twin with three-speed transmission and magneto ignition

20-JA: "A" motor F-head V-twin with three-speed transmission and electrical system

20-JD: 74ci F-head V-twin with three-speed transmission and electrical system

20-JDS: 74ci F-head V-twin with three-speed transmission, electrical system, and sidecar gearing

Sidecars and Chassis

20-L: right-hand single-passenger sidecar

20-LC: right-hand single-passenger sidecar chassis

20-LR: right-hand single-passenger Roadster sidecar

20-LX: right-hand Speedster Sidecar

L-20-L: left-hand single-passenger sidecar

L-20-LC: left-hand single-passenger sidecar chassis

L-20-LR: left-hand single-passenger Roadster Sidecar

20-M: standard commercial sidecar

20-Q: two-passenger sidecar chassis, 56in tread

20-QA: standard closed commercial van, 56in-tread chassis

20-QB: standard open commercial van, 56in-tread chassis

20-WD: two-compartment Parcel Car, 56in-tread chassis

20-QL: right-hand two-passenger sidecar

20-QC3: three-stake platform Parcel Car, 56in-tread chassis

20-QC4: four-stake platform Parcel Car, 56in-tread chassis

20-PC: double-bar chassis

Retail Prices

Model WF: $335

Model WJ: N/A

Model F: $370

Model FS: $370

Model J: $395

Model JS: $395

Production Totals

Model F: 7,579

Model J: 14,192

Model WF: 4,459

Model WJ: 810

Options

Dealers racing frame; open at bottom; used with FCA-motor
Schebler Deluxe carburetor
Acetylene lighting
Flat front mudguard
Rear brake, hand-operated
Mesinger Air Cushion saddle
All-weather tread, Goodyear Blue Streak tires
Firestone Non-Skid tires
Goodrich Safety-Tread tires
Pennsylvania Vacuum Cup black tread tires
Speedometer
Front stand
Luggage carrier

Paint Colors

Olive Green with Pullman Coach Green broad striping edged in Pea Green pinstripes with a Black center pinstripe

Series F and J Big Twins

First Year

Revised front and rear cylinders
Inlet pushrods, from "500" motors
Pushrod-spring covers
Clutch dust ring
Revised rear brake band
Revised brake lever on drum
Revised headlight body
Revised headlight reflector
Headlight placed above horn
Clear headlight lens
Red taillight lens
Generators and coils made by H-D (late year, Series J only)

Only Year

Revised headlight body style (early year) that was revised again midyear

Series W Sport Twins

First Year

Electric lighting offered starting midyear, with the introduction of the Model WJ
Battery case and revised tool-box cover and locks (Model WJ)
Headlight body (Model WJ)
Clear headlight lens (Model WJ)
Headlight placed above the horn (Model WJ)
Generators and coils built by H-D (Model WJ)
3-3/8in front motor-clamp-plate studs
Front motor-clamp spacer
Revised front footboard support
Revised foot-clutch lever
Revised foot-clutch-lever friction spring
Revised clutch operating-rod end
Starter-crank bracket bolt
Luggage carrier brace

First Year

"E" motor classification for the "Fast Motors"
"E" motors feature aluminum pistons and drilled connecting rods
Revised right and left flywheels on "E" motors
"E" motor cylinders stamped with "E" on left side

Motor Company Minutes, 1920

2,400 employees.
April, completion of Juneau Avenue Factory, now giving a total of 542,258sq-ft.
After completion of the new building addition, the H-D company becomes the largest motorcycle factory in the world.
Increase of 5,000 percent in sales this year.
George Appel is hired to supervise development of H-D batteries. Appel is a former electrical engineer for Remy.
Last year H-D Wrecking Crew dominates the 300-Mile Dodge City Race.
The company has established H-D dealerships in 67 countries.
50,000 subscribers to *The Enthusiast*.
Famous "Hog" story starts because of the H-D Race Team riding their winning lap with a pet pig sitting on the gas tank. From this exhibition, the name "Hog" became synonymous with H-D.

Racing Notes

Otto Walker wins 100-Mile International Road Race Championship, Marion, Indiana, with record 77.25mph.
Ray Weishaar wins National Motorcycle Road Race with record 71mph.
Domingos Lopez wins Brazilian Kilometer Championship Side-Car Race with record 80.77mph.
Hap Scherer sets new 1,224-mile Denver-to-Chicago record of 47.5 hours, averaging 26.4mph.
Fred Ludlow wins 25-Mile World Record over 1-Mile Dirt Track with record 19 minutes and 1/5 seconds, September 19.
Jim Davis wins 300-mile Dodge City Race.

Model Year 1921

1921 J. *The Littlest Biker, Inc., Christopher Freeman*

Main Models

21-CD Commercial: 37ci F-head single with three-speed transmission and magneto ignition

21-WF Solo: 35.64ci (584.03cc) horizontally opposed twin with three-speed transmission and magneto ignition

21-WJ Solo: 35.64ci (584.03cc) horizontally opposed twin with three-speed transmission and electrical system

21-F Solo: 61ci F-head V-twin with three-speed transmission and magneto ignition

21-FS Sidecar Twin: 61ci F-head V-twin with three-speed transmission, magneto ignition, and sidecar gearing

21-J Solo: 61ci F-head V-twin with three-speed transmission and electrical system

21-JS Sidecar Twin: 61ci F-head V-twin with three-speed transmission, electrical system, and sidecar gearing

21-FD Solo: 74ci F-head V-twin with three-speed transmission and magneto ignition

21-FDS Sidecar Twin: 74ci F-head V-twin with three-speed transmission, sidecar gearing, and magneto ignition

21-JD Solo: 74ci F-head V-twin with three-speed transmission and electrical system

21-JDS Sidecar Twin: 74ci F-head V-twin with three-speed transmission, electrical system, and sidecar gearing

Specialty Models

21-FCA: "T" motor F-head V-twin with three-speed transmission and magneto ignition

21-FA: "A" motor 61ci F-head V-twin with three-speed transmission and magneto ignition

21-FDA: "A" motor 74ci F-head V-twin with three-speed transmission and magneto ignition

21-FE: "E" motor F-head V-twin with three-speed transmission and magneto ignition

21-JA: "A" motor F-head V-twin with three-speed transmission and electrical system

21-JDA: "A" motor 74ci F-head V-twin with three-speed transmission and electrical system

21-JE: "E" motor F-head V-twin with three-speed transmission and magneto ignition

Sidecars and Chassis

21-L: right-hand single-passenger sidecar

21-LC: right-hand single-passenger sidecar chassis

21-LR: right-hand single-passenger Roadster Sidecar

21-LX: right-hand Speedster Sidecar

L-21-L: left-hand single-passenger sidecar

L-21-LR: Roadster, Single Passenger, left-hand

21-M: standard commercial sidecar

21-Q: two-passenger sidecar chassis, 56in tread

21-QA: standard closed commercial van, 56in-tread chassis

21-QB: standard open commercial van, 56in-tread chassis

21-QD: two-compartment Parcel Car, 56in-tread chassis

21-QL: right-hand two-passenger sidecar

Retail Prices

Model WF: $415
Model WJ: $445
Model CD: $430
Model F: $450
Model FS: $450
Model J: $485
Model JS: $485
Model FD: $485
Model FDS: $485
Model JD: $520
Model JDS: $520

Production Totals

Model WF: 1,100
Model WJ: 823
Model F: 2,413
Model FD: 277
Model J: 4,526
Model JD: 2,321

Options

Schebler Deluxe carburetor
Flat front mudguard and skirt
Hand brake (Sport Model)
Heel brake (Big Twins)
Front stand (Big Twins)
Luggage carrier (Big Twins)
Ammeter, complete
Speedometer by Corbin Brown
Speedometer by Johns-Manville
Firestone Non-Skid tires
All-weather tread Goodyear Blue Streak tires
Goodrich Safety-Tread tires

Paint Colors

Olive Green with Pullman Coach Green broad striping edged in Pea Green pinstripes with a Black center pinstripe

Series CD Big Singles

First Year

The CD is a new Big Single model for commercial use
Engine: 37ci single made by removing one cylinder from the 74ci Big Twin motor
Chassis: standard chassis used on the V-twin models

Only Year

Olive-painted crankcases
Spoked flywheels

Series F and J 61ci Big Twins

First Year
> Solid flywheels (late year)
> Revised connecting rods, pistons, piston pins, and piston rings
> Front stand
> One-piece tubular steel handlebars
> New front and rear fenders with center rib and side panels on front fender
> Concave section on front fender for forks
> Revised tanks
> Revised toolbox cover (electric models)
> Revised rear hub shell
> Revised front footboard support rod

Only Year
> No compression plates (solo models)

Series FD and JD 74ci Big Twins

First Year
> The Series FD and JD 74ci F-head Big Twins are new models created by boring and stroking the engine used in the Series F and J Big Twins
> Engine: 74.66ci F-head V-twin with 3-7/16x4in bore and stroke and output of 18hp
> 1-1/4in Schebler carburetor
> Silichrome-alloy exhaust valves
> New right and left crankcases
> New cylinders and heads
> Solid flywheels
> Front and rear exhaust pipes

Only Year
> Olive-painted crankcases
> Coach Green broad stripe down middle of front fender

Series W Sport Twins

First Year
> Big Twin-style tank trim
> Fenders both center ribbed
> Side panels on front fender
> Brake-lever guide
> Revised headlight body

Specialty Notes
> The "A" V-twin motor is now a special high-speed motor for police use.
> The "B" V-twin motor is now a special high-compression motor for high altitudes.
> The "E" V-twin motor is now a special racing motor.

Motor Company Minutes, 1921
> Mid-March to mid-April, the factory was temporarily closed down due to low sales.
> H-D officers receive a 15 percent cut in pay.
> An H-D catalogue is printed in seven foreign languages.

Racing Notes
> H-D wins all eight National Championship Races.
> Douglas Davidson (no relation) sets new record at Brooklands, England, at 100.76 mph.
> Otto Walker wins a 25-mile board track race in Beverly Hills at a record 104.4 mph.

Model Year 1922

Main Models
> 22-CD Commercial: 37ci F-head single with three-speed transmission
> 22-WF Sport Model Solo: 35.64ci (584.03cc) horizontally opposed twin with three-speed transmission and magneto ignition
> 22-WJ Solo: 35.64ci (584.03cc) horizontally opposed twin with three-speed transmission and electrical system
> 22-F Solo: 61ci F-head V-twin with three-speed transmission and magneto ignition
> 22-FS Sidecar Twin: 61ci F-head V-twin with three-speed transmission, magneto ignition, and sidecar gearing
> 22-J Solo: 61ci F-head V-twin with three-speed transmission and electrical system
> 22-JS Sidecar Twin: 61ci F-head V-twin with three-speed transmission, electrical system, and sidecar gearing
> 22-FD Solo: 74ci F-head V-twin with three-speed transmission and magneto ignition
> 22-FDS Sidecar Twin: 74ci F-head V-twin with three-speed transmission, sidecar gearing, and magneto ignition
> 22-JD Solo: 74ci F-head V-twin with three-speed transmission and electrical system
> 22-JDS Sidecar Twin: 74ci F-head V-twin with three-speed transmission, electrical system, and sidecar gearing

Specialty Models
> 22-FA: "A" motor 61ci F-head V-twin with three-speed transmission and magneto ignition
> 22-FDA: "A" motor 74ci F-head V-twin with three-speed transmission and magneto ignition
> 22-FCA: "T" motor F-head V-twin with three-speed transmission
> 22-FE: "E" motor F-head V-twin with three-speed transmission and magneto ignition
> 22-JA: "A" motor F-head V-twin with three-speed transmission and electrical system
> 22-JDA: "A" motor 74ci F-head V-twin with three-speed transmission and electrical system
> 22-JE: "E" motor F-head V-twin with three-speed transmission and magneto ignition

Sidecars and Chassis
> 22-L: right-hand single-passenger sidecar
> 22-LR: right-hand single-passenger Roadster Sidecar
> 22-LT: right-hand single-passenger Tourist Sidecar
> 22-LX: right-hand Speedster Sidecar
> L-22-L: left-hand single-passenger sidecar
> L-22-LR: left-hand single-passenger Roadster Sidecar
> L-22-LT: left-hand single-passenger Tourist Sidecar
> 22-LC: right-hand single-passenger sidecar chassis
> L-22-LC: left-hand single-passenger sidecar chassis
> 22-M: standard commercial sidecar
> 22-Q: two-passenger sidecar chassis, 56in tread
> 22-QA: standard closed commercial van, 56in-tread chassis
> 22-QB: standard open commercial van, 56in-tread chassis
> 22-QD: two-compartment Parcel Car, 56in-tread chassis
> 22-QL: right-hand two-passenger sidecar
> 22-QT: right-hand two-passenger Tourist Sidecar

Retail Prices

Model WF: $310
Model WJ: $340
Model CD: $315
Model F: $335
Model FD: $360
Model FS: $335
Model FDS: $360
Model J: $365
Model JS: $365
Model JD: $390
Model JDS: $390
Bicycles: $35–$45

Production Totals

Model WF: 388
Model WJ: 455
Model F: 1,824
Model CD: 39
Model FD: 909
Model J: 3,183
Model JD: 3,988

Options

Schebler Deluxe carburetor
Flat front mudguard and skirt
Ammeter, complete
Firestone Non-Skid tires
All-weather tread, Goodyear Blue Streak tires
Goodrich Safety tread tires
U.S. Traxion tread tires
Heel brake (Big Twins)
Hand brake (Sport Model)
Luggage carrier (Big Twins)
Front stand (Big Twins)
Speedometer by Corbin-Brown
Speedometer by Johns-Manville
Olive Drab paint

Paint Colors

Brewster Green edged with Gold double pinstriping

Series CD Big Singles

First/Only Year

Solid flywheels
(Model CD was discontinued at the end of the model year)

Series F and J 61ci Big Twins

First Year

Twelve long roller bearings for male connecting rod (late year)
New inlet and exhaust valve springs of "longer life"
Revised right and left crankcases
Revised gearbox and cover
Revised front forks
Double-plunger oil pump (late year)
Manual battery-cutout switch with automatic alarm (midyear)
Brewster Green-painted crankcases
A 1/16in compression plate beneath each cylinder on solo models; a 1/8in and a 1/16in compression plate beneath each cylinder on sidecar models

Series FD and JD 74ci Big Twins

First Year

Twelve long roller bearings for male connecting rod (late year)
New inlet and exhaust valve springs of "longer life"
Revised right and left crankcases
Revised gearbox and cover
Revised front forks
Double-plunger oil pump (late year)
Manual battery-cutout switch with automatic alarm (midyear)
Brewster Green-painted crankcases
Revised cylinders that are 1/16in longer (engines after 22JD6649)
A 1/8in and a 1/16in compression plate beneath each cylinder on sidecar models (engines 22JD6649 and under); a 1/8in plate for each cylinder, after engine 22JD6649

Only Year

1/16in thick compression plates (engines 22JD6649 and under)

Series W Sport Twins

First Year

31/64in rollers for the connecting rod big end (late year)
Revised crankshaft and counterweight
Detail changes in frame, luggage carrier, front and rear fenders, chain guard, magneto gear, battery case, and toolbox cover

Specialty Notes

74ci DCA engine fitted with aluminum pistons and drilled connecting rods

Motor Company Minutes, 1922

H-D management meets with Indian's top management to set equal retail pricing between the two. Arthur Davidson has lunch with Frank Weschler (Indian general manager) at New York Astoria Hotel.

Alfred Rich Child, export sales representative, signs contract in spring with Baron Okura, representing Tokyo import firm. Import shipment by Baron Okura of Model Js, with full electrics, delivered.

Special delivery stamp issued picturing a H-D V-Twin motorcycle.

Racing Notes

George Ellis and his teammate, J. T. Blandford, ride the Kentucky hills to win the Sidecar Trade Team Award held at the second National Six Days Trail.

George Ellis and his teammate, J. T. Blandford, set national Boston-to-Chicago record.

Model Year 1923

Main Models

23-WF Sport Model Solo: 35.64ci (584.03cc) horizontally opposed twin with three-speed transmission and magneto ignition

23-WJ Sport Model Solo: 35.64ci (584.03cc) horizontally opposed twin with three-speed transmission and electrical system

23-J Solo: 61ci F-head V-twin with three-speed transmission and electrical system

23-JS Sidecar Twin: 61ci F-head V-twin with three-speed transmission, electrical system, and sidecar gearing

23-F Solo: 61ci F-head V-twin with three-speed transmission and magneto ignition

23-FS Sidecar Twin: 61ci F-head V-twin with three-speed transmission, magneto ignition, and sidecar gearing

23-JD Solo: 74ci F-head V-twin with three-speed transmission and electrical system

23-JDS Sidecar Twin: 74ci F-head V-twin with three-speed transmission, electrical system, and sidecar gearing

23-FD Solo: 74ci F-head V-twin with three-speed transmission and magneto ignition

23-FDS Sidecar Twin: 74ci F-head V-twin with three-speed transmission, sidecar gearing, and magneto ignition

Specialty Models

23-FA: "A" motor 61ci F-head V-twin with three-speed transmission and magneto ignition

23-FDA: "A" motor 74ci F-head V-twin with three-speed transmission and magneto ignition

23-FE: "E" motor 61ci F-head V-twin with three-speed transmission and magneto ignition

23-FDCA: 74ci F-head V-twin with three-speed transmission and magneto ignition

23-FCA: 61ci F-head V-twin with three-speed transmission and magneto ignition

23-JDA: "A" motor 74ci F-head V-twin with three-speed transmission and electric ignition

23-JE: "E" motor 61ci F-head V-twin with three-speed transmission and electric ignition

23-JDCA: 74ci F-head V-twin with three-speed transmission and electric ignition

23-S Track Racer: F-head single with magneto ignition

23-T Track Racer: F-head V-twin with magneto ignition

Sidecars and Chassis

23-LT: right-hand Tourist Sidecar

23-LX: right-hand Speedster Sidecar

23-M: right-hand standard commercial sidecar

23-LC: right-hand standard chassis, 42-1/2in tread

L-23-LT: left-hand Tourist Sidecar

L-23-LC: left-hand standard chassis, 46-1/2in tread

23-Q: right-hand two-passenger sidecar, 56-1/4in tread

23-QT: right-hand two-passenger Tourist Sidecar

L-23-LQ: left-hand two-passenger sidecar chassis

L-23-LQT: left-hand two-passenger sidecar body

Retail Prices

Model WF: $275
Model WJ: $295
Model J: $305
Model JS: $305
Model F: $285
Model FS: $285
Model JD: $330
Model JDS: $330
Model FD: $310
Model FDS: $310
Bicycles: $35–$45

Production Totals

Model WF: 614
Model WJ: 481
Model F: 2,822
Model FD: 869
Model J: 4,802
Model JD: 7,458

Options

Schebler Deluxe carburetor
Acetylene lighting
Flat front mudguard and skirt
Ammeter, complete
Corbin-Brown speedometer
Johns-Manville speedometer
Firestone Non-Skid tires
Goodyear All-Weather tires
U.S. Traxion tread tires
Heel brake (Big Twins)
Hand brake (Sport Model)
Luggage carrier (Big Twins)
Front stand (Big Twins)

Paint Colors

Brewster Green edged with Gold triple-line pinstriping

Series F and J 61ci Big Twins

First Year

Silichrome exhaust valves
Improved brake-pedal control
Roller-bearing rear hub
Larger-size generator (Models J and JS only)
Staylit shock-absorbing taillight (Models J and JS only)
Hinged rear mudguard

Series FD and JD 74ci Big Twins

First Year
Improved silichrome exhaust valves
Improved cylinder heads with squarer cooling fins and seven cooling fins on the exhaust manifold
Larger-size generator (Models JD and JDS only)
Staylit shock-absorbing taillight (Models JD and JDS only)
Improved brake-pedal control
Roller-bearing rear hub
Staylit shock-absorbing taillight
Hinged rear mudguard

Specialty Notes

First Year
Bean-shaped timing case cover on Two-Cam Racers

Motor Company Minutes, 1923
All racing efforts set on the back burner, putting the extra effort into an aggressive sales campaign instead.

Business arrangement with Kilbourn Finance Corporation to form a financing company.

Around this time, H-D stressed the importance of a quiet motorcycle and termed other riders on noisy bikes as "Boobs."

Walter and Arthur Davidson meet with Frank Weschler, Indian's General Manager, to talk about evicting all other motorcycle brands from their showrooms.

First H-D agency in Japan is established and is managed by Alfred Rich Child.

A second order of the Model Js are exported to Baron Okura, of Tokyo import firm.

July, Alfred Rich Child meets with the Sankyo Company of Japan. From this meeting, Sankyo Company orders 350 Big Twins with replacement parts and repair tools.

September 1, the road system in the eastern part of Japan is destroyed by an earthquake. Imported H-D motorcycles play major part in crossing over roads that cars and trucks can't.

Racing Notes
Freddie Dixon wins 1,000cc Championship Race on 8-valve (100.10mph).

Freddie Dixon wins Flying Kilometer Record at Bois DeBoulogne, France, with record 108.6mph.

Model Year 1924

Main Models
24-FE: 61ci F-head V-twin with three-speed transmission, magneto ignition, and aluminum-alloy pistons

24-FES Sidecar Twin: 61ci F-head V-twin with three-speed transmission, magneto ignition, sidecar gearing, and aluminum-alloy pistons

24-JE: 61ci F-head V-twin with three-speed transmission, electrical system, and aluminum-alloy pistons

24-JES Sidecar Twin: 61ci F-head V-twin with three-speed transmission, electrical system, and aluminum-alloy pistons

24-FD: 74ci F-head V-twin with three-speed transmission, magneto ignition, and cast-iron pistons

24-FDS Sidecar Twin: 74ci F-head V-twin with three-speed transmission, sidecar gearing, and magneto ignition and cast-iron pistons

24-JD: 74ci F-head V-twin with three-speed transmission, electrical system, and cast-iron pistons

24-JDS Sidecar Twin: 74ci F-head V-twin with three-speed transmission, electrical system, sidecar gearing, and cast-iron pistons

24-FDCA: 74ci F-head V-twin with three-speed transmission, magneto ignition, and aluminum-alloy pistons

24-FDSCA Sidecar Twin: 74ci F-head V-twin with three-speed transmission, magneto ignition, and aluminum-alloy pistons

24-JDCA: 74ci F-head V-twin with three-speed transmission, electrical system, and aluminum-alloy pistons

24-JDSCA Sidecar Twin: 74ci F-head V-twin with three-speed transmission, electrical system, sidecar gearing, and aluminum-alloy pistons

Sidecars and Chassis
24-LT: right-hand single-passenger Royal Tourist Sidecar
24-LX: right-hand single-passenger Racer Sidecar
24-QT: right-hand two-passenger Family Delight sidecar
24-M: Parcel Car with hinged cover
L-24-LT: left-hand single-passenger Royal Tourist Sidecar
L-24-LX: left-hand single-passenger Racer Sidecar
L-24-QT: left-hand two-passenger Family Delight sidecar

Retail Prices
Model FE: $300
Model FES: $300
Model JE: $320
Model JES: $320
Model FD: $315
Model FDS: $315
Model JD: $335
Model JDS: $335
Model FDCA: $325
Model FDSCA: $325
Model JDCA: $345
Model JDSCA: $345

Production Totals

Model FE: 2,708
Model FD: 502
Model FDCB: 90
Model FDCA: 351
Model JE: 4,994
Model JD: 2,955
Model JDCB: 3,034
Model JDCA: 3,014

Options

Iron-alloy pistons with three narrower and deeper rings (74ci)
Zenith carburetor
Schebler Deluxe carburetor
Muffler brackets designed to fit box-shaped mufflers back to 1915 Models
Corbin-Brown speedometer
Acetylene lighting
Flat front mudguard and skirt
Ammeter
Goodyear All Weather tires
Firestone Non-Skid tires
U.S. Traxion tread tires
Heel brake for Big Twins
Front stand for Big Twins
Luggage carrier for Big Twins

Paint Colors

Olive Green with Maroon broad striping edged in Black with a Gold center pinstriping

Series FE and JE 61ci Big Twins

First Year

Aluminum-alloy piston with four unevenly spaced rings
Four-plate battery
Revised flywheels with different balance factor
New front exhaust pipe
5/16in square generator brushes
Larger generator body
Fender center rib more prominent in height
Front fender main section extends farther ahead of the side panels

Only Year

Aluminum pistons with four slot-cut rings
Large box-shaped muffler
Twelve Alemite grease fittings

Series FD and JD 74ci Big Twins

First Year

Revised flywheels with different balance factor
New front and rear exhaust pipes
5/16in square generator brushes
Larger generator body
Four-plate battery
Fender center rib more prominent in height
Front fender main section extends farther ahead of the side panels
Running gear lubricated by an Alemite gun

Only Year

Large box-shaped muffler
Twelve Alemite grease fittings

Specialty Notes

First Year

Valves now operating with direct action from lobes on Two-Cam racer
Roller tappets on Two-Cam racer
Hollow pushrods on Two-Cam racer
Removable lifter blocks bolted to crankcase on Two-Cam racer

Motor Company Minutes, 1924

Everett DeLong is hired to work on designing a new four-cylinder engine. William A. Davidson scraps project as too expensive. Everett had been the chief design engineer for Ace Motorcycles.

The work force is trimmed from 2,500 down to 1,000 employees.

The company shows $119,143 loss.

6,194 motorcycles exported overseas.

H-D exports nearly half of all motorcycles manufactured.

Sales reach 3,257 for sidecars.

At least 1,400 various law enforcement agencies nationwide are equipped with H-D motorcycles.

The Soviet Union, represented by a Mr. Karsov, purchases on credit 1,200 sidecar units, through the sales efforts of Charles Cartwright, the New England sales representative.

Model Year 1925

1925 JD. *Doug Mitchel*

Main Models

25-FE: 61ci F-head V-twin with three-speed transmission, magneto ignition, and iron-alloy pistons

25-FES Sidecar Twin: 61ci F-head V-twin with three-speed transmission, magneto ignition, and iron-alloy pistons

25-JE: 61ci F-head V-twin with three-speed transmission, electrical system, and iron-alloy pistons

25-JES Sidecar Twin: 61ci F-head V-twin with three-speed transmission, electrical system, and iron-alloy pistons

25-FDCB: 74ci F-head V-twin with three-speed transmission, magneto ignition, and iron-alloy pistons

25-FDCBS Sidecar Twin: 74ci F-head V-twin with three-speed transmission, magneto ignition, and iron-alloy pistons

25-JDCB: 74ci F-head V-twin with three-speed transmission, electrical system, and iron-alloy pistons

25-JDCBS Sidecar Twin: 74ci F-head V-twin with three-speed transmission, electrical system, and iron-alloy pistons

Sidecars and Chassis

25-LT: right-hand single-passenger Royal Tourist Sidecar
25-LX: right-hand single-passenger Racer Sidecar
25-QT: right-hand two-passenger Family Delight sidecar
25-MA: Parcel Car chassis only
L-25-LT: left-hand single-passenger Royal Tourist Sidecar
L-25-LX: left-hand single-passenger Racer Sidecar
L-25-QT: left-hand two-passenger Family Delight sidecar

Retail Prices

Model FE: $295
Model FES: $295
Model JE: $315
Model JES: $315
Model FDCB: $315
Model FDCBS: $315
Model JDCB: $335
Model JDCBS: $335

Production Totals

Model F: 1,318
Model FD: 433
Model J: 4,114
Model JD: 9,506

Options

Schebler Deluxe carburetor with low-speed button
Zenith carburetor
Acetylene lighting
Tandem seat by Mesinger
Yoke springs
Loose-wound hooked coil springs
Tandem yoke bracket with fender hump
Tandem-seat passenger pegs mounted on pair of long straps clamped to the rear axle's upper and lower stays
Winter windshield. A large shield
27x3.5in Goodyear tires
27x3.5in Firestone tires
27x3.5in United States tires
Heel brake
Luggage carrier
Front stand
Ammeter
Corbin-Brown speedometer
Johns-Manville speedometer
Light color finish

Paint Colors

Olive Green with Maroon broad striping edged in Black with Gold center pinstriping

Series FE, JE, FDCB, and JDCB Big Twins

First Year

Wider frame that lowers saddle 3in
Front downtube is double-butted
Cylindrical toolbox mounted across front fork
Iron-alloy pistons with narrower and deeper piston rings. Standard
Oil drain plug allows case to be flushed without removing transmission
Two-piece step-down transmission bushing mounted and keyed to mainshaft
Waterproof metal cover on spark coil of generator
14in seat post cushion spring
Alemite-lubricated mainshaft roller bearing
Drop-forged steel frame fittings
Battery placed in lower position and sits in upright position
Teardrop-style streamlined tanks (5.3gal)
Longer rear fender
Steel channel running under the motor
Rear chainguard lengthened and widened
New shape handlebars
Softer cushion and recoil springs on front fork
Bucket-type concave saddle, adjustable to six positions
Longer headlight switch
Shorter rear stand
Long tube-shaped one-piece "Speedster" muffler
Offset rear sprocket
Transmission widened by 5/8in
10-5/8in transmission mainshaft
Transmission main gear receives longer roller bearing
Sixteen Alemite fittings
Shrouded-style taillight
Front fender braces mount through fork rockers
27x3.50in tires standard
20in wheel size
Tire tubes use automobile-size valves
Foot-operated compression release
Rear fender taillight cable clip

Extended gearbox tube on the left side for Alemite grease gun
Primary chain spaced outward 5/8in
Lower transmission bracket redesigned to allow a lower kick-start position
Headlight with flat diffusing lens
Adjustable headlight bracket supports

Only Year
No transmission lockout

Motor Company Minutes, 1925
Last year sidecars are supplied by the Rogers Company of Chicago, Illinois.

A new separate building is built to manufacture H-D sidecars.

The H-D riding Maine State Police is founded. Motorcycle officers earn a weekly pay of $25.

First of the Sankyo Company-ordered motorcycle shipment is sent to Japan.

Racing Notes
Joe Petrali wins National Championship.

July 4, Joe Petrali on pocket-valve wins the 300-Mile Board Track Race held in Altoona, Pennsylvania, with average recorded speed of 100.36mph.

Joe Petrali wins 100-Mile Board Track Race with record 100.36mph, July 4 in Altoona, Pennsylvania.

Joe Petrali wins 10-Mile Board Track Race with record 111.18mph, September 7 in Laurel, Maryland. This is Petrali's first win under his H-D contract.

Model Year 1926

1926 21-ci "Peashooter" board track racer. *Gene Robbins*

Main Models
26-A Solo: 21ci flathead single with three-speed transmission and magneto

26-B Solo: 21ci flathead single with three-speed transmission and electrical system

26-AA Sport Solo: 21ci OHV single with three-speed transmission and magneto

26-BA Sport Solo: 21ci OHV single with three-speed transmission and magneto

26-S Racer: 21ci OHV racing single with magneto

26-J Solo: 61ci F-head V-twin with three-speed transmission and lighting system

26-JS Sidecar Twin: 61ci F-head V-twin with three-speed transmission, electrical system, and sidecar gearing

26-JD Solo: 74ci F-head V-twin with three-speed transmission and lighting system

26-JDS Sidecar Twin: 74ci F-head V-twin with three-speed transmission and lighting system

Sidecars and Chassis
26-LT: right-hand Tourist Sidecar

26-LX: right-hand Speedster Sidecar

26-M: right-hand commercial side van

26-MO: right-hand commercial side van with open body

26-LC: right-hand chassis for LT body

26-MC: right-hand chassis for M body

26-QT: right-hand two-passenger Tourist Sidecar

26-Q: right-hand chassis to fit QT body

26-Q: right-hand chassis to fit QT body

Retail Prices
Model A: $210

Model B: $235

Model AA: $250

Model BA: $275

Model S: $300

Model J: $315

Model JS: $315

Model JD: $335

Model JDS: $335

Production Totals

Model A: 1,128
Model AA: 61
Model AAE: 146
Model B: 5,979
Model BA: 515
Model BAE (export): 161
Model F: 760
Model FD: 232
Model J: 3,749
Model JD: 9,544

Options

Speedster handlebars
Acetylene lighting
Mesinger tandem seat
Tandem-seat passenger pegs
Tandem-seat yoke bracket with fender hump
Yoke springs
Corbin-Brown speedometer
Johns-Manville speedometer
27x3.85 Balloon Cord tires
27x3.5 High Pressure Fabric tires
Luggage carrier
Hand brake
Jiffy stand
Ammeter, complete
Winter windshield
Light color finish

Paint Colors

Big Twin: Olive Green with Maroon broad striping edged in Black with Gold center pinstriping. Fenders with Maroon broad striping edged in Black; available at extra cost are White or Cream

Singles: Olive Green with Maroon broad striping with Gold center pinstriping

Series S OHV Singles

First Year

The Model S Racing Single is a new model
Engine: 21ci OHV single
Single-speed transmission
Magneto ignition
27in tires
Sager fork
Rectangular folding footboards

Series A and B Peashooter Singles

First Year

The Models A, AA, B, and BA singles were all-new lightweight models that offered the choice of flathead or OHV motors

Engine (Models A and B): 21ci flathead single with 2-7/8x3-1/4in bore and stroke and output of 8hp

Engine (Models AA and BA): 21ci OHV single with 2-7/8x3-1/4in bore and stroke and output of 12hp

Ricardo cylinder heads
Black-painted Klaxon horn
Fully sprung front fender
26x3.30in balloon tires
Teardrop-style tank
Rectangular folding footboards
Single-tube mufflers
Large centrally mounted coil-spring for clutch
Single-tube starter pedal
Three-speed transmission
Switch panel with key lock and control levers (Models B and BA)
Single-row primary chain
Thirteen-tooth cushioned motor sprocket
Thirty-six tooth clutch sprocket
Toolbox mounts under the seat onto the frame, ahead of the rear fender
Two cam gears acting with direct action on mushroom tappets
Each cam gear ported to vent crankcase pressure out of crankcase
Sheet metal chain guard
Single unit electrical system

Series J and JD Big Twins

First Year

Muffler with a cutout to deflect gases away from the rider
Switch panel with key lock and control levers
Wider fenders
Twelve-tooth starter clutch gear
26x3.30in balloon tires
Rust-proofing on nipples and wheel spokes
Long horizontal motion clutch arm
Clutch actuating fork using pushing motion
Gearbox filler plug placed on gearbox front right side
No transmission lockout
No gearshift lock gate
Higher output generator
Automatic-relay generator cutout
Battery with twice the capacity

Motor Company Minutes, 1926

First year production sidecars of H-D design and manufacture.

A separate office is established to handle fleet sales to various law enforcement agencies.

More than 2,500 law agencies are using H-D motorcycles.

1927 B. *Doug Mitchel*

Main Models

27-A Solo: 21ci flathead single with three-speed transmission and magneto

27-B Solo: 21ci flathead single with three-speed transmission and electrical system

27-AA Sport Solo: 21ci OHV single with three-speed transmission and magneto

27-BA Sport Solo: 21ci OHV single with three-speed transmission and electrical system

27-S Racer: OHV racing single with magneto

27-J Solo: 61ci F-head V-twin with three-speed transmission and electrical system

27-JS Sidecar Twin: 61ci F-head V-twin with three-speed transmission and electrical system

27-JD Solo: 74ci F-head V-twin with three-speed transmission and lighting system

27-JDS Sidecar Twin: 74ci F-head V-twin with three-speed transmission with light iron-alloy pistons

Specialty Models

27-SM Racer: OHV single with multiple-speed transmission and magneto ignition

27-T Racer: V-twin racer with magneto ignition

27-SA Racer: single with single-speed transmission and electric ignition

27-SMA Racer: single with multiple-speed transmission and electric ignition

27-AAE Export: OHV single with magneto ignition

27-BAE Export: OHV single with electric ignition

27-F Solo: 61ci V-twin with light iron-alloy pistons and magneto ignition

27-FS Sidecar Twin: 61ci V-twin with light iron-alloy pistons and magneto ignition

27-FK Special Solo: 61ci V-twin with magneto ignition

27-FHAC Hill-Climber Export: 61ci V-twin with magneto ignition

27-FHAD Hill-Climber Domestic: 61ci V-twin with magneto ignition

27-JK Special Solo: 61ci V-twin with generator ignition

27-8-V Special Racer: eight-valve V-twin with Dow-metal pistons and magneto ignition

27-FD Solo: 74ci V-twin with light iron-alloy pistons and magneto ignition

27-FDS Sidecar Twin: 74ci V-twin with light iron-alloy pistons and magneto ignition

27-FDL Special Solo: 74ci V-twin with magneto ignition

27-JDL Special Solo: 74ci V-twin with generator ignition

Sidecars and Chassis

27-LT: Tourist Sidecar

27-LX: Speedster Sidecar

27-M: commercial side van

27-MO: commercial side van with open body

27-LC: chassis for LT body

27-LC: chassis for LT body

27-MC: chassis for M box

27-QT: two-passenger Tourist Sidecar

27-Q: chassis to fit QT body

27-Q: chassis to fit QT body

Retail Prices

Model A: $210

Model B: $235

Model AA: $250

Model BA: $275

Model S: $300

Model J: $310

Model JS: $310

Model JD: $320

Model JDS: $320

Production Totals

Model A: 444

Model B: 3,711

Model AA: 32

Model BA: 481

Model S: 6

Model SM: 26

Model AAE: 66

Model BAE: 43

Model SMA: 8

Model F: 246

Model FD: 209

Model J: 3,561

Model JD: 9,691

Model FHAD: 8

Model FHAC: 11

Model T: 1

Model 8V: 2

Options

Mesinger tandem seat

Tandem-seat yoke bracket with fender hump

Tandem-seat passenger pegs

Yoke springs

Loose-wound hooked coil springs

Winter windshield

Luggage carrier

Hand brake for singles

Hand control for foot brake for Big Twins

Jiffy stand

Ammeter, complete

Corbin speedometer

27x3.85 Balloon Cord tires

25x3.85 Balloon Cord tires

27x3.50 High Pressure Fabric tires

Paint Colors

Twins: Olive Green with Maroon broad striping edged in Black with a Gold center pinstriping; available at extra cost are White or Cream

Singles: Olive Green with Maroon broad striping and a Gold center pinstriping

Series A and B Peashooter Singles

First Year

New Ricardo cylinder heads (Models AA and BA)
Reinforced frame
Hinged-band brake
Adjustable foot clutch pedal
Reinforced fuel tanks
Deeper bucket-shaped saddle
Heavier duty clutch spring
Larger crankcase mounting tabs
Muffler designed to reduce back pressure
Transmission oil drain plug redesigned for easier maintenance
Alemite grease gun, tire pump, and adjustable wrench are standard equipment

Series J and JD Big Twins

First Year

"Wasted-spark" distributorless ignition using a circuit breaker and a single coil firing both spark plugs at once
Headlight wiring simplified to remove four connections
Angle-tooth sprockets
Ventilated motor inlet-housing caps

Motor Company Minutes, 1927

The H-D riding Utah Highway Patrolmen is founded.
October, first public announcement of the "Twin 45" model by President Walter Davidson at stockholder's meeting.

Model Year 1928

Main Models

28-B Solo: 21ci flathead single with three-speed transmission and electrical system

28-BA Sport Solo: 21ci OHV single with three-speed transmission and electrical system

28-J Solo: 61ci F-head V-twin with three-speed transmission and electrical system

28-JS Sidecar Twin: 61ci F-head V-twin with three-speed transmission and electrical system

28-JX Sport Solo: 61ci F-head V-twin with three-speed transmission and electrical system

28-JXL Special Sport Solo: 61ci F-head V-twin with three-speed transmission, electrical system, and Dow-metal pistons

28-JH Solo: 61ci F-head Two-Cam V-twin with three-speed transmission, electrical system, and Dow-metal pistons

28-JD Solo: 74ci F-head V-twin with three-speed transmission and electrical system

28-JDS Sidecar Twin: 74ci F-head V-twin with three-speed transmission and electrical system

28-JDX Sport Solo: 74ci F-head V-twin with three-speed transmission

28-JDXL Special Sport Solo: 74ci F-head V-twin with three-speed transmission, electrical system, and Dow-metal pistons

28-JDH Solo: 74ci F-head Two-Cam V-twin with three-speed transmission and Dow-metal pistons

Specialty Models

28-A: single with magneto ignition

28-AA: OHV single with magneto ignition

28-AAE Export: OHV single with magneto ignition

28-F Solo: 61ci V-twin with magneto ignition and light iron-alloy pistons

28-FS Sidecar Twin: 61ci V-twin with magneto ignition and light iron-alloy pistons

28-FH Special Solo: 61ci V-twin with magneto ignition, small wheels, and solo bars

28-FHAD Hill-Climber Domestic: 61ci V-twin with magneto ignition

28-FD Solo: 74ci V-twin with light iron-alloy pistons and magneto ignition

28-FDS Sidecar Twin: 74ci V-twin with light iron-alloy pistons and magneto ignition

28-FDH Special Solo: 74ci V-twin with magneto ignition, small wheels, and solo bars

28-FHAC Hill-Climber Export: 61ci V-twin with magneto ignition

28-S Racer: single with magneto ignition

28-SA Special Racer: single with magneto ignition

28-SM Racer: single with multiple-speed transmission and magneto ignition

28-SMA Racer: single with multiple-speed transmission and magneto ignition

28-T Racer: V-twin with magneto ignition

28-8-V Racer: eight-valve V-twin with magneto ignition

28-BAE Export: OHV single with electric ignition

Sidecars and Chassis

28-LC: chassis for LT body
28-LC: chassis for LT body
28-LT: Tourist Sidecar
28-LX: Speedster Sidecar
28-Q: chassis to fit QT body
28-Q: chassis to fit QT body
28-QT: two-passenger Tourist Sidecar
28-M: commercial side van
28-MC: chassis for M body
28-MO: commercial side van with open body
28-MW: commercial side van, 56in tread
28-MWC: chassis to fit MWB body
28-MWX: commercial express van with screens, extra wide
28-MWXP: commercial express van with panels, extra wide
28-MX: commercial express van with screens, standard width
28-MXP: commercial express van with panels, standard width

Retail Prices

Model B: $235
Model BA: $255
Model J: $310
Model JS: $310
Model JX: $310
Model JXL: $325
Model JD: $320
Model JDS: $320
Model JDX: $320
Model JDXL: $335
Model JH: $360
Model JDH: $390

Production Totals

Model A: 519
Model AA: 65
Model AAF: 4
Model B: 3,483
Model BA: 943
Model BAF: 207
Model F: 141
Model FD: 131
Model J: 4,184
Model JD: 11,007

Options

Tandem-seat yoke bracket with fender hump
27x3.85 Balloon Cord tires
26x3.30 Balloon Cord tires
25x3.85 Balloon Cord tires
27x3.5 High Pressure Fabric tires
Wicker sidecar
Left-hand throttle control for Big Twins
Police plate on front fender for police only
Schebler Deluxe carburetor
Model H Schebler carburetor
Luggage carrier
Jiffy stand
Ammeter, complete
Corbin speedometer
Speedometer light
Air cleaner (with Schebler Deluxe carburetor only)
Mesinger tandem seat
Tandem-seat passenger pegs
Yoke springs
Winter windshield
Front wheel brake for Big Twins
Solo bars for Twins
Speedster bars for Singles
Retrofit four-tube muffler-bracket kit

Paint Colors

Twins: Olive Green with broad Maroon striping edged in Black pinstripes with a Gold center pinstriping; available at extra cost are Black, Fawn Gray, Azure Blue, Maroon, Coach Green, White, Cream, or Police Blue

Singles: Olive Green with broad Maroon striping and a Gold center pinstriping

Models B and BA

First Year

Two-ring Dow-metal pistons standard (Model B)
Lighter flywheels and connecting rods
Throttle-controlled oil pump
Hinged rear fender
Wider fenders
Front wheel brake
5/16in-wide front and rear chains
Larger size wheel spokes
Air cleaner
23-1/2in clutch sprocket with 47 teeth
Guide rings on the piston (Model BA)
Expander "cushion" ring behind guide ring (Model BA)
19-tooth cushion motor sprocket
Cushion sprocket using eight rubber blocks placed between the sprocket and sprocket hub
46-tooth clutch sprocket
19-tooth transmission sprocket
47-tooth rear sprocket

Series J and JD Big Twins

First Year
Air cleaner
25x3.85 tires standard
Larger capacity fuel pump connected to the throttle
Oil-control cover (late year)
Front-wheel brake
Second return spring on front wheel brake (late year)
Control coil for brake adjusted by 15/16in hollow bolt
Larger size wheel spokes
Addition of gussets at frame points
Gearshift interlock on transmission reintroduced
Gearshift lock gate reintroduced
Cooling fins designed around both the valve pocket and cylinder
Inlet rocker arms redesigned for a larger bushing

Only Year
No oil-control cover (early year)

Series JH and JDH Two-Cam Big Twins

First Year
The Models JH (61ci) and (JDH (74ci) are variants of the Models J and JD with the high-performance Two-Cam motor and a slimmer sport chassis
Engine (JH): 61ci F-head Two-Cam V-twin with 3-5/16x3-1/2in bore and stroke
Engine (JDH): 74.66ci F-head Two-Cam V-twin with 3-7/16x4in bore and stroke
Direct-action valve gear with cam lobes moving tappets rather than roller arms
Removable lifter blocks routing oil back to the crankcase
Dow-metal domed pistons
Narrow 4.75gal tanks
18in wheels standard
Throttle-controlled oil pump
Air cleaner
No oil-control cover
Cooling fins designed around both the valve pocket and cylinder
Inlet rocker arms redesigned for a larger diameter bushing (late year)
Larger size wheel spokes
Roadster handlebars standard
Two pair thick guide rings on each piston
Expander ring behind each guide ring
Front-wheel brake
Second return spring on front brake (late year)
Public sale of Road Model "Two-Cam 61"

Series JX, JXL, JDX, and JDXL Special Sport Solo Big Twins

First Year
The Models JX, JXL, JDX, and JDXL combine the slimmer, lower chassis of the JH and JDH with a high-performance version of the J and JD motors
Engines have larger inlet valves and valve cages
Dow-metal pistons (Models JXL and JDXL)
Two pair thick guide rings on each piston (Models JXL and JDXL)
Expander ring behind each guide ring (Models JXL and JDXL)
Narrow 4.75gal tanks
Air cleaner
18in wheels standard
Roadster handlebars standard
Racing-style tapered cylinder cooling fins
Front-wheel brake
Second return spring on front brake (late year)
Larger size wheel spokes
Throttle-controlled oil pump
Oil control cover (late year)
Cooling fins designed around both the valve pocket and cylinder
Inlet rocker arms redesigned for a larger bushing than standard

Only Year
No oil-control cover (early year)

Specialty Notes
Limited number of specially built Ricardo F-head cylinders with a compression ratio of 10:1 sold to dealers for racing and hill climbing.
Experimental prototype V-Four Model. 90ci; flathead V-Four; 1,475cc; side-valve; shaft-driven. No further details available.
Experimental prototype V-Four Model. 80ci; flathead V-Four; 1,300cc; side-valve; chain-driven. No further details available.

Motor Company Minutes, 1928
William H. Davidson, son of William A. Davidson, joins the company.
The Department of the Interior orders 25 sidecars for use by National Park Rangers.
Dudley Perkins honored as the largest dealer in United States for Package Truck sales.

Model Year 1929

1929 JDH. *Randy Leffingwell*

Main Models

29-B Solo: 21ci flathead single cylinder with three-speed transmission

29-BA Sport Solo: 21ci flathead single with three-speed transmission

29-C Solo: 30.50ci flathead single with three-speed transmission

29-D Solo: 45ci low-compression flathead V-twin with three-speed transmission and Dow-metal pistons

29-DL Sport Solo: 45ci high-compression flathead V-twin with three-speed transmission and Dow-metal pistons

29-J Solo: 61ci F-head V-twin with three-speed transmission and electrical system

29-JH Two-Cam Solo: 61ci Two-Cam F-head V-twin with three-speed transmission and Dow-metal pistons

29-JS Sidecar Twin: 74ci F-head V-twin with three-speed transmission and Dow-metal pistons

29-JD Solo: 74ci F-head V-twin with three-speed transmission and iron-alloy pistons

29-JDS Sidecar Twin: 74ci F-head V-twin with three-speed transmission and iron-alloy pistons

29-JDH Two-Cam Solo: 74ci Two-Cam F-head V-twin with three-speed transmission and Dow-metal pistons

Specialty Models

29-A: single with magneto ignition

29-AA: OHV single with magneto ignition

29-F Solo: 61ci V-twin with light iron-alloy pistons and magneto ignition

29-FS Sidecar Twin: 61ci V-twin with light iron-alloy pistons and magneto ignition

29-FL Solo: 61ci "L-motor" V-twin with Dow-metal pistons

29-FD Solo: 74ci V-twin with light iron-alloy pistons and magneto ignition

29-FDS Sidecar Twin: 74ci V-twin with light iron-alloy pistons and magneto ignition

29-FDH Special Solo: 74ci "H-motor" Two-Cam V-twin

29-FDL Solo: 74ci "DL-motor" V-twin with Dow-metal pistons

29-FHAC Racer: 61ci V-twin with three-speed transmission

29-FHAD Hill-Climber: 61ci V-twin

29-SA Special Racer: single with single-speed transmission

29-SMA Special Racer: single with multiple-speed transmission

29-T Racer: V-twin with single-speed transmission

29-BAF Export: OHV two-port single

29-JXL Solo: "L-motor" 61ci V-twin with Dow-metal pistons

29-JDXL Solo: "DL-motor" 74ci V-twin with Dow-metal pistons

29-JDF: 74ci V-twin with Two Unit system

Sidecars and Chassis

29-LC: chassis for LT body with 46-1/8in tread

29-LC: chassis for LT body with 46-1/8in tread

29-LT: single-passenger sidecar, 46-1/8in tread

29-Q: chassis for QT body, 56in tread

29-QT: two-passenger sidecar, 56in tread

29-Q: chassis for QT body, 56in tread

29-M: side van with cover with 49in tread

29-MC: chassis for M box with 49in tread

29-MO: side van without cover, for 49in tread

29-MW: side van without cover, for 56in tread

29-MWC: chassis for MW body, for 56in tread

29-MWP: side van with panels, for 56in tread

29-MXP: side van with panels, for 49in tread

29-LX: Speedster Sidecar

29-LS: single-passenger sidecar for 45ci Twin

29-MX: Commercial Express with screens-standard width

29-MDC: dryer's and cleaner's side van with 49in tread

29-MNP: newspaper side van with 49in tread

Retail Prices

Model B: $235

Model BA: $255

Model C: $255

Model D: $290

Model DL: $290

Model J: $310

Model JS: $310

Model JD: $320

Model JDS: $320

Model JDH: $370

Production Totals

    Model D: 4,513
    Model DL: 2,343
    Model F: 191
    Model FD: 73
    Model J: 2,886
    Model JD: 10,182
    Model A: 197
    Model AA: 21
    Model AAF: 5
    Model B: 1,592
    Model BA: 191
    Model BAF: 213
    Model C: 1,570
    Model CM: 12

Options

    Air cleaner
    Mesinger tandem seat
    Tandem-seat yoke bracket with fender hump
    Tandem-seat passenger pegs
    Yoke springs
    Solo handlebars
    Speedster handlebars
    Cadmium-plated wheel rims
    Accessory lighting
    Retrofit four-tube muffler kits
    Model D high-performance kit
    Winter windshield
    Luggage carrier
    Jiffy stand
    Front stand
    Commercial motor
    Dow-metal pistons for Models J and JD
    Speedometer light
    Corbin speedometer
    26x.30 Balloon Cord Tires
    27x3.85 Balloon Cord Tires
    25x3.85 Balloon Cord Tires
    27x3.50 High Pressure Fabric Tires

Paint Colors

Big Twins: Olive Green with broad Maroon striping edged in Black pinstripes with a Gold center pinstriping; available at extra cost are Black, Coach Green, Fawn Gray, Azure Blue, Orange, Maroon, Cream, Police Blue (police only), or any colors ordered in a two-color combination

Singles and 45 Twins: Olive Green with broad Maroon striping and a Gold center pinstriping

Series B 21ci Singles

First Year

Dow-metal pistons standard on Model AA
Dual bullet headlights, except on Model B Export
Fourteen longer and smaller coil springs placed around clutch circumference (late year)
3/8in thick steel collar used as clutch pushrod guide (early year)
Two friction discs added to the clutch

Only Year

Clutch has twelve small coil springs placed around its circumference (early year)
Four tube "Pipes O' Pan" muffler, except on Model B Export
Dow-metal pistons standard on Model BA

Series C 30.50ci Singles

First Year

The Model C is a new model featuring a 30.50ci (500c) single engine in the chassis of the Model B 21ci single
Engine: 30.50ci (500cc) flathead single with 3-3/32x4in bore and stroke and an output of 10hp
Cylindrical toolbox mounted across front fork
Cup-and-cone style rear axle bearings
Wheelbase measures 57.5in
Black-painted Klaxon horn
Dual-bullet headlights
Six-volt electrical system
Double-row primary chain drive
Shrouded-style taillight
Rectangular folding footboards

Only Year

Clincher wheel rims
5-1/4gal tanks
Four-tube "Pipes O' Pan" muffler
Tubular front forks
Model B frame on Model C
Twelve small coil springs designed around clutch circumference (early year)

Series D 45ci V-Twins

First Year

The Model D was an all-new model 45ci V-twin

Engine: 45ci flathead V-twin with 2-3/4x3-13/16in bore and stroke

Battery and coil ignition

Dow-metal pistons

Removable Ricardo heads

Seven-bolt-hole cylinders

Rear crankcase baffle drilled with three holes in each baffle side (late year)

Roller bearings on the drive side with a plain journal bearing on the pinion gear side

Four-dowel-pin gear-case cover matching up to a four-pin right crankcase (late year)

Four cam gears, each gear having its own lobe

Connecting rod little ends run, without bushings, directly on the piston wrist pin

Fourteen-spring clutch (late year)

Three-speed sliding-gear transmission

Manual kickstarter

Dry clutch

Fiber discs riveted to the clutch sprocket (early year)

Throw-out bearing made of a three-piece sandwiched bearing assembly

Duplex-chain primary drive

Rectangular folding footboards

Streamlined fuel/oil tanks

Cup-and-cone-style rear axle bearing

Black-painted Klaxon horn

Dual bullet headlights

Cushion sprocket uses eight rubber blocks between the sprocket hub and sprocket

Front fork extended 1in (midyear)

18in wheels

Front fender bracing geometry redesigned (midyear)

Plunger-type crankcase oil drain

Sheet-metal chainguard

Gearbox mounted directly onto the frame

Removable side cover on transmission

Only Year

Front chain lubricated by the air-oil mist of crankcase blow-by

Clincher wheel rims

4-3/8gal tanks (early year)

Four-tube "Pipes O' Pan" muffler

Twelve-spring "Singles" clutch

Two-dowel-pin-hole gear-case cover matching up to a two-pin right crankcase (early year)

Tubular-type front forks

Full baffles under each cylinder (early year)

Straight front, single downtube frame

3/16in thick steel collar used as clutch pushrod guide (very early year)

No toolbox mounted across front fork

Series J and JD Big Twins

Only Year

Dual bullet headlights

Electrical-switch panel with ammeter mounted to canter of bars

Four-tube "Pipes O' Pan" muffler

New, high-frequency horn

Adjustable generator output controller

Cover for throttle-controlled oiler

Inlet rocker arms with a larger diameter bushing

Felt washer along with a retainer cap on the lower end of inlet pushrod assemblies

(F-head Big Twin models discontinued at the end of the 1929 model year)

Motor Company Minutes, 1929

H-D's only real competition came from the Excelsior motorcycle and the Indian motorcycle, the last few of a long line of H-D competitors left.

Charles "Red" Wolverton opens his H-D dealership in Reading, Pennsylvania.

H-D has now supplied over 2,900 law enforcement agencies across the country.

Joining the family business are Walter C. Davidson, his brother Gordon Davidson, and William J. Harley.

The California Highway Patrol's first order, some Model JDs.

A nationwide drop in motorcycle sales this year. Due to the Great Depression, many other motorcycle companies go out of business.

CHAPTER 4

1930-1939

Model Year 1930

1930 V. *Doug Mitchel*

Main Models

30-B Solo: 21ci flathead single with three-speed transmission and electrical system

30-C Solo: 30.50ci flathead single with three-speed transmission

30-D Solo: 45ci low-compression flathead V-twin with three-speed transmission and Dow-metal pistons

30-DS Sidecar Twin: 45ci low-compression flathead V-twin with three-speed transmission

30-DL Sport Solo: 45ci high-compression flathead V-twin with three-speed transmission and Dow-metal pistons

30-DLD Special Sport Solo: 45ci high-compression flathead V-twin with three-speed transmission

30-V Solo: 74ci medium-compression flathead V-twin with three-speed transmission and Dow-metal pistons

30-VL Sport Solo: 74ci high-compression flathead V-twin with three-speed transmission and Dow-metal pistons

30-VS Sidecar Twin: 74ci flathead V-twin with three-speed transmission and Dow-metal pistons

30-VC Commercial: 74ci flathead V-twin with three-speed transmission and nickel-iron pistons

Specialty Models

30-A: single with magneto ignition

30-AA: single with overhead valve

30-CM: 30.50ci flathead single

30-VCM: 74ci V-twin with nickel-iron pistons

30-VLM: 74ci V-twin with magneto

30-VM Solo: 74ci V-twin with magneto

30-VMS Sidecar Twin: 74ci V-twin with magneto

30-VMG: 74ci V-twin with magneto

30-BR Special: 21ci flathead single

30-BAF: Two-Port 21ci OHV single

Sidecars and Chassis

30-LC: chassis for LT body, 47-7/8in tread

30-LT: single-passenger sidecar, 47-7/8in tread

30-LS: single-passenger sidecar for 45ci twin

30-LSC: chassis for LS body

30-Q: chassis for QT body, 58-1/8in tread

30-QT: two-passenger sidecar, 58-1/8in tread

30-M: side van with cover, 49-3/4in tread

30-MC: chassis for M box, 49-3/4in tread

30-MO: side van without cover, 49-3/4in tread

30-MXP: double-compartment side van, 49-3/4in tread

30-MDC: dryer's and cleaner's side van, 49-3/4in tread

30-MNP: newspaper side van, 49-3/4in tread

30-MW: side van without cover, 56-3/4in tread

30-MWC: chassis for MW body, 56-3/4in tread

30-MWP: double-compartment side van, 56-3/4in tread

30-MT: mail Package Truck, 49-3/4in tread

30-GM: Goulding side van with cover

30-GMC: Goulding chassis with commercial check strap

Retail Prices

Model B: $235

Model C: $260

Model D: $310

Model DS: $310

Model DL: $310

Model BA: $255

Model DLD: $310

Model V: $340

Model VL: $340

Model VS: $340

Model VC: $340

Model VM: $340

Model VLM: $340

Production Totals

Model A: 4
Model AA: 1
Model B: 577
Model BA: 9
Model BAF: 86
Model BR: 95
Model C: 1,483
Model CM: 11
Model CR: 135
Model D: 2,000
Model DS: 213
Model DL: 3,191
Model DLD: 206
Model VMS: 13
Model VMG: 19
Model V: 1,960
Model VS: 3,612
Model VL: 3,246
Model VC: 1,174
Model VM: 1

Options

Solo bars
Retrofit four-tube-muffler kit
Steering damper
Speedometer light
80mph plain speedometer
100mph hand speedometer
Police Special speedometer
Model D high-performance kit
Left foot clutch
Front stand
Hand clutch control
Jiffy stand
Luggage carrier
Fancy dual ignition keys
20x3.30in balloon tires for Model B
18x4in balloon tires for Models D and C
19x4in balloon tires for Models V
19x4.40 balloon tires for Models V
Narrow-bucket tandem seat of H-D design
Tandem-seat yoke bracket with fender hump
Mesinger tandem seat
Tandem-seat passenger pegs
Yoke springs
Winter windshield
Air cleaner

Paint Colors

Twins: Olive Green with broad Vermilion striping edged in Maroon with a Gold center pinstriping; available at extra cost are Maroon, Cream, Azure Blue, Fawn Gray, Coach Green, or Police Blue; any combination of colors could be ordered in a two-color combination

Singles: Olive Green with broad Vermilion striping and Gold center pinstriping

Series B 21ci Singles

First Year

Lever actuated steering damper optional
New handlebars, except on Export Model B
Drop-center wheel rims, except on Export Model B
Coil-spring type contact points, except on Export Model B
Generator with two independent field coils, except on Export Model B
Two-tube muffler, except on Export Model B, which has four-tube muffler

Only Year

Single headlight on Export Model Two-Port only

Series C 30.50ci Singles

First Year

Chassis from the Model D 45ci twin
New frame that lowers saddle height, increases ground clearance, and allows easier access to battery
Drop-forged I-beam front forks
Tool box mounted on the forks
Bullet-shaped tanks
Theft-proof lock on steering head
Automatic oiling of primary chain
Larger clutch
Front brake drum is built integral with wheel hub
Drop-center wheel rims
Dual-key tank-top panel
Two-tube muffler
Double-chain primary drive

Series D 45ci V-Twins

First Year

New frame that lowers saddle height, increases ground clearance, and allows easier access to battery
Drop-forged I-beam front forks
Tool box mounted on the forks
Bullet-shaped tanks
Theft-proof lock on steering head
Automatic oiling of primary chain
Larger clutch
Front brake drum is built integral with wheel hub
Drop-center wheel rims
Dual-key tank-top panel
Generator with two independent field coils; one coil is cut out until the headlight switch is turned on
Double-chain primary drive

Only Year

Banjo fitting installed under oil pump's oil chamber screw bleeding oil to front chain
Cylindrical toolbox mounted across front forks
Two-tube muffler

Series V 74ci Big Twins

First Year

The Model V is the new Big Twin, replacing the F-head Models J and JD
Engine: 74ci (1,200cc) flathead (side-valve) V-twin with bore and stroke of 3-7/16inx4in

Ricardo removable heads

Magnesium-alloy pistons

New valve springs and covers

Three-piece valve covers (midyear)

Cylinder heads designed with oil deflector to prevent fouled spark plugs

Ported rear exhaust cam gear shaft

Each valve has individual cam and cam gears

Down-draft intake manifold

Total-loss oiling/lubrication system

Breather of a new design, starting with engine number 7290

Stiff-action nine-spring clutch with 220.89sq-in of friction surface

Double-chain primary drive

Automatic oiling of primary chain

Three-speed sliding-gear transmission

Oil deflector designed into the left side of three-speed transmission

Front and rear cast-in mounting "ears" on transmission housing

Frame 25 percent heavier, with front fork lock built in

Drop-forged I-beam front forks

Shifter gate on three-speed Models

Rectangular folding footboards

Interchangeable stepped-hub front and rear wheels

Internal-expanding shoe rear brake

Drop-center wheel rims

Dual-key tank top panel

Tank indented on right side for rear spark plug (late year)

Two mounting brackets riveted on twin-lead coil body

Three-brush generator

Generator with two independent field coils; one coil is cut out until the headlight switch is turned on

New seat-post springs

Only Year

Two-piece valve covers (early year)

Tank on right side not indented by rear spark plug (early year)

Dual bullet headlights

Cylindrical toolbox mounted across front forks

Two-piece step-down transmission bushing mounted and keyed to mainshaft

Light-action six-spring clutch (early year)

Black-painted Klaxon horn

Two-tube muffler

Specialty Notes

First experimental commercial street painter sidecar rig for painting street and highway lines; the striping rig was designed for the wrong side, putting the driver in the flow of traffic.

Motor Company Minutes, 1930

Foreign sales total 7,630 motorcycles.

The Buffalo, New York, Police Department orders 17 Model VLs.

Over 3,000 law enforcement agencies around the United States are now riding H-Ds.

An aggressive sales campaign is launched to export markets. Foreign markets are sought due to Depression back in United States.

Racing Notes

William H. Davidson wins 20th Anniversary Jack Pine Endurance Race riding a Model 30-DLD.

Olle Virgil wins Dirt Track Series of Sweden and Denmark with record 111.78mph, riding H-D Model 45.

Model Year 1931

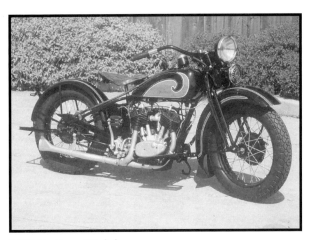

1931 D. *Doug Mitchel*

Main Models

31-C Solo: 30.50ci flathead single with three-speed transmission

31-D Solo: 45ci low-compression flathead V-twin with three-speed transmission

31-DS Sidecar Twin: 45ci low-compression flathead V-twin with three-speed transmission and sidecar gearing

31-DL Sport Solo: 45ci high-compression flathead V-twin with three-speed transmission

31-DLD Special Sport Solo: 45ci high-compression flathead V-twin with three-speed transmission

31-V Solo: 74ci medium-compression flathead V-twin with three-speed transmission

31-VS Sidecar Twin: 74ci medium-compression flathead V-twin with three-speed transmission and sidecar gearing

31-VL: Sport Solo 74ci high-compression flathead V-twin with three-speed transmission

31-VC Commercial: 74ci low-compression flathead V-twin with three-speed transmission

Specialty Models

31-VMS Sidecar Twin: 74ci flathead V-twin with three-speed transmission and magneto

31-VLM: 74ci high-compression flathead V-twin with three-speed transmission and magneto

31-VMG: 74ci flathead V-twin with three-speed transmission and magneto

31-VCR: 74ci low-compression flathead V-twin with three-speed transmission for road-marking

31-RM: no details available

31-CH: single; no details available

31-B: flathead single with generator ignition

31-BA: OHV single

31-CMG: single; no details available

31-CC: single; no details available

31-DC: no details available

Sidecars and Chassis

31-LT: single-passenger sidecar, without apron
31-LS: sidecar for 45ci twin
31-QT: two-passenger sidecar
31-M: Package Truck, complete with cover
31-MO: Package Truck, without cover
31-MXP: Package Truck (panel type)
31-MT: Package Truck (panel type, built over springs)
31-MDC: Package Truck for dryers and cleaners
31-MNP: Package Truck for newspapers
31-MW: Package Truck with 56in road tread
31-MWP: Package Truck (panel type), 56in tread
31-LC: chassis for LT sidecar bodies
31-LSC: chassis for LS sidecar bodies
31-Q: chassis for QT sidecar bodies
31-MC: chassis for M, MO, MXP, MDC, MNP, and MT truck bodies
31-MWC: chassis for MW and MWP truck bodies
31-LT: body only
31-LS: body only
31-QT: body only
31-M: body only
31-MO: body only
31-MXP: body only
31-MDC: body only
31-MT: body only
31-MNP: body only
31-MW: body only
31-MWP: body only

Retail Prices

Model V: $340
Model VL: $340
Model VM: $340
Model VS: $340
Model VC: $340
Model D: $310
Model DS: $310
Model DL: $310
Model DLD: $325
Model C: $260

Production Totals

Model C: 874
Model CH: 180
Model B: 2
Model BA: 1
Model CMG: 2
Model CC: 3
Model D: 715
Model DS: 276
Model DL: 1,306
Model DLD: 241
Model DC: 11
Model V: 825
Model VS: 1,994
Model VL: 3,477
Model VS: 465
Model VMS: 1
Model VLM: 1
Model VMG: 17
Model VSR: 10
Model RM: 6

Options

Many optional colors
Cadmium-plated wheel rims
Special scroll pattern on tank panels
Dual headlights
Catalog listed extra cost color options
Narrow-bucket tandem seat of H-D design
Tandem-seat yoke bracket with fender hump
Model D high-performance kit
Fancy dual ignition keys
Air cleaner
Luggage carrier
Jiffy stand
Front stand
Front-wheel siren
Pyrene extinguishers and brackets
80mph plain speedometer
100mph hand speedometer
Police special speedometer
Solo bars
First aid kit and box
Speedometer light
Steering damper
Hand clutch control for Models C and D only
Cadmium-plated rims
18x4in balloon tires for Models C and D
19x4in balloon tires for Models V
19x4.50in balloon tires for Models V
Mesinger tandem seat
Yoke springs
Tandem-seat passenger pegs
Winter windshield

Paint Colors

All models: Olive Green with broad Vermilion striping edged in Maroon with a Gold center pinstriping; available at extra cost are Solid White with Gold broad striping edged with Gold pinstripes, Maroon and Cream with Vermilion broad striping and Gold center pinstripe, Black and Vermilion with one Gold broad stripe and one Gold pinstripe, Olive Green and Vermilion with one Gold broad stripe and one Gold pinstripe, or Police Blue and Fawn Gray with one Vermilion broad stripe and one Gold pinstripe

Series B 21ci Singles

First/Only Year

Series B singles are for foreign sales only

First Year

Piston-pin lock rings
Gear lock installed in the transmission
Big Twin rear wheel brake
Chrome plating of small parts

Series C 30.50ci Singles

First Year
- Gear lock installed in transmission
- F-head Big Twin rear brake
- Chrome plating of small parts
- Wedge-shaped toolbox mounted across front fork
- John Brown Motolamp 7in headlight with a flat diffusing lens
- Horn with "Sunburst Face"; horn body gloss black paint and cover is chrome plated; mounted below the headlight
- New piston-pin lock rings (midyear)
- New standard handlebars
- Shorter Speedster handlebars optional

Series D 45ci V-Twins

First/Only Year
- Horn with "Sunburst Face"; horn body gloss black paint and cover is chrome plated; mounted below the headlight
- Die-cast Schebler Deluxe carburetor
- "Sifton Treatment" of frames. Reinforcement welded to the frame
- Wedge-shaped toolbox mounted across front fork
- John Brown Motolamp 7in headlight with a flat diffusing lens
- Gear lock installed in transmission
- F-head Big Twin rear brake
- Installation of a new generator drive gear set containing a new generator drive gear, generator drive shaft and generator drive shaft bevel gear with pin (midyear)
- Revised oil-pump assembly with a bleeder line leading directly from pump body
- Fishtail muffler
- Revised valve spring covers
- Revised seat-post cushion springs
- Chrome plating of small parts
- Piston-pin bushings
- New piston-pin lock rings (midyear)
- Revised gear cover and oiler
- Revised crankcase relief pipe
- Revised police sirens
- New clutch assembly having a different sprocket, inner roller race and bearing washers, key ring and outer clutch disc, with an additional fiber plate and steel plate (Model DLD only)
- New standard handlebars
- Shorter Speedster handlebars optional
- (The Series D 45ci twins were discontinued at the end of the model year)

Series V 74ci Big Twins

First Year
- Horn with "Sunburst Face"; horn body gloss black paint and cover is chrome plated; mounted below the headlight
- Constant mesh starter (prevents gear jamming and makes starting easier)
- Die-cast Schebler Deluxe carburetor
- Cadmium-plated brake and clutch pedals
- Thicker piston cushion rings made of vanadium steel matched to thinner guide rings
- New piston-pin lock rings (midyear)
- New brake linings
- Three-speed-with reverse transmission optional (midyear)
- Wedge-shaped toolbox mounted across front fork
- Pistons 1/16in shorter than standard (Model VC and VCR only)
- John Brown Motolamp 7in headlight with a flat diffusing lens
- Burgess-brand single-tube muffler with fishtail
- A removable viewing plug on left side of crankcase added, which allows the flywheel to be seen to adjust the ignition timing
- Chrome plating of small parts

Motor Company Minutes, 1931
- William H. Davidson named to the company board of directors.
- Factory runs at only 10 percent of its total capacity.
- Gross revenue is $4,173,000.
- The company loss is $17,000.
- Engineering Department receives approval to design a sump oiler engine, the 61ci OHV V-twin.
- H-D's only competition left is the Indian motorcycle manufactured by Hendee Manufacturing.

Racing Notes
- H-D wins Daytona Grand National Championship.
- Joe Petrali wins 10-Mile Race, Hamilton Speedway, June 21, 69.88mph.
- Joe Petrali wins 5-Mile Race at Hamilton Speedway, June 21 with record 69.75mph.

Model Year 1932

Main Models

32-B Solo: 21ci flathead single with three-speed transmission and electrical system

32-C Solo: 30.50ci flathead single with three-speed transmission

32-R Solo: 45ci low-compression flathead V-twin with three-speed transmission

32-RS Sidecar Twin: 45ci low-compression flathead V-twin with three-speed transmission

32-RL Sport Solo: 45ci high-compression flathead V-twin with three-speed transmission and Dow-metal pistons

32-RLD Special Sport Solo: 45ci high-compression flathead V-twin with three-speed transmission

32-V Solo: 74ci medium-compression flathead V-twin with three-speed transmission

32-VS Sidecar Twin: 74ci medium-compression flathead V-twin with three-speed transmission and sidecar gearing

32-VL Sport Solo: 74ci high-compression flathead V-twin with three-speed transmission

32-VC Commercial: 74ci low-compression flathead V-twin with three-speed transmission

32-G Servi-Car with tow bar: 45ci flathead V-twin with three-speed transmission (late-year introduction)

32-GA Servi-Car without tow bar: 45ci flathead V-twin with three-speed transmission (late-year introduction)

32-GD large-compartment Servi-Car without tow bar: 45ci flathead V-twin with three-speed transmission (late-year introduction)

32-GE large-compartment Servi-Car with air tank: 45ci flathead V-twin with three-speed transmission (late-year introduction)

Specialty Models

32-CC: single; no details available

32-CR: single; no details available

32-CS: single; no details available

Sidecars and Chassis

32-LT: single-passenger sidecar, without apron

32-LS: sidecar for 45ci twin

32-QT: two-passenger sidecar

32-M: Package Truck, complete with cover

32-MO: Package Truck, without cover

32-MXP: Package Truck (panel type)

32-MT: Package Truck (panel type, built over springs)

32-MDC: Package Truck for dryers and cleaners

32-MNP: Package Truck for newspapers

32-MW: Package Truck, 56in tread

32-MWP: Package Truck (panel type), 56in tread

32-LC: chassis for LT sidecar bodies

32-LSC: chassis for LS sidecar bodies

32-Q: chassis for QT sidecar bodies

32-MC: chassis for M, MO, MXP, MDC, MNP, and MT truck bodies

32-MWC: chassis for MW and MWP truck bodies

32-LT: body only

32-LS: body only

32-QT: body only

32-M: body only

32-MO: body only

32-MXP: body only

32-MDC: body only

32-MT: body only

32-MNP: body only

32-MW: body only

32-MWP: body only

Retail Prices

Model B: $195

Model C: $235

Model R: $295

Model RS: $295

Model RL: $295

Model RLD: $310

Model V: $320

Model VS: $320

Model VL: $320

Model VC: $320

Model G: $450

Production Totals

Model C: 213

Model CC: 7

Model CR: 220

Model CS: 100

Model B: 535

Model V: 478

Model VS: 1,233

Model VL: 2,684

Model VC: 239

Model VMG: 1

Model RM: 1

Model GE: 5

Model GD: 36

Model R: 410

Model RS: 111

Model RL: 628

Model RLD : 98

Model G and GA: 219

Options

Safety guards

Tandem-seat yoke bracket with fender hump

Tandem seat, H-D design, narrow bucket seat

Scrollwork, two-color paint schemes, and decals for gas tanks

Chrome plating on selected parts

Cadmium plating on selected parts

Luggage carrier

Jiffy stand

Pyrene extinguishers and brackets

Front-wheel siren

First aid kit and box

Speedometer light

80mph plain speedometer

100mph hand speedometer

Solo bars

Steering damper

Front stand

Hand clutch control for Models C and D only

Police special speedometer

20x3.30in balloon tires for Model B

18x4in balloon tires for Models C and R

19x4in balloon tires for Models V

19x4.50in balloon tires for Models V

Mesinger tandem seat

Tandem-seat passenger pegs

Yoke springs

Winter windshield

Reverse gear

Air cleaner

Ride Control for forks (late-year introduction)

Paint Colors

Olive Green with broad Vermilion striping edged in Maroon with a Gold center pinstripe; available at extra cost are Delft Blue and Turquoise, Vermilion with Gold striping, Vermilion and Black, White with Gold striping, Police Blue and Cream, Police Blue, or Delft Blue with Gold striping

Series B 21ci Singles

First Year

Model B reintroduced onto the domestic market
Bicycle style starter pedal
Only ignition and light switches on switch panel; no ammeter
Exhaust pipes painted with a special high-temperature black paint
Mufflers painted with a special high-temperature black paint
Seat-post tube 1in shorter
Seat lowered 1in
Heavier-duty rear axle
Two-tube muffler
Tapered roller bearings in rear axle

Only Year

Schebler carburetor

Series C 30.50ci Singles

First Year

Exhaust pipes painted with a special high-temperature black paint
Mufflers painted with a special high-temperature black paint
Heavier forged frame and tubing
Reinforced oil pump
Redesigned oil pump internals
Oil pump designed to be removable without removing gear case cover
Gear case air-oil mist controlled by centrifugal force
Two tapered roller bearings in rear axle
Rear brake anchorage redesigned to make wheel easy to remove
Rear wheel readily removable

Only Year

Plain graphics

Series R 45ci V-Twins

First Year

New Model

The Series R 45ci twins replace the discontinued Series D 45ci twins
Stronger valve springs
Cylinders now designed with air space between the barrels and exhaust ports
Full baffle under each cylinder; rear baffle has six holes
Larger flywheels
New crankcases
Aluminum pistons
Thicker cushion rings made of vanadium steel matched to thinner guide rings
New piston-pin lock rings
Longer connecting rods with bronze bush upper bearings
Crankcase breathing redesigned and improved (rear exhaust cam gear shaft now used to help vent crankcase pressure)
New inlet and exhaust cam gears and shafts
Gear case cover designed with an air-venting section
Gear case cover redesigned around new oil-pump body

Heavier duty oil-pump body
New oil pump assembly with a stronger disk hinge pin and a lighter plunger spring
Oil pump mounting redesigned so pump is removable without removing gear case cover
Horizontally mounted generator with larger brushes, producing a more uniform current
Oil bath for gear-side ball bearing of generator
Four-plate clutch using a splined outer disc
Throw-out bearing made of a three-piece sandwiched bearing assembly
New front chainguard
Longer chrome-plated air intake pipe
M11 1in Linkert carburetor; M16 1in Linkert carburetor (Model RLD)
Gas strainer on carburetor
Double-curved bowed front downtube frame with heavier forging and tubing
2-1/2in diameter muffler with full fishtail
Rear brake anchorage redesigned to make wheel easy to remove
Rear wheel readily removable
Exhaust pipes painted with a special high-temperature black paint
Mufflers painted with a special high-temperature black paint
Front header pipe not squashed in midsection
Dual key tank-top panel
Two mounting brackets riveted on twin-lead coil body
Molded anti-score front brake lining
Heavier front fork forging

Only Year

Plain tank graphics
John Brown Motolamp 7in headlight with a flat diffusing lens

Series V 74ci Big Twins

First Year

Cylinders redesigned allowing airflow between exhaust ports and the barrels
New piston-pin lock rings
New oil pump assembly with a stronger disc hinge pin and a lighter plunger spring
Improved oil sealing between cam case and generator
New transmission countershaft and gear
New generator with larger brushes producing a more uniform current, making it also run cooler
Exhaust pipes painted with a special high-temperature black paint
Muffler painted with a special high-temperature black paint
Longer chrome-plated air intake pipe
Burgess muffler in a longer, narrower style
Oil slinger drive gears with lock pin holes and use of lock pins securing gear to armature shaft of generator
Front cast-in "ear" on gearbox removed; substituted with a stamped metal bracket
Gas strainer on carburetor
Molded anti-score front brake lining
Constant-mesh starter
Heavier duty front forks

Series G Servi-Cars

First Year

Series G Servi-Car is a new three-wheeled version of the Series R 45ci twins

Empty space between front of box and battery box

Combination loose ball-bearing hub and brake drum

Single drum brake, inside rear axle housing

Front wheel noninterchangeable

Both rear brakes internal-expanding, two-shoe, adjustable, fixed pivot, mechanical-type brakes

Sheet metal boxes

Parking-brake lock

One pair trunk latches to secure box cover

Horizontal hand rails

Rectangular folding footboards

Motor Company Minutes, 1932

Operating loss of $321,670.

Alfred Rich Child, H-D Japanese Sales Representative, signs a contract with Japanese businessmen for the sale of current blueprints, along with tools dies and machinery to the Sankyo Company of Japan to produce motorcycles under the name Rikuo, "King of the Road." An interesting footnote is that during World War II, the U.S. forces rode American H-Ds against the Japanese forces, who rode Japanese RTII Rikuo H-Ds. Under agreement of the $32,320 sale, an annual royalty fee payment structure is arranged until 1936.

Overseas export of 1,974 motorcycles.

Racing Notes

Joe Petrali wins National Hill-Climb Championship.

H-D wins Daytona Grand National Championship.

Model Year 1933

Main Models

33-B: 21ci flathead single with three-speed transmission

33-C: 30.50ci flathead single with three-speed transmission

33-R Solo: 45ci low-compression flathead V-twin with three-speed transmission

33-RS Sidecar Twin: 45ci low-compression flathead V-twin with three-speed transmission

33-RL Sport Solo: 45ci high-compression flathead V-twin with three-speed transmission

33-RLD Special Sport Solo: 45ci high-compression flathead V-twin with three-speed transmission

33-V Solo: 74ci medium-compression flathead V-twin with three-speed transmission

33-VS Sidecar Twin: 74ci medium-compression flathead V-twin with three-speed transmission and sidecar gearing

33-VL Sport Solo: 74ci high-compression flathead V-twin with three-speed transmission

33-VLD Special Sport Solo: 74ci high-compression flathead V-twin with three-speed transmission and magnesium-alloy pistons

33-VC Commercial: 74ci flathead V-twin with three-speed transmission

33-G Servi-Car with tow bar: 45ci flathead V-twin with three-speed-and-reverse transmission

33-GA Servi-Car without tow bar: 45ci flathead V-twin with three-speed-and-reverse transmission

33-GD large-compartment Servi-Car without tow bar: 45ci flathead V-twin with three-speed-and-reverse transmission

33-GDT large-compartment Servi-Car with tow bar: 45ci flathead V-twin with three-speed-and-reverse transmission

33-GE large-compartment Servi-Car with air tank: 45ci flathead V-twin with three-speed-and-reverse transmission

Specialty Models

33-CB: 30.50ci flathead single with three-speed transmission in the chassis from the Series B 21ci single

33-CS: 30.50ci flathead single for export to Japan

33-RE: 45ci flathead V-twin with magnesium-alloy pistons

33-RLE: 45ci high-compression flathead V-twin with magnesium-alloy pistons

33-RLDE: 45ci special high-compression flathead V-twin with magnesium-alloy pistons

33-RS Sidecar Twin: 45ci V-twin with sidecar gearing

33-VE Solo: 74ci flathead V-twin with magnesium-alloy pistons

33-VF Solo: 74ci flathead V-twin with nickel-iron pistons

33-VFS Sidecar Twin: 74ci flathead V-twin with nickel-iron pistons

33-VLE: 74ci high-compression flathead V-twin with magnesium-alloy pistons

33-VSE Sidecar Twin: 74ci flathead V-twin with magnesium-alloy pistons

Sidecars and Chassis

33-LT: single-passenger sidecar
33-LS: sidecar for 45ci twin
33-QT: two-passenger sidecar
33-M: Package Truck with cover
33-MO: Package Truck without cover
33-MXP: Package Truck, double compartment
33-MT: mail Package Truck
33-MWP: Package Truck, 56-3/4in road tread
33-LC: chassis for LT sidecar body
33-LSC: chassis for LS sidecar body
33-Q: chassis for QT sidecar body
33-MC: chassis for M box
33-MWC: chassis for MW body
33-LT: body only
33-LS: body only
33-QT: body only
33-M: body only
33-MO: body only
33-MXP: body only
33-MT: body only
33-MWP: body only

Retail Prices

Model B: $187.50
Model C: $225.00
Model R: $280.00
Model RS: $280.00
Model RL: $280.00
Model RLD: $290.00
Model V: $310.00
Model VS: $310.00
Model VL: $310.00
Model VLD: $320.00
Model VC: $310.00

Production Totals

Model C: 112
Model B: 123
Model CB: 51
Model CR: 20
Model R: 162
Model RS: 37
Model RL: 264
Model RLD: 68
Model G: 80
Model GA: 12
Model GD: 60
Model GDT: 18
Model GE: 12
Model RESX: 5
Model RLEX: 8
Model V: 233
Model VS: 164
Model VL: 886
Model VLD: 780
Model VC: 106
Model VCE: 3
Model UFS: 499

Options

Fancy dual ignition keys
Buddy seat; standard black model only
Buddy-seat cover
Left and right footboard extensions for Big Twins
Fully chromed motorcycle for $15 extra
Chrome-plated package. Oiler cover, timer cover, handlebars, valve spring covers, generator end cover, coil clamp, intake pipe clamp nuts, chainguard cover, muffler, tailpipe, front brake control clamp, exhaust pipes, and seat bar assembly
Tandem seat, H-D design
Mesinger tandem seat
Tandem-seat yoke bracket with fender hump
Tandem-seat passenger pegs
Safety guard
Handlebar crossbar
Fancy gearshift ball—Onyx or glass
Flashy two-tone and three-tone paint jobs
Front-fender eagle
Little King spotlight
Yoke springs
Winter windshield
Air cleaner
20x3.30in balloon tires for Model B
18x4in balloon tires for Models C and R
19x4in balloon tires for Models V
19x4.50in balloon tires for Models V
Reverse gear
Luggage carrier
Front stand
Ride Control
Speedometer light
80mph plain speedometer
100mph hand speedometer
Police special speedometer
Siren—front or rear
Steering damper
Solo bars
Windshield and leg shield, complete
First aid kit and box
Pyrene extinguisher and bracket
Pair parking lamps
First year: standard buddy seat in full hide smooth black leather over sponge rubber

Paint Colors

Singles (except Model CB) and Servi-Cars: Silver and Turquoise with Black and Gold striping with a stylized bird motif tank panel

CB single: Olive Green with Black tank panels and fender sides with a stylized bird motif tank panel

Twins (except Servi-Car): Sunshine Blue and White with Gold striping, Silver and Turquoise with Black and Gold striping, Olive and Brilliant Green with Brilliant Green striping; Black and Mandarin Red with Gold striping, or Police Blue and White with Gold striping—all with a stylized bird motif tank panel

Series B 21ci Singles

First Year
>Linkert carburetor (late year)
>Black-painted frames standard
>Black-painted forks standard

Only Year
>Art deco stylized eagle design on gas tanks

Series C 30.50ci Singles

First Year
>Black-painted frames standard
>Black-painted forks standard

Only Year
>Art Deco stylized eagle design on gas tank

Series CB 30.50ci Singles

First Year
>Model CB 30.50ci single is a new model made by fitting the 30.50ci motor from the Series C into the chassis from the Series B 21ci single
>>Black-painted frames standard
>>Black-painted forks standard

Only Year
>Art Deco stylized eagle design on gas tanks

Series R 45ci V-Twins

First Year
>Pair stamped steel foot pegs for buddy seat footrests, optional
>Convex headlight lens
>Black-painted frames standard
>Black-painted forks standard
>Black-painted chain guards standard
>Linkert carburetor (late year)

Only Year
>Art deco stylized eagle design on gas tanks

Series V 74ci Big Twins

First Year
>Model VLE: fitted with magnesium-alloy pistons
>Model VLD: fitted with magnesium-alloy pistons and a Y-shaped intake manifold
>Linkert carburetor (late year)
>Convex headlight lens
>Left and right footboard extensions optional, clamped to the rear of footboard, as buddy-seat footrests
>>Black-painted chainguard standard
>>Black-painted frame standard
>>Black-painted forks standard
>>New bleeder pipe on oiler
>>New generator oil retainer

Only Year
>Art deco stylized eagle design on gas tanks
>M-21 1-1/4in Linkert carburetor (Model VLD)

Series G Servi-Cars

First Year
>Linkert carburetor (late year)
>Convex headlight lens
>Safety guards optional
>Black-painted frame standard
>Black-painted forks standard
>Constant-mesh three-speed-with-reverse transmission
>Black-painted chain guards standard
>Removable side cover on transmission

Only Year
>Art deco stylized eagle design on gas tanks

Motor Company Minutes, 1933
The first royalty fee of $3,000 is paid by the Sankyo Company of Japan, in accordance with their purchase agreement for blueprints, tools, dies, and machinery.

During the Spanish Civil War, Loyalist military cadets defending Alcazar make use of a Model 33-VL. Stripped of the fender and rear wheel and using a belt, it ran the generator before Franco's Forces completely overtook them.

The H-D is designated the official California Highway Patrol motorcycle.

The California Highway Patrol motorcycle fleet now totals 437 H-Ds.

Racing Notes
>Joe Petrali wins National Hill-Climb Championship.
>H-D wins Daytona 200-Mile Expert Championship.

Model Year 1934

1934 VLD. *Doug Mitchel*

Main Models

34-B: 21ci flathead single with three-speed transmission

34-C: 30.50ci flathead single with three-speed transmission

34-CB: 30.50ci flathead single with three-speed transmission

34-RL Sport Solo: 45ci flathead V-twin with three-speed transmission

34-R Solo: 45ci low-compression flathead V-twin with three-speed transmission

34-RLD Special Sport Solo: 45ci extra-high-compression flathead V-twin with three-speed transmission

34-VLD Special Sport Solo: 74ci high-compression flathead V-twin with three-speed transmission

34-VD Solo: 74ci low-compression flathead V-twin with three-speed transmission

34-VDS Sidecar Twin: 74ci low-compression flathead V-twin with three-speed transmission, sidecar bars, and sidecar gearing

34-VFDS Sidecar Twin: 74ci flathead V-twin with three-speed transmission, sidecar bars, sidecar gearing, and nickel-iron pistons

34-G Servi-Car with tow bar: 45ci flathead V-twin with three-speed-and-reverse transmission

34-GA Servi-Car without tow bar: 45ci flathead V-twin with three-speed-and-reverse transmission

34-GD large-compartment Servi-Car without tow bar: 45ci flathead V-twin with three-speed-and-reverse transmission

34-GDT large-compartment Servi-Car with tow bar: 45ci flathead V-twin with three-speed-and-reverse transmission

34-GE large-compartment Servi-Car with air tank: 45ci flathead V-twin with three-speed-and-reverse transmission

Specialty Models

34-VFD Solo: 74ci flathead V-twin with nickel-iron pistons

34-RX: 45ci V-twin with aluminum pistons for export to Germany

34-RLX: 45ci high-compression V-twin with aluminum pistons for export to Germany

34-RLDX: 45ci special-high-compression V-twin with aluminum pistons for export to Germany

34-RS Sidecar Twin: 45ci V-twin with aluminum pistons

34-RSX Sidecar Twin: 45ci V-twin with aluminum pistons for export to Germany

Sidecars and Chassis

34-LT: single-passenger sidecar

34-LS: single-passenger sidecar for 45ci twin

34-M: side van with cover

34-MO: side van without cover

34-MXP: side van-double compartment

34-MT: mail Package Truck

34-LC: chassis for LT body

34-LSC: chassis for LS body

34-MC: chassis for M box

34-MWC: chassis for MW box

34-LT: body only

34-LS: body only

34-M: body only

34-MO: body only

34-MXP: body only

34-MT: body only

Retail Prices

Model B: $187.50

Model C: $225.00

Model CB: $197.50

Model R: $280.00

Model RL: $280.00

Model RLD: $290.00

Model VLD: $310.00

Model VD: $310.00

Model VDS: $310.00

Model VFDS: $310.00

Model G: $430.00

Model GA: $415.00

Model GD: $430.00

Model GDT: $445.00

Model GE: $485.00

Production Totals

Model B: 424

Model CB: 310

Model C: 220

Model CR: 165

Model R: 450

Model RS: 302

Model RL: 743

Model RLD: 240

Model G: 317

Model GA: 40

Model GD: 104

Model GDT: 58

Model GE: 27

Model RX: 5

Model RLX: 36

Model RSR: 215

Model RLDX: 1

Model VFD: 5

Model VFDS: 1,330

Model VD: 664

Model VDS: 1,029

Model VLD: 4,527

Options

Fancy dual ignition keys
Chrome-plating package
Mirrors
Black handlebar grips
Air cleaner
Mesinger tandem seat
Yoke springs
Tandem-seat passenger pegs
Winter windshield

Paint Colors

Singles: Silver and Teak Red; available without cost is Olive Green and Black

CB single: Olive Green with Black tank panels and fender sides

Twins: Silver with Teak Red tank panels and fender sides or Teak Red with Black tank panels and fender sides; available without cost are Black with Orlando Orange tank and fender centers, Seafoam Blue with Silver tank and fender centers, or Black with Olive Green tank and fender centers; a Summer Color Special (limited time) was available without cost for twins—Vermilion tank and fender centers with a Copper enameled main section

Series B 21ci Singles

First/Only Year

Tanks have Art Deco bars and stylized logo in a diamond shape on tank panel

(The Series B singles were discontinued at the end of the model year)

Series C 30ci Singles

First/Only Year

Tanks have Art Deco bars and stylized logo in a diamond shape on tank panel

(The Series C singles were discontinued at the end of the model year)

Series CB Singles

First/Only Year

Tanks have Art Deco bars and stylized logo in a diamond shape on tank panel

(The Series CB singles were discontinued at the end of the model year)

Series R 45ci V-Twins

First Year

Low-expansion aluminum-alloy pistons
New oil pump
New gear case cover
Twelve-spring clutch
New clutch gear
New outer clutch disc
New clutch spring collar
New clutch thrust cap
Airflow taillight
High-Flo muffler
Tanks have Art Deco bars and stylized logo in diamond shape on tank panel

Front stand (export models)
New shifting arm for low and reverse (three-speed-with-reverse transmission)
Shifting arm for second and high (three-speed-with-reverse transmission)
Airflow taillight
High-Flo muffler
Solo bucket saddle having shiny rivets
Streamlined fenders (three-piece construction)
Straight-bore cylinders and T-slot pistons (late year)

Only Year

Front fender lamp is short-bodied and chrome-plated

Series V 74ci Big Twins

First Year

Low-expansion aluminum-alloy pistons
Airflow taillight
High-Flo muffler
Tanks have Art Deco bars and stylized logo in diamond shape on tank panel
Front stand (export models)
Airflow taillight
High-Flo muffler
Solo bucket saddle having shiny rivets
Streamlined fenders (three-piece construction)
Straight-bore cylinders and T-slot pistons (late year)

Only Year

Front fender lamp is short-bodied and chrome-plated

Series G Servi-Cars

First Year

Straight-bore cylinders and T-slot pistons (late year)
Three-piece fender construction
Seat leather is horsehide
Seat padding is sponge rubber
Taillight lens bucket chrome-plated
Front fender lamp bodies chrome-plated
Tanks have Art Deco bars and stylized logo in diamond shape on tank panel

Only Year

Front fender lamp is short-bodied and chrome-plated

Motor Company Minutes, 1934

Second royalty fee due of $5,000 is paid from the 1932 contract agreement for the sale of blueprints, tools, dies, and machinery to the Sankyo Company of Japan.

Net profit is $373,000.

Direct mail program starts. Postcards announce the new models.

Racing Notes

H-D wins Daytona 200-Mile Expert Championship.
Joe Petrali wins National Hill-Climb Championship.
H-D wins Miniature TT Race National Championship.

Main Models

35-RL Solo: 45ci high-compression flathead V-twin with three-speed transmission

35-R Solo: 45ci low-compression flathead V-twin with three-speed transmission

35-RS Sidecar Twin: 45ci low-compression flathead V-twin with three-speed transmission and sidecar gearing

35-RLD Special Sport Solo: 45ci flathead V-twin with three-speed transmission

35-RLDR Competition Special: 45ci flathead V-twin with three-speed transmission

35-VLD Special Sport Solo: 74ci high-compression flathead V-twin with three-speed transmission

35-VD Solo: 74ci low-compression flathead V-twin with three-speed transmission

35-VDS Sidecar Twin: 74ci low-compression flathead V-twin with three-speed transmission and sidecar gearing

35-VLDJ Competition Special: 74ci flathead V-twin with three-speed transmission

35-VLDD Sport Solo: 80ci flathead V-twin with three-speed transmission and solo bars

35-VDDS Sidecar Twin: 80ci flathead V-twin with three-speed transmission and sidecar bars

35-G Servi-Car with tow bar: 45ci flathead V-twin with three-speed-and-reverse transmission

35-GA Servi-Car without tow bar: 45ci flathead V-twin with three-speed-and-reverse transmission

35-GD large-compartment Servi-Car without tow bar: 45ci flathead V-twin with three-speed-and-reverse transmission

35-GDT large-compartment Servi-Car with tow bar: 45ci flathead V-twin with three-speed-and-reverse transmission

35-GE large-compartment Servi-Car with air tank: 45ci flathead V-twin with three-speed-and-reverse transmission

Specialty Models

35-VFD Solo: 74ci flathead V-twin with nickel-iron pistons

35-VFDS Sidecar Twin: 74ci flathead V-twin with nickel-iron pistons

35-RSR: 45ci V-twin for export to Japan

Sidecars and Chassis

35-LT: single-passenger sidecar

35-LS: single-passenger sidecar for 45ci twin

35-M: side van with cover

35-MO: side van without cover

35-LC: chassis for LT body

35-LSC: chassis for LS body

35-MC: chassis for M box

35-MWC: chassis for MW box

35-LT: body only

35-LS: body only

35-M: body only

35-MO: body only

Retail Prices

Model VLD: $320.00

Model VD: $320.00

Model VDS: $320.00

Model VLDJ: $333.50

Model VLDD: $347.00

Model VDDS: $347.00

Model RL: $295.00

Model R: $295.00

Model RS: $295.00

Model RLD: $305.00

Model RLDR: $322.00

Model G: $440.00

Model GA: $425.00

Model GD: $440.00

Model GDT: $455.00

Model GE: $495.00

Production Totals

Model R: 543

Model RS: 392

Model RSR: 50

Model RL: 819

Model RLD: 177

Model RLDR: 29

Model G: 323

Model GA: 64

Model GD: 91

Model GDT: 72

Model GE: 17

Model VD: 585

Model VDS: 1,189

Model VFDS: 327

Model VLD: 3,963

Model VLDJ: 102

Model VLDD: 179

Options

Solo Group No. 1
Deluxe Solo Group
Police Group No. 1
Deluxe Police Group
Servi-Car Group No. 1
Deluxe Servi-Car Group for G
Deluxe Servi-Car Group for GD
LT Sidecar Group No. 1
Deluxe Group for LT sidecar
Deluxe Truck Group
Motorcycle safety bars
Four-speed transmission for sidecar use
Black rubber handlebar grips
Sidecar fender lamp
Air cleaner with removable cover, 6in diameter, chrome plated with H-D logo stamped on face
Fancy dual ignition keys

Paint Colors

Egyptian Ivory and Regent Brown, Teak Red and Black, Olive Green and Black, Verdant Green and Black, Venetian Blue and Silver, or Silver and Black (police only); available at extra cost are Cameo Cream with Dawn Gray panels or Potomac Blue striping (limited time)

Series R 45ci V-Twins

First Year

Constant-mesh three-speed transmission
Quick-detach rear wheel with hub-driven speedometer and internal-expanding brake
Adjustable brake-shoe pivot stud
Carburized brake drums
Harder brake linings
Gas-deflecting muffler end
Improved carburetor air intake
Larger filler caps for gas and oil
New, rectangular tool box on left side of frame
Shorter handlebar grips
Beehive taillight lens
Revised horn position on front forks

Series V 74ci and 80ci Big Twins

First Year

Carburized brake drums
Harder brake linings
Gas-deflecting muffler end
Improved carburetor air intake
Larger filler caps for gas and oil
New, rectangular tool box on right side of frame
Shorter handlebar grips
Beehive taillight lens
Revised horn position on front forks
Adjustable circuit-breaker stop screw
The Series V 80ci flathead Big Twins are new models
Engine: 80ci flathead V-twin with 3.422x4-1/4in bore and stroke
Chassis: same as used for the Series V 74ci Big Twins

Only Year

Air intake is box-like with three horizontal ribs and slash-cut at the rear

Series G Servi-Cars

First Year

Carburized brake drums
Harder brake linings
Gas-deflecting muffler end
Improved carburetor air intake
Larger filler caps for gas and oil
New, rectangular tool box on Servi-Car body (only on models without a tow bar)
Shorter handlebar grips
Beehive taillight lens
Revised horn position on front forks
Rear axle housing tie rod

Motor Company Minutes, 1935

Production increases 250 percent over last year.
Net profit is $300,354.
Third royalty fee of $8,000 is paid from the 1932 contract agreement for the sale of blueprints, tools, dies, and machinery to the Sankyo Company of Japan.
First year that the Japanese Rikuo/H-D is being manufactured out of entirely Japanese-made parts.

Racing Notes

Jim Young wins Oakland 200-Mile National Speedway Championship.
Joe Petrali wins all 13 National Championship Dirt Track Races.
Joe Petrali wins 3-Mile National Race at Reading, Pennsylvania.
Joe Petrali wins 10-Mile Race, Syracuse, New York, August 31, 81.65mph.
Joe Petrali wins 15-Mile Race, Syracuse, New York, August 31, 80.50mph.
Joe Petrali wins 25-Mile Race, Syracuse, New York, August 31, 80.11mph.
Joe Petrali sets four new AMA records.
Joe Petrali wins National Hill-Climb Championship.
H-D wins Daytona 200-Mile Expert Championship.
H-D wins Miniature TT Races National Championship.
Joe Petrali crowned Dirt Track Champion.

Model Year 1936

1936 VL. *Drag Specialties*

Main Models

36-RL Sport Solo: 45ci high-compression flathead V-twin with three-speed transmission and solo bars

36-RLD Special Sport Solo: 45ci extra-high-compression flathead V-twin with three-speed transmission and solo bars

36-RLDR Competition: 45ci flathead V-twin with three-speed transmission and solo bars

36-R Solo: 45ci low-compression flathead V-twin with three-speed transmission and solo bars

36-RS Sidecar Twin: 45ci low-compression flathead V-twin with three-speed transmission and sidecar gearing

36-EL Special Sport Solo: 61ci high-compression Knucklehead OHV V-twin with four-speed transmission

36-E Solo: 61ci medium-compression Knucklehead OHV V-twin with four-speed transmission

36-ES Sidecar Twin: 61ci medium-compression Knucklehead OHV V-twin with four-speed transmission and sidecar gearing

36-VLD Special Sport Solo: 74ci high-compression flathead V-twin with three-speed transmission

36-VD Solo: 74ci low-compression flathead V-twin with three-speed transmission

36-VDS Sidecar Twin: 74ci low-compression flathead V-twin with three-speed transmission, sidecar bars, and sidecar gearing

36-VLH Sport Solo: 80ci flathead V-twin with three-speed transmission and solo bars

36-VHS Sidecar Twin: 80ci low-compression flathead V-twin with three-speed transmission, sidecar gearing, and sidecar bars

36-G Servi-Car with tow bar: 45ci flathead V-twin with three-speed-and-reverse transmission

36-GA Servi-Car without tow bar: 45ci flathead V-twin with three-speed-and-reverse transmission

36-GD large-compartment Servi-Car without tow bar: 45ci flathead V-twin with three-speed-and-reverse transmission

36-GDT large-compartment Servi-Car with tow bar: 45ci flathead V-twin with three-speed-and-reverse transmission

36-GE large-compartment Servi-Car with air tank: 45ci flathead V-twin with three-speed-and-reverse transmission

Specialty Models

36-VFD Solo: 74ci V-twin with nickel-iron pistons

36-VFDS Sidecar Twin: 74ci V-twin with nickel-iron pistons and sidecar gearing

36-VMG: 74ci V-twin with Bosch magneto

36-VFH Solo: 80ci V-twin with nickel-iron pistons

36-VFHS Sidecar Twin: 80ci V-twin with nickel-iron pistons and sidecar gearing

36-RSR: 45ci V-twin for export to Japan

36-EM: 61ci V-twin motor for midget car racing

Specialty Notes

First Year

All sidecar doors have H-D logo

Axle shared by Goulding and LE sidecars

Package truck bodies, Servi-Car boxes, and Big Twin sidecars built by Abresh Body Company, Milwaukee

Two horizontal stainless steel stripes on each side of Big Twin sidecar body

Sidecars and Chassis

36-K: single-passenger sidecar for 74ci Twin

36-LE: single-passenger sidecar for 61ci Twin

36-LS: single-passenger sidecar for 45ci Twin

36-M: side van with cover

36-MO: side van without cover

36-KC: chassis for K body

36-LEC: chassis for LE body

36-LSC: chassis for LS body

36-MC: chassis for M box

36-MWC: chassis for MW box

36-K: body only

36-LE: body only

36-LS: body only

36-M: body only

Retail Prices

Model RL: $295

Model RLD: $295

Model RLDR: $320

Model R: $295

Model RS: $295

Model EL: $380

Model E: $380

Model ES: $380

Model VLD: $320

Model VD: $320

Model VDS: $320

Model VLH: $340

Model VHS: $340

Model G: $440

Model GA: $425

Model GD: $440

Model GDT: $455

Model GE: $495

Production Totals

Model G: 382
Model GA: 55
Model GD: 96
Model GDT: 85
Model GE: 30
Model R: 539
Model RS: 437
Model RSR: 30
Model RL: 355
Model RLD: 540
Model RLDR: 79
Model E: 152
Model EL: 1,526
Model ES: 26
Model VFDS: 600
Model VD: 176
Model VDS: 623
Model VLD: 1,577
Model VLH: 2,046
Model VHS: 305
Model VMG: 118
Model VFHS: 35

Options

Accessories now sold in groups
Standard Solo Group for 45ci, 74ci, and 80ci Models: $28.00
Standard Solo Group for 61ci Models: $14.00
Deluxe Solo Group for 45ci, 74ci and 80ci Models: $49.50
Deluxe Solo Group for 61ci Models: $34.50
Standard Police Group for 45ci, 74ci, and 80ci Models: $53.00
Standard Police Group for 61ci Models: $44.00
Deluxe Police Group for 45ci, 74ci, and 80ci Models: $90.50
Deluxe Police Group for 61ci Models: $80.50
Standard Group for all Servi-Cars: $29.75
Deluxe Group for G Servi-Car: $59.90
Deluxe Group for GD Servi-Car: $62.90
Standard Group for Sport Sidecars: $15.75
Deluxe Group for Sport Sidecars: $39.50
Deluxe Truck Group: $26.90

Paint Colors

Sherwood Green with Silver panels and rims, Dusk Gray with Royal Buff panels and rims, Teak Red with Black panels and Red rims, Venetian Blue with Croydon Cream panels and rims, and Maroon with Nile Green panels and rims

Series R 45ci V-Twins

First and Only Year

Deep-finned cylinder heads fastened by eight bolt studs
Deep-finned cylinders
Redesigned combustion chambers
Streamlined air intake streamlined
Y-type intake manifold
1-1/4in carburetors on RL and RLD models
Spring shield for fork springs
Chrome-plated horn face and horn brackets
Revised rake and offset of steering head
Tubular rear stand
Improved ammeter with damped needle
Convex-shaped gear lever
Oil-pump guard revised for improved air flow to the condenser
Revised rear chain guard
Chrome cover for chain adjustment port

Guard over the clutch release
Brake linings 7/32in thick
Revised transmission-oil-seal retainers
Classic art deco tank transfers
(Series R 45ci twins discontinued at end of model year)

Series E 61ci Knucklehead Big Twins

First Year

The Series E OHV Big Twins were all-new models
Engine: 61ci OHV V-twin with 3-5/16x3-1/2in bore and stroke
Dry-sump recirculating oiling system
Four-speed constant-mesh transmission
Heavy-duty clutch of new design
Saddle-type twin gas tanks
Oil in separate U-shaped tank behind the motor and below seat with battery in the center of the U
"Skull-face" teardrop-style built-in instrument cover with oil-pressure gauge, ammeter, and ignition switch; instrument cover painted Black
"White-face" Stewart-Warner 120mph speedometer is standard equipment
Art deco tank transfers
Front safety guards standard
18in wheels standard
Single-check-valve feed oil pump
Rectangular folding footboards
Motors having rockers and shafts in two separate pieces with the rocker pivoting on shaft
Rocker shafts are adjustable for oil flow
Intake manifold made up of an inlet pipe with two inlet nuts and two inlet nut bushings
Toolbox is rectangular and mounted on right rear side and uses a lock and key
Two mounting brackets on twin-lead coil body
"Star" hub wheels, interchangeable on both front and rear
"Beehive" taillight
Manual-advance single-point timer
"Winged-face" horn
2-1/2in diameter muffler with a full fishtail
Three-piece header pipe set has front header pipe, S-pipe, and rear header pipe
Front header pipe fits inside the exhaust port
Seven-tooth speedometer drive gear
Horn switch placed near top of left handlebar with headlight switch directly below
Aluminum "knuckle" rocker boss on each cylinder head

Changes During the Year

Early 1936 dashes lack the holes for the speedometer trip-meter and speedometer lamp switch; mid- and late-year dashes have the tripmeter hole but still lack the lamp-switch hole
120mph speedometer without tripmeter; tripmeter became optional in mid-1936
Frame was reinforced on right side, under the transmission
Rocker-shaft cover nuts replace domed covers
Air fitting added to front rocker boss
Pinion-gear shaft revised to improve oil mileage
Kickstarter gears changed to 16-tooth mainshaft and 24-tooth crank gear
Two updates of the gear-case cover
Three types of oil tanks and fittings
Cylinder-head-casting changes
Cylinder updates

Only Year

Air intake is box-like with three horizontal ribs and slash-cut at the rear

Double downtube cradle frame with sidecar mounts brazed on to continuous frame downtubes

Series V 74ci and 80ci Flathead Twins

First and Only Year

Deep-finned heads fastened by nine studs

Deep-finned cylinders

New design combustion chamber

Lightened upper connecting-rod bushings

Streamlined air intake with chrome-plated steel cover, slash cut at the rear, measuring 9-5/8in long, 3-3/4in high at carburetor, and 2-1/4in high at rear

Spring shield on fork springs

Chrome-plated horn face and horn brackets

Four-speed transmission optional

First gear is full forward on the shifting lever with optional four-speed

Improved ammeter with damped needle

Convex-shaped gearshift lever

Classic Art Deco transfer on tanks

Tubular rear stand

Note: Series V big twins discontinued at end of model year

Series G Servi-Cars

First Year

Deep-finned cylinders fastened by eight bolt studs

Redesigned combustion chambers

Streamlined air intake streamlined

Y-type intake manifold

Spring shield for fork springs

Chrome-plated horn face and horn brackets

Revised rake and offset of steering head

Tubular rear stand

Improved ammeter with damped needle

Convex-shaped gear lever

Oil-pump guard revised for improved air flow to the condenser

Revised rear chain guard

Chrome cover for chain adjustment port

Guard over the clutch release

Brake linings 7/32in thick

Revised transmission-oil-seal retainers

Classic art deco tank transfers

One chrome-plated spring latch securing small body box cover

Two chrome-plated spring latches securing the large body box cover

Note: 1936 is the last year for Servi-Cars based on the Series R 45ci twins

Motor Company Minutes, 1936

The Denver Police Department receives six new H-D Servi-Cars. Experimental police radio receivers begin their testing.

Fourth and final royalty fee due of $10,000 is paid from the 1932 contract agreement for the sale of blueprints, tools, dies, and machinery to the Sankyo Company of Japan.

Because the shape of the rocker boxes with big nuts resembled knuckles, the 61ci OHV engine was nicknamed Knucklehead.

First year of the Jack Pine Gypsies Motorcycle Club, organized by J.C. "Pappy" Hoel. The Jack Pine Gypsies are credited with starting the Black Hills Rally in Sturgis, South Dakota.

Net profit is $381,227.

Racing Notes

H-D wins Miniature TT Race National Championship. Joe Petrali wins National Dirt Track Championship.

Model Year 1937

1937 EL. *Doug Mitchel*

Main Models

37-WL Sport Solo: 45ci high-compression flathead V-twin with three-speed transmission

37-WLD Special Sport Solo: 45ci extra-high-compression flathead V-twin with three-speed transmission

37-WLDR Competition Special: 45ci flathead V-twin with three-speed transmission

37-W Solo: 45ci low-compression flathead V-twin with three-speed transmission

37-WS Sidecar Twin: 45ci low-compression flathead V-twin with three-speed transmission and sidecar gearing

37-EL Special Sport Solo: 61ci high-compression Knucklehead OHV V-twin with four-speed transmission

37-E Solo: 61ci medium-compression Knucklehead OHV V-twin with four-speed transmission

37-ES Sidecar Twin: 61ci medium-compression Knucklehead OHV V-twin with four-speed transmission and sidecar gearing

37-UL Special Sport Solo: 74ci high-compression flathead V-twin with four-speed transmission

37-U Solo: 74ci medium-compression flathead V-twin with four-speed transmission

37-US Sidecar Twin: 74ci medium-compression flathead V-twin with four-speed transmission and sidecar gearing

37-ULH Special Sport Solo: 80ci high-compression flathead V-twin with four-speed transmission

37-UH Solo: 80ci medium-compression flathead V-twin with four-speed transmission

37-UHS Sidecar Twin: 80ci medium-compression flathead V-twin with four-speed transmission and sidecar gearing

37-GE large-compartment Servi-Car with air tank: 45ci flathead V-twin with three-speed-and-reverse transmission

37-G Servi-Car with tow bar: 45ci flathead V-twin with three-speed-and-reverse transmission

37-GA Servi-Car without tow bar: 45ci flathead V-twin with three-speed-and-reverse transmission

37-GD large-compartment Servi-Car without tow bar: 45ci flathead V-twin with three-speed-and-reverse transmission

37-GDT large-compartment Servi-Car with tow bar: 45ci flathead V-twin with three-speed-and-reverse transmission

Specialty Models
37-WSR: 45ci V-twin for export to Japan
37-UMG: 74ci V-twin with Bosch magneto

Sidecars and Chassis
37-LE: single-passenger sidecar for 61ci, 74ci, and 80ci twins
37-LS: single-passenger sidecar for 45ci twin
37-M: side van with cover
37-MO: side van without cover
37-LEC: chassis for LE body
37-LSC: chassis for LS body
37-MC: chassis for M box
37-LE: body only
37-M: body only
37-MO: body only

Retail Prices
Model WL: $355
Model WLD: $355
Model WLDR: $380
Model W: $355
Model WS: $355
Model EL: $435
Model E: $435
Model ES: $435
Model UL: $395
Model U: $395
Model US: $395
Model ULH: $415
Model UH: $415
Model UHS: $415
Model G: $515
Model GA: $500
Model GD: $515
Model GDT: $530
Model GE: $570

Production Totals
Model W: 509
Model WS: 232
Model WL: 560
Model WLD: 581
Model WLDR: 145
Model WSR: 5
Model G: 491
Model GA: 55
Model GD: 112
Model GDT: 136
Model GE: 22
Model E: 126
Model EL: 1,829
Model ES: 70
Model U: 612
Model US: 1,080
Model UL: 2,861
Model ULH: 1,513
Model UH: 185
Model UHS: 400
Model UMG: 150

Options
Standard Solo Group: $21.75
Deluxe Solo Group: $49.00
Standard Police Group: $49.50
Deluxe Police Group: $83.50
Standard Group for Sidecar or Commercial: $20.00
Standard Group for Servi-Car: $21.90
Deluxe Group for G or GA Servi-Car: $48.00
Deluxe Group for GA or GDT Servi-Car: $53.00
Standard Group for Sport sidecars: $17.50
Deluxe Group for Sport sidecars: $44.00
Deluxe Truck Group: $29.00

Paint Colors
Teak Red with Black striping (edged in Gold), Bronze Brown with Delphine Blue striping (edged in yellow), Police Silver with Black striping (edged in Gold, police only), Delphine Blue with Teak Red striping (edged in Gold, export), and Olive Green with Black striping (edged in Gold, export)

Series W 45ci V-Twins

First Year
The Series W 45ci twins are all-new models with styling like the Model E 61ci OHV
Redesigned motor with a recirculating oil system and roller bearings throughout
Vane-type feed pump driven by the rear exhaust cam gear shaft
Oil pump mounted on outside of gear case cover
Twin saddle tanks: left tank for gas and right tank for oil
Instrument panel on top of tanks with speedometer, oil-pressure gauge, ammeter, ignition switch, and speedometer light switch
"White-face" Stewart-Warner 120mph speedometer standard; tripmeter included with Deluxe and Standard accessory groups
Upright ignition timer with chrome cover
Front chain lubricated automatically
Horizontal fins on left crankcase and timing case
Patent decal placed on toolbox door
Revised flywheel counterweights

Series E 61ci Knucklehead Twins

First Year
Reinforced frame with revised sidecar mounts
Flat-sided gearshift lever
120mph speedometer
Oil-tank screen deleted
Patent decal located on both sides of the oil tank
Clevis ends added to brake rod
Larger rear brake
Revised shifter gate with positive stops
Terminal post added to seat-post mast
Balancing spring added to clutch-release pedal
Shaft bushing added to rear brake, midyear

Series U 74ci and 80ci Flathead Big Twins

First Year

Series U and UH Big Twins were all-new flathead big twins restyled like the Model E 61ci OHV twin

Redesigned motor with a recirculating oil system and roller bearings throughout

Four-speed transmission and clutch from the Model E OHV

Frame, suspension, and running gear same as on the Model E OHV

Vane-type feed pump driven by the rear exhaust cam gear shaft

Oil pump mounted on outside of gear case cover

Twin saddle gas tanks similar to those on the Model E OHV

Instrument panel on top of tanks with speedometer, oil-pressure gauge, ammeter, ignition switch, and speedometer light switch

"White-face" Stewart-Warner 120mph speedometer standard; tripmeter included with Deluxe and Standard accessory Groups

Upright ignition timer with chrome cover

Front chain lubricated automatically

U-shaped oil tank mounted under the seat with battery in the center of the U

Series G Servi-Cars

First Year

All-new model with styling like the Model E 61ci OHV and the new motor of the Series W 45ci twins

Redesigned motor with a recirculating oil system and roller bearings throughout

Vane-type feed pump driven by the rear exhaust cam gear shaft

Oil pump mounted on outside of gear case cover

Twin saddle tanks: left tank for gas and right tank for oil

Instrument panel on top of tanks with speedometer, oil-pressure gauge, ammeter, ignition switch, and speedometer light switch

"White-face" Stewart-Warner 100mph speedometer standard

Upright ignition timer with chrome cover

Patent decal placed on toolbox door

Front chain lubricated automatically

Revised flywheel counterweights

Separate rear brakes for each wheel

Stronger brake lock

Large hub caps

Speedometer drive enclosed from the differential forward

Motor Company Minutes, 1937

William H. Davidson named vice president.

April 21, William A. Davidson, production head, passes away.

Noted actor and H-D rider Clark Gable purchases his first Model UL.

Racing Notes

First year the 200-Mile National Championships held at Daytona Beach, Florida.

Joe Petrali on Model EL alcohol/benzoyl-burning special twin-carburetor engine, sets new World Speed Record with 136.183mph at Daytona.

Joe Petrali wins National Hill-Climbing Championship.

1938 U. *Doug Mitchel*

Main Models

38-WLD Sport Solo: 45ci flathead V-twin with extra-high-compression and four-speed transmission

38-WL Solo: 45ci flathead V-twin with high-compression and four-speed transmission

38-WLDR Competition: 45ci flathead V-twin with four-speed transmission

38-EL Special Sport Solo: 61ci high-compression Knucklehead OHV V-twin with four-speed transmission

38-ES Sidecar Twin: 61ci Knucklehead OHV V-twin with four-speed transmission

38-UL Special Sport Solo: 74ci high-compression flathead V-twin with four-speed transmission

38-U Solo: 74ci medium-compression flathead V-twin with four-speed transmission

38-US Sidecar Twin: 74ci medium-compression flathead V-twin with four-speed transmission and sidecar gearing

38-ULH Special Sport Solo: 80ci high-compression flathead V-twin with four-speed transmission

38-UH Solo: 80ci medium-compression flathead V-twin with four-speed transmission

38-UHS Sidecar Twin: 80ci medium-compression flathead V-twin with four-speed transmission and sidecar gearing

38-G Servi-Car with tow bar: 45ci flathead V-twin with three-speed-and-reverse transmission

38-GA Servi-Car without tow bar: 45ci flathead V-twin with three-speed-and-reverse transmission

38-GD large-compartment Servi-Car without tow bar: 45ci flathead V-twin with three-speed-and-reverse transmission

38-GDT large-compartment Servi-Car with tow bar: 45ci flathead V-twin with three-speed-and-reverse transmission

Specialty Models

38-GE large-compartment Servi-Car with air tank: 45ci flathead V-twin with three-speed transmission

38-UMG: 74ci V-twin with Bosch magneto

38-W: 45ci V-twin with 6.8ci head volume

38-WS Sidecar Twin: 45ci V-twin

Sidecars and Chassis

38-LE: right-hand single-passenger sidecar
38-LS: right-hand single-passenger sidecar for 45ci twin
38-M: right-hand side van with cover
38-MO: right-hand side van without cover
38-LEC: right-hand chassis for LE body
38-LSC: right-hand chassis for LS body
38-MC: right-hand chassis for M box
38-MWC: wide chassis

Retail Prices

Model WL: $355
Model WLD: $355
Model WLDR: $380
Model EL: $435
Model ES: $435
Model UL: $395
Model U: $395
Model US: $395
Model ULH: $415
Model UH: $415
Model UHS: $415
Model G: $515
Model GA: $500
Model GD: $515
Model GDT: $530

Production Totals

Model W: 302
Model WS: 247
Model WL: 309
Model WLD: 402
Model WLDR: 139
Model G: 259
Model GA: 83
Model GD: 81
Model GDT: 102
Model EL: 2,289
Model ES: 189
Model U: 504
Model US: 1,193
Model UL: 1,099
Model ULH: 579
Model UH: 108
Model UHS: 132
Model UMG: 141

Options

Standard Solo Group: $16.70
Deluxe Solo Group: $49.75
Standard Police Group: $52.25
Standard Group for sidecar or package truck: $14.25
Standard Group for Servi-Car: $18.25
Deluxe Group for G or GA Servi-Car: $49.00
Deluxe Group for GD or GDT Servi-Car: $54.00
Standard Group for Sport sidecars: $17.50
Deluxe Group for Sport sidecars: $44.00
Deluxe Package Truck Group: $29.00

Paint Colors

Hollywood Green with Gold striping (edged in Black), Teak Red with Black striping (edged in Gold), Venetian Blue with White striping (edged in Burnt Orange), Police Silver with Black stripe (police only), Silver Tan with Sunshine Blue striping (edged in Gold-Export), and Olive Green with Black striping (edged in Gold-Export)

Series W 45ci V-Twins

First Year

Deep pocket under rear exhaust cam in right crankcase used as oil bath for the gears
Shaved timing gears
Eight-ball clutch thrust bearing
Clutch throw-out bearing made as a one-piece assembly
Gearbox similar to the Big Twins'
Shifter cams have four oval-shaped holes around the shaft hole
Reinforced mainshaft second gear
Second- and high-gear shifter clutches made of better steel
Shifter gate pattern for three-speed with reverse transmission models, front to back: R-1-N-2-3
Big-twin-style clutch pedal and footboards
Foot clutch rod 13-3/4in long
Return lines use nipple fittings at tank end
Diaphram-type oil signal switch
2mph calibrations on speedometer
New-type seals for the valve covers
Oil and generator indicator warning lights in tank-mounted dash
Revised horn and light wiring
Black horn brackets
Zerk-Alemite grease fittings
Synthetic-rubber valve-enclosure rings
Optional 6in round chrome air cleaner with four "J" slots
Must be ordered with one of the option groups

Series E 61ci Knucklehead Big Twins

First Year

Completely enclosed rocker arm assemblies
Shaved timing gears
Diaphram-type oil signal switch
Compression-type oil-pipe connections on the oil tank
Oil tank vent pipes enlarged to 3/8in
Strengthened frame
Steering head redesigned with a lower self-aligning head cone having a convex base
Black horn brackets
Zerk-Alemite grease fittings
Oil and generator warning lights in dash
Speedometer with 2mph hash marks and tripmeter
Transmission improvements: 10-ball thrust bearing, new starter cover, new clutch pushrod, and redesigned third and fourth gears
Rerouted horn and light wiring
Repositioned handlebars for greater legroom
Interconnected brake shoes on rear brakes
Rex-Hide brake linings on front brake
Chain-inspection cover painted Black
Timer cover is cadmium-plated
All bolts and nuts are Parkerized
Spot lamp terminal post, optional
Lighter rear stand
Magnetic speedometer hand stop (police)
Streamlined aluminum siren (police)
Optional chrome air cleaner with four J-slots
Must be ordered with one of the option groups

Series U and UH 74ci and 80ci Big Twins

First Year

Shaved timing gears
Compression-type oil-pipe connections on the oil tank
Oil tank vent pipes enlarged to 3/8in
Strengthened frame
Steering head redesigned with a lower self-aligning head cone having a convex base
Black horn brackets
Zerk-Alemite grease fittings
Oil and generator warning lights in dash
Speedometer with 2mph hash marks and tripmeter
Transmission improvements: 10-ball thrust bearing, new starter cover, new clutch pushrod, and redesigned third and fourth gears
Rerouted horn and light wiring
Repositioned handlebars for greater legroom
Interconnected brake shoes on rear brakes
Rex-Hide brake linings on front brake
Chain-inspection cover painted Black
Timer cover is cadmium-plated
All bolts and nuts are Parkerized
Spot lamp terminal post, optional
Lighter rear stand
Magnetic speedometer hand stop (police)
Streamlined aluminum siren (police)
Optional chrome air cleaner with four J-slots
Must be ordered with one of the option groups

Series G Servi-Cars

First Year

Deep pocket under rear exhaust cam in right crankcase used as oil bath for the gears
Shaved timing gears
Eight-ball clutch thrust bearing
Clutch throw-out bearing made as a one-piece assembly
Gearbox similar to the Big Twins'
Shifter cams have four oval-shaped holes around the shaft hole
Reinforced mainshaft second gear
Second- and high-gear shifter clutches made of better steel
Big-twin-style clutch pedal and footboards
Foot clutch rod 13-3/4in long
Return lines use nipple fittings at tank end
Diaphram-type oil signal switch
New-type seals for the valve covers
Oil and generator indicator warning lights in tank-mounted dash
Revised horn and light wiring
Black horn brackets
Zerk-Alemite grease fittings
Synthetic-rubber valve-enclosure rings
Optional 6in round chrome air cleaner with four "J" slots
Enclosed rear chain
Larger Burgess muffler
Jaw-type tow-bar clamp
59-tooth clutch sprocket and 24-tooth engine sprocket
Rex-Hide linings in rear brakes
Must be ordered with one of the option groups

Motor Company Minutes, 1938

The AMA sanctions the Black Hills Rally in Sturgis. The rally is originally started by the Jack Pine Gypsies Motorcycle Club, who put up a $300 first-prize purse.

The California Highway Patrol installs radio receivers on their H-Ds.

Racing Notes

Ben Campanale wins Daytona 200-Mile Expert Championship with record 73.99mph.

Joe Petrali wins National Hill-Climb Championship.

Sam Arena wins 200-Mile National Speedway Championship, Oakland, California, with record 83mph.

H-D wins National Miniature TT Races.

Joe Petrali retires from H-D racing team to work for Howard Hughes.

Model Year 1939

1939 EL. Wheels are period-correct aftermarket items.
Greg Field

Main Models

39-WLD Sport Solo: 45ci extra-high-compression flathead V-twin with four-speed transmission

39-WL Solo: 45ci high-compression flathead V-twin with four-speed transmission

39-WLDR Competition: 45ci flathead V-twin with four-speed transmission

39-EL Special Sport Solo: 61ci high-compression Knucklehead OHV V-twin with four-speed transmission

39-ES Sidecar Twin: 61ci medium-compression Knucklehead OHV V-twin with four-speed transmission and sidecar gearing

39-UL Sport Solo: 74ci high-compression flathead V-twin with four-speed transmission

39-U Solo: 74ci medium-compression flathead V-twin with four-speed transmission

39-US Sidecar Twin: 74ci medium-compression flathead V-twin with four-speed transmission and sidecar gearing

39-ULH Special Sport Solo: 80ci high-compression flathead V-twin with four-speed transmission

39-UH Solo: 80ci medium-compression flathead V-twin with four-speed transmission

39-UHS Sidecar Twin: 80ci medium-compression flathead V-twin with four-speed transmission and sidecar gearing

39-G Servi-Car with tow bar: 45ci flathead V-twin with three-speed-and-reverse transmission

39-GA Servi-Car without tow bar: 45ci flathead V-twin with three-speed-and-reverse transmission

39-GD large-compartment Servi-Car without tow bar: 45ci flathead V-twin with three-speed-and-reverse transmission

39-GDT large-compartment Servi-Car with tow bar: 45ci flathead V-twin with three-speed-and-reverse transmission

Specialty Models

39-GE large commercial Servi-Car with air tank: 45ci V-twin with air gauge, air hose, rear bumper, and tow bar

39-W: 45ci V-twin with 6.8ci head volume

39-WS Sidecar Twin: 45ci V-twin

39-UMG: 74ci V-twin with Bosch magneto

Sidecars and Chassis

39-LE: right-hand single-passenger sidecar

39-M: right-hand side van with cover

39-MO: right-hand side van without cover

Retail Prices

Model WL: $355

Model WLD: $355

Model WLDR: $380

Model EL: $435

Model ES: $435

Model UL: $395

Model U: $395

Model US: $395

Model ULH: $415

Model UH: $415

Model UHS: $415

Model G: $515

Model GA: $500

Model GD: $515

Model GDT: $530

Production Totals

Model W: 260

Model WS: 170

Model WL: 212

Model WLD: 326

Model WLDR: 173

Model WLDD: 273

Model G: 320

Model GA: 126

Model GD: 90

Model GDT: 114

Model EL: 2,695

Model ES: 214

Model U: 421

Model US: 1,327

Model UL: 902

Model ULH: 384

Model UH: 92

Model UHS: 109

Model UMG: 82

Options

Standard Solo Group: $15.50

Deluxe Solo Group: $47.00

Standard Police Group: $41.00

Standard Group for sidecar or package truck: $14.00

Standard Group for Servi-Car: $12.50

Deluxe Group for G or GA Servi-Car: $39.50

Deluxe Group for GD or GDT Servi-Car: $44.50

Standard Group for Sport sidecar: $17.75

Deluxe Group for Sport sidecar: $47.00

Deluxe Package Truck Group: $31.75

Paint Colors

Black with Ivory panel, Airway Blue with White panel, Teak Red with Black panel, Police Silver with Black striping (police stripes are one narrow, one wide)

Series W 45ci V-Twins

First Year

Revised pistons with a 1/8in lower ring groove

Front piston has three compression rings, and the rear piston has two compression rings and a lower oil-control ring

Long-life valve springs

Crankcase main bearings lapped straight through

Manifold has cadmium-plated unpolished pipes and nuts

Needle roller bearings on kickstarter side of transmission countershaft

Steering heads feature self-aligning head cones

Improved optional ride control for forks

Stainless steel fender strips

"Cat's-eye" streamlined instrument console; painted to match the color of the tank panel

Round, cadmium-plated panel light switch on instrument panel

"Boattail" taillight, painted the main color of the fender

Fuel filter with a compression type-fitting and gas line, feeding through the bottom

Extra-large oil cup on front brake cable

Drain plug in carburetor bowl

Lighter, stamped foot-brake lever

Russet, rhino-grain leather on saddles

Reshaped steering damper lever and new-type steering-damper pressure disc

Neoprene-covered spark plug cables

Mechanical brake stop lamp switch with a permanent bracket

Series E 61ci Knucklehead Big Twins

First Year

Front pistons have three compression rings; rear pistons, two compression rings and an oil-control ring

New pistons with more stock behind the third ring grooves

One-piece pinion gear shaft

Improved valve springs

Self-tapping screws used on rocker arm covers

Perforated screen on the breather valve

Oil pump and pinion gears are spline-fit

Oil-pump bypass spring pressure reduced by 4 to 6 pounds

Manifold has cadmium-plated unpolished pipes and nuts

Carburetor bowls have drain plugs

Fiber clutch discs riveted to the steel discs

Stronger clutch springs

Clutch pushrod thrust bearing is of the radial-thrust type

New, optional three-speed and three-speed-with-reverse transmissions with sliding-gear first

"Boattail" taillight; painted the main color of the fender

Steering head features self-aligning head cones

"Cat's-eye" streamlined dash console with round, cadmium-plated panel light switch knob; dash painted to match the color of the tank panel

Improved front chain oil deflector

Voltage regulator on radio-equipped bikes

Extra-large push ball oil cup on front brake

Mechanical brake stop lamp switch with a permanent bracket

Fuel filter with compression-type fitting and gas line

Front safety guard redesigned for more ground clearance

Neoprene-covered spark plug cables

Improved springing on front forks

Stainless steel fender strips

Russett, rhino-grain leather on seats

Optional chromed exhaust pipe covers

New four-speed transmission with sliding-gear second

Smaller high-speed notch on shifter gate

Revised shift pattern with neutral between second and third

Seat leather color is reddish-brown

Series U 74ci and 80ci Flathead Big Twins

First Year

Two compression rings and a lower oil-control ring on each piston

Intake manifold lengthened 3/4in to keep carburetor cooler

Wire and asbestos gasket fitted between carburetor and manifold to reduce vapor lock

Spring-equipped rear mounting bolts for the primary cover

Interchanged front and rear connecting rods

Closed boss on lower end of forked connecting rod

Thinner cylinder walls on 80ci models

Screen added to scavenger passage

Improved valve-spring covers

Carburetor bowls have drain plugs

Fiber clutch discs riveted to the steel discs

Stronger clutch springs

Clutch pushrod thrust bearing is of the radial-thrust type

New, optional three-speed and three-speed-with-reverse transmissions with sliding-gear first

"Boattail" taillight; painted the main color of the fender

Steering head features self-aligning head cones

"Cat's-eye" streamlined dash console with round, cadmium-plated panel light switch knob; dash painted to match the color of the tank panel

Improved front chain oil deflector

Voltage regulator on radio-equipped bikes

Extra-large push ball oil cup on front brake

Mechanical brake stop lamp switch with a permanent bracket

Fuel filter with compression-type fitting and gas line

Front safety guard redesigned for more ground clearance

Neoprene-covered spark plug cables

Improved springing on front forks

Stainless steel fender strips

Russett, rhino-grain leather on seats

Optional chromed exhaust pipe covers

Only Year

New four-speed transmission with sliding-gear second

Smaller high-speed notch on shifter gate

Revised shift pattern, with neutral between second and third

Seat leather color is reddish-brown

Series G Servi-Cars

First Year

Revised pistons with a 1/8in lower ring groove

Front piston has three compression rings, and the rear piston has two compression rings and a lower oil-control ring

Long-life valve springs

Crankcase main bearings lapped straight through

Needle roller bearings on kickstarter side of transmission countershaft

Steering heads feature self-aligning head cones

Stainless steel fender strips

"Cat's-eye" streamlined instrument console, painted to match the color of the tank panel

Round, cadmium-plated panel light switch on instrument panel

"Boattail" taillight, painted the main color of the fender

Fuel filter with a compression type fitting and gas line, feeding through the bottom

Extra-large oil cup on front brake cable

Drain plug in carburetor bowl

Lighter, stamped foot-brake lever

Russet, rhino-grain leather on saddles

Reshaped steering damper lever and new-type steering-damper pressure disc

Neoprene-covered spark plug cables

Mechanical brake stop lamp switch with a permanent bracket

Permanently attached tow bar

Extra-wide jaw clamp on tow bar

Stronger safety cable on tow bar

Larger Servi-Car body with box cover ribs perpendicular to the bumper

Chrome bumper optional

Stainless trim strip where rear apron joins body

Rear bumper is chrome-plated

Dual tail/stop lamps standard

Spring-loaded saw-toothed lever attached by pivot bolt to brake pedal as parking brake

Only Year

Stainless steel polished trim pieces on rear panel of Servi-car box on Models G and GD

Seat leather color is reddish-brown

Racing Notes

Ben Campanale wins Daytona 200-Mile Expert Championship with record 76.68mph.

Jack Cottrell wins Oakland 200-Mile National Speedway Championship on Model WLDR.

Armando Magri places second Oakland 200-Mile National Speedway Championship on Model WLDR.

H-D wins the National Miniature TT Races.

CHAPTER 5
1940-1949

Model Year 1940

1940 E. *Jeff Hackett*

Main Models

40-WLD Special Sport Solo: 45ci flathead V-twin with four-speed transmission and aluminum cylinder heads

40-WL Sport Solo: 45ci high-compression flathead V-twin with four-speed transmission

40-WLDR Competition: 45ci flathead V-twin racer with four-speed transmission and aluminum heads

40-EL Special Sport Solo: 61ci high-compression Knucklehead OHV V-twin with four-speed transmission

40-ES Sidecar Twin: 61ci medium-compression Knucklehead OHV V-twin with four-speed transmission and sidecar gearing

40-UL Special Sport Solo: 74ci high-compression flathead V-twin with four-speed transmission

40-U Solo: 74ci medium-compression flathead V-twin with four-speed transmission

40-US Sidecar Twin: 74ci medium-compression flathead V-twin with four-speed transmission and sidecar gearing

40-ULH Special Sport Solo: 80ci high-compression flathead V-twin with four-speed transmission

40-UH Solo: 80ci medium-compression flathead V-twin with four-speed transmission

40-UHS Sidecar Twin: 80ci medium-compression flathead V-twin with four-speed transmission and sidecar gearing

40-G Servi-Car with tow bar: 45ci flathead V-twin with three-speed-and-reverse transmission

40-GA Servi-Car without tow bar: 45ci flathead V-twin with three-speed-and-reverse transmission

40-GD large-compartment Servi-Car without tow bar: 45ci flathead V-twin with three-speed-and-reverse transmission

40-GDT large-compartment Servi-Car with tow bar: 45ci flathead V-twin with three-speed-and-reverse transmission

Specialty Models

40-W: 45ci V-twin with 6.8ci head volume

40-WS Sidecar Twin: 45ci V-twin

40-WLA: 45ci V-twin for the U.S. Army

40-UMG: 74ci V-twin with Bosch magneto

Sidecars and Chassis

40-LE: right-hand single-passenger sidecar

40-LEC: right-hand chassis for LE body

40-LS: right-hand single-passenger sidecar for 45ci twin

40-LSC: right-hand chassis for LS body

40-LLE: left-hand single-passenger sidecar

40-LLEC: left-hand chassis for LE body

40-LLS: left-hand single-passenger sidecar for 45ci twin

40-LLSC: left-hand chassis for LLS body

40-M: right-hand side van with cover

40-MC: right-hand chassis for M box

40-MO: right-hand side van without cover

40-MWC: right-hand chassis—57-7/8in tread

40-LMC: left-hand chassis

Retail Prices

Model WL: $350
Model WLD: $365
Model WLDR: $395
Model EL: $430
Model ES: $430
Model UL: $385
Model U: $385
Model US: $385
Model ULH: $410
Model UH: $410
Model UHS: $410
Model G: $515
Model GA: $500
Model GD: $515
Model GDT: $530

Production Totals

Model W: 439
Model WL: 569
Model WS: 202
Model WLD: 567
Model WLDR: 87
Model G: 468
Model GA: 156
Model GD: 158
Model GDT: 126
Model EL: 3,893
Model ES: 176
Model U: 260
Model US: 1,516
Model UL: 822
Model ULH: 672
Model UH: 187
Model UHS: 163

Options

Sport Solo Group: $22.50
Utility Solo Group: $11.00
Deluxe Solo Group: $46.00
Standard Police Group: $39.50
Utility Group for sidecar or package truck: $8.50
Utility Group for Servi-Car: $13.50
Deluxe Group for G or GA Servi-Car: $39.75
Deluxe Group for GD or GDT Servi-Car: $44.75
Deluxe Group for Sport sidecar: $50.00

Paint Colors

Black with Flight Red stripe, Clipper Blue with white stripe, Squadron Gray with Bittersweet stripe, Flight Red with Black stripe, and Police Silver with Black stripe (police only)

Series W 45ci V-Twins

First Year

Aluminum heads, large manifold, deep-finned cylinders, and large carburetor on WLD and WLDR
Two compression rings and one oil-control ring per piston
Rear crankcase baffle removed
Positions of male and female connecting rods interchanged, and lower-boss slot on female rod is half filled in for better oiling
Clutch key ring with six flat springs
Spring-loaded chrome-moly steel ball shift lock in transmission
Rollers fitter to gearshift fingers
Redesigned clutch foot-lever bearing cover
Tubular front forks; heat-treated
Teardrop tank nameplate is chrome-plated, stamped brass, embossed with the company name and a speed-line above and below; the name letters are painted Red, and the speed-lines are painted Black
Gas tank with instant-on fuel valve
Copper flange-type wire ends for horn and headlight
Forged flange on drive side of rear wheel hub
Half-moon footboards
Solo seat in brown smooth-grained cowhide
Optional 5.00x16in tires

Only Year

M-64 1-1/4in Linkert carburetor (Model WLA)
Air cleaner painted glossy olive drab (military models)

Series E 61ci Knucklehead Big Twins

First Year

Two compression rings and one oil-control ring on each piston
Rear crankcase baffle removed
Positions of male and female connecting rods interchanged, and lower-boss slot on female rod is half filled in for better oiling
Larger, 1-1/4in main bearing with 54 rollers
Straight-through-lapped main bearings
Ribbed gear cover with eight cooling fins
Five-fin cylinders
Larger intake ports in cylinder head
Manifold bore increased to 1-9/16in and is T-shaped
Larger, 1-1/2in carburetor with 1-5/16in venturi
Four-slotted spring keys on each lined clutch disc
Nonadjustable rocker-arm shafts
Four-speed constant-mesh transmission with neutral between first and second
Heat-treated front forks
Interconnected tanks; left gas tank features the instant-on fuel valve
Teardrop tank nameplate is chrome-plated, stamped brass, embossed with the company name and a speed-line above and below; the name letters are painted Red, and the speed-lines are painted Black
Toolbox designed in a streamline teardrop shape, with speed lines on cover, mounted at the right rear frame stay; uses a lock and key
Redesigned clutch foot-lever bearing cover
Half-moon footboards
Copper flange-type wire ends for horn and headlight
Flange on drive side of interchangeable wheels is now a forging
Cast nickel-iron front brake drum
Solo seat in brown smooth-grained cowhide
Redesigned front stand
5.00x16in tires optional
Whipped latex padding on optional Buddy Seat

Series U 74ci and 80ci Flathead Big Twins

First Year

Larger, 1-1/4in main bearing with 54 rollers

Straight-through-lapped main bearings

Ribbed gear cover with nine cooling fins

Four-slotted spring keys on each lined clutch disc

Four-speed constant-mesh transmission with neutral between first and second

Heat-treated front forks

Interconnected tanks; left gas tank features the instant-on fuel valve

Teardrop tank nameplate is chrome-plated, stamped brass, embossed with the company name and a speed-line above and below; the name letters are painted Red, and the speed-lines are painted Black

Toolbox designed in a streamlined teardrop shape, with speed lines on cover, mounted at the right rear frame stay; uses a lock and key

Redesigned clutch foot-lever bearing cover

Half-moon footboards

Copper flange-type wire ends for horn and headlight

Flange on drive side of interchangeable wheels is now a forging

Cast nickel-iron front brake drum

Solo seat in brown smooth-grained cowhide

Redesigned front stand

5.00x16in tires optional

Whipped latex padding on optional Buddy Seat

Aluminum cylinder heads 80ci twins

Series G Servi-Cars

First Year

Two compression rings and one oil-control ring per piston

Rear crankcase baffle removed

Positions of male and female connecting rods interchanged, and lower-boss slot on female rod is half filled in for better oiling

Clutch key ring with six flat springs

Spring-loaded chrome-moly steel ball shift lock in transmission

Rollers fitter to gear-shift fingers

Redesigned clutch foot-lever bearing cover

Tubular front forks; heat-treated

Teardrop tank nameplate is chrome-plated, stamped brass, embossed with the company name and a speed-line above and below; the name letters are painted Red, and the speed-lines are painted Black

Gas tank with instant-on fuel valve

Copper flange-type wire ends for horn and headlight

Half-moon footboards

Solo seat in brown smooth-grained cowhide

Optional 5.00x16in tires

Strengthened axle housing

Rear chain guard clearance increased 3/4in

Cast, nickel-iron rear brake drums with turnbuckle adjusters

Forged flange on drive side of rear wheel hubs

Tow-bar jaw clamp reinforced and fitted with a ratchet lock

Motor Company Minutes, 1940

Over 3,500 law enforcement agencies around the United States are using H-Ds for patrol use

Racing Notes

Babe Tancrede wins 200-Mile Expert Championship Classic with record 75.11mph.

H-D wins seven-place sweep at the Oakland 200-Mile National Championship.

1941 WLDR. *Gibson Keller*

Main Models

41-WLD Sport Solo: 45ci flathead V-twin with four-speed transmission

41-WL: 45ci flathead V-twin with four-speed transmission

41-WLDR Special Sport Solo: 45ci flathead V-twin with four-speed transmission

41-EL Special Sport Solo: 61ci high-compression Knucklehead OHV V-twin with four-speed transmission

41-ES Sidecar Twin: 61ci medium-compression Knucklehead OHV V-twin with four-speed transmission and sidecar gearing

41-UL Special Sport Solo: 74ci high-compression flathead V-twin with four-speed transmission

41-U Solo: 74ci medium-compression flathead V-twin with four-speed transmission

41-US Sidecar Twin: 74ci medium-compression flathead V-twin with four-speed transmission and sidecar gearing

41-FL Special Sport Solo: 74ci high-compression Knucklehead OHV V-twin with four-speed transmission

41-FS Sidecar Twin: 74ci medium-compression Knucklehead OHV V-twin with four-speed transmission and sidecar gearing

41-ULH Special Sport Solo: 80ci high-compression flathead V-twin with four-speed transmission

41-UH: 80ci medium-compression flathead V-twin with four-speed transmission

41-UHS Sidecar Twin: 80ci medium-compression flathead V-twin with four-speed transmission and sidecar gearing

41-G Servi-Car with tow bar: 45ci flathead V-twin with three-speed-and-reverse transmission

41-GA Servi-Car without tow bar: 45ci flathead V-twin with three-speed-and-reverse transmission

41-GD large-compartment Servi-Car without tow bar: 45ci flathead V-twin with three-speed-and-reverse transmission

41-GDT large-compartment Servi-Car with tow bar: 45ci flathead V-twin with three-speed-and-reverse transmission

Specialty Models

41-WLA: 45ci V-twin for the U.S. Army

41-WLS Sidecar Twin: 45ci V-twin with 4.75:1 compression ratio

41-WR Special: 45ci V-twin race model

41-UA: 74ci flathead V-twin for the U.S. Army

Sidecars and Chassis

41-LE: right-hand single-passenger sidecar

41-LEC: right-hand chassis for LE body

41-LS: right-hand single-passenger sidecar for 45ci twin

41-LSC: right-hand chassis for LS body

41-LLE: left-hand single-passenger sidecar

41-LLEC: left-hand chassis for LE body

41-LLS: left-hand single-passenger sidecar for 45ci twin

41-LLSC: left-hand chassis for LLS body

41-M: right-hand side van with cover

41-MC: right-hand chassis for M box

41-MO: right-hand side van without cover

41-MWC: right-hand chassis with 57-7/8in tread

41-LMC: left-hand chassis

Retail Prices

Model WL: $350

Model WLD: $365

Model WLDR: $385

Model EL: $425

Model E: $425

Model US: $385

Model U: $385

Model ULH: $410

Model UH: $410

Model FL: $465

Model F: $465

Model G: $515

Model GA: $500

Model GD: $515

Model GDT: $530

Production Totals

Model W45: 4,095

Model WLA: 2,282

Model WLC: 149

Model WL: 4,277

Model WLA: 2,460

Model WLD: 455

Model WLDR: 171

Model WR: 36

Model WLC: 205

Model G: 607

Model GA: 221

Model GD: 195

Model GDT: 136

Model EL: 2,280

Model ES: 261

Model FL: 2,452

Model FS: 156

Model U: 884

Model US: 1,888

Model UL: 715

Model ULH: 420

Model UH: 126

Model UHS: 112

Options

Standard Solo accessory Group
Deluxe Solo accessory Group
Sport Solo Group
Deluxe Solo Group
Utility Solo Group
Standard Police Group
Utility Group for Sidecar or Package Truck
Utility Group for Servi-Car
Deluxe Group for Servi-Car
Deluxe Group for Sport Sidecar

Paint Colors

Brilliant Black, Skyway Blue, Flight Red, Cruiser Green, or Police Silver (police only)

Series W 45ci V-Twins

First Year

Oxide-coated piston rings
Redesigned valve springs
Centrifugally controlled oil feed pump
Larger, 7in-diameter air cleaner
Redesigned clutch with two fiber discs, two steel discs, one spring disc, and a larger hub that is splined to the mainshaft
Larger clutch pushrod bearing
Longer, straight clutch release lever
Multistranded clutch cable
New, synchromesh transmission
Revised inner and outer primary covers
Frame redesigned for the new transmission and toolbox location; transmission mounts to the frame using three studs
Streamlined teardrop-shaped toolbox with speed-lined cover; toolbox now mounted on the right rear frame stay; uses a lock and key
"Plain-type" hand lever, polished aluminum
"Airplane-style" speedometer
1940-style tank badges but with a gasket underneath and chrome strips extending to the front and rear of the tank
Taillight body painted Black
16in wheels standard
Combination loose ball bearing hub and brake drum (all 45ci solos, except WLC)
Wider rear brake drum
Redesigned optional rear safety guard
Starter spring 9/16in-wide x 2-5/8in diameter
Front brake drum and hub one unit
Rear chainguard clamped to frame
WLDR is now a regular road model
Gearshift cyanide-hardened
Battery grounded to frame
Front fender light is "Blacked out" (WLA)
Blackout ignition switch covers painted olive drab (WLA)
"Cat's-eye" lenses Blacked out (WLA)
2-1/2in-diameter muffler with half fishtail venting exhaust back and up (WLA)
Twin taillights (WLA)
Oil-bath air cleaner (WLA)

Series E and F 61ci and 74ci Knucklehead Big Twins

First Year

Series F 74ci OHV engine; bore is 3-7/16in and stroke is 3-31/32in
Larger, heavier, 8-1/2in flywheels
Oxide-coated piston rings
Mainshaft thrust bearings redesigned and fitted with shields on both sides
Redesigned crankcases
Revised gear-case cover (breather passage "hump" protrudes diagonally across the cover)
Centrifugal-bypass oil pump
Intake manifold 1/2in longer to prevent vapor lock
Larger, 7in air cleaner (Sport Solo and Deluxe Solo accessory Groups)
Redesigned clutch with three friction discs, three steel discs, and one spring disc; the clutch hub is also larger in diameter, has 10 driving pins, and has 36 ball bearings
Frame has 29deg neck angle
1gal reserve gas supply
"Airplane-style" speedometer
Taillight body painted Black
Redesigned transmission main nut
"Plain-type" hand lever, polished aluminum
16in wheels standard
Carburetor venturi on 61ci models increased to 1-1/8in
New speed-lined muffler
Gearshift cyanide-hardened
Battery grounded to frame
1940-style tank badges but with a gasket underneath and chrome strips extending to the front and rear of the tank
Redesigned clutch-foot-lever bearing
One-piece clutch release lever
Heavier clamping ring on horn

Series U and UH 74ci and 80ci Big Twins

First Year

Oxide-coated piston rings
Mainshaft thrust bearings redesigned and fitted with shields on both sides
Redesigned crankcases
Centrifugal-bypass oil pump
Larger, 7in air cleaner (Sport Solo and Deluxe Solo accessory groups)
Redesigned clutch with three friction discs, three steel discs, and one spring disc; the clutch hub is also larger in diameter, has 10 driving pins and has 36 ball bearings
Frame has 29deg neck angle
1gal reserve gas supply
"Airplane-style" speedometer
Taillight body painted Black
Redesigned transmission main nut
"Plain-type" hand lever, polished aluminum
16in wheels standard
New speed-lined muffler
Gearshift cyanide-hardened
Battery grounded to frame
1940-style tank badges but with a gasket underneath and chrome strips extending to the front and rear of the tank
Redesigned clutch-foot-lever bearing
One-piece clutch release lever
Heavier clamping ring on horn

Series G Servi-Cars

First Year

Oxide-coated piston rings
Redesigned valve springs
Centrifugally controlled oil feed pump
Larger, 7in-diameter air cleaner (optional)
Redesigned clutch with two fiber discs, two steel discs, and one spring disc and a larger hub that is splined to the mainshaft
Larger clutch pushrod bearing
Longer, straight clutch release lever
Multistranded clutch cable
New, synchromesh transmission
Revised inner and outer primary covers
Frame redesigned for the new transmission; transmission mounts to the frame using three studs
"Plain-type" hand lever, polished aluminum
"Airplane-style" speedometer
1940-style tank badges, but with a gasket underneath and chrome strips extending to the front and rear of the tank
Taillight shell painted Black
16in wheels standard
Stronger starter spring
Gearshift cyanide-hardened
Battery grounded to frame
Welded rear axle tube
New recoil strap guide
Big Twin interchangeable front wheel and brake
Big twin front axle

Motor Company Minutes, 1941

Civilian sales nationwide drop to around 6,000 motorcycles.
Suspended production of civilian motorcycles, due to the war.
Last year H-D Service School, first started in 1917.

Model Year 1942

1942 XA. *Randy Leffingwell*

Main Models

42-WLD Special Sport Solo: 45ci flathead V-twin with four-speed transmission and aluminum cylinder heads

42-WL Solo: 45ci high-compression flathead V-twin with four-speed transmission

42-EL Special Sport Solo: 61ci high-compression Knucklehead OHV V-twin with four-speed transmission

42-E Solo: 61ci medium-compression Knucklehead OHV V-twin with four-speed transmission

42-UL Special Sport Solo: 74ci high-compression flathead V-twin with four-speed transmission

42-U Solo: 74ci medium-compression flathead V-twin with four-speed transmission, medium compression

42-FL Special Sport Solo: 74ci high-compression Knucklehead OHV V-twin with four-speed transmission

42-F Solo: 74ci medium-compression Knucklehead OHV V-twin with four-speed transmission

42-G Servi-Car with tow bar: 45ci flathead V-twin with three-speed-and-reverse transmission

42-GA Servi-Car without tow bar: 45ci flathead V-twin with three-speed-and-reverse transmission

Specialty Models

42-WLA: 45ci V-twin for the U.S. Army
42-WLS Sidecar Twin: 45ci V-twin
42-WLC: 45ci V-twin for the Canadian Army
42-ELC: 61ci V-twin for the Canadian Army
42-US Sidecar Twin: 74ci flathead V-twin
42-XA Solo Twin: 45ci flathead opposed twin with shaft drive and foot shift for the U.S. Army

Sidecars and Chassis

42-LE: right-hand single-passenger sidecar
42-LEC: right-hand chassis for LE body
42-LS: right-hand single-passenger sidecar for 45ci twin
42-LSC: right-hand chassis for LS body
42-LLE: left-hand single-passenger sidecar
42-LLEC: left-hand chassis for LE body
42-LLS: left-hand single-passenger sidecar for 45ci twin
42-LLSC: left-hand chassis for LLS body
42-M: right-hand side van with cover
42-MC: right-hand chassis for M box
42-MWC: right-hand chassis-57-7/8in tread
42-LMC: left-hand chassis

Retail Prices

Model WLD: $365
Model WL: $350
Model UL: $385
Model U: $385
Model EL: $425
Model E: $425
Model FL: $465
Model F: $465
Model G: $525
Model GA: $510

Production Totals

Army U: 41
Army USA: 426
Army WLC: 9,820
Army WLA: 13,051
Army XA: 1,000
Model U: 421
Model US: 978
Model UL: 405
Model EL: 620
Model ELA: 8
Model ES: 164
Model ELC: 45
Model FS: 107
Model FL: 799
Model WL: 142
Model WLA: 13,460
Model WLC: 9,825
Model WLD: 133
Model WR: 36
Model G: 138
Model GA: 261
Model XA: 1,011

Options

Sport Solo Group: $27.00
Deluxe Solo Group: $60.00
Utility Solo Group: $14.50
Standard Police Group: $42.50
Utility Group for sidecar or package truck: $12.00
Utility Group for Servi-Car: $18.50
Deluxe Group for Servi-Car: $44.00
Deluxe Group for Sport sidecar: $54.00

Paint Colors

Brilliant Black, Skyway Blue, Flight Red, Cruiser Green, and Police Gray (police only)

Series W 45ci V-Twins

First Year

Blackout drive lamps (WLA)
Radio frequency feedback suppresser ends, on fabric covered plug cables (WLA, late year)
Set of two Blackout lamps, taillight and stoplight (WLA)
Blackout lamp painted a flat light Olive Drab (WLA)
Horn body and cover painted gloss Black (WLA)
Tappet guides painted White
Transmission side cover painted White
Oil-pump body painted white
Positions of headlight and horn swapped (WLA and WLC)

Series E and F 61ci and 74ci Knucklehead Big Twins

First Year

Tappet guides painted White
Oil-pump body painted White
Fuel filter featuring a tapered flair nut fitting and gas line, feeding through the side

Series U 74ci Flathead Twins

First Year

Tappet guides painted White
Oil-pump body painted White
Fuel filter featuring a tapered flair nut fitting and gas line, feeding through the side

Series G Servi-Cars

First Year

Box-cover ribs parallel to rear bumper
Shock absorbers
Tappet guides painted white
Oil-pump body painted white
Fuel filter featuring a tapered flair nut fitting and gas line, feeding through the side

Motor Company Minutes, 1942

February 7, Walter Davidson, president, passes away.
February 23, William H. Davidson named president.

Model Year 1943

Main Models

43-E Solo: 61ci medium compression Knucklehead OHV V-twin with four-speed transmission

43-EL Special Sport Solo: 61ci high-compression Knucklehead OHV V-twin with four-speed transmission

43-U Solo: 74ci medium-compression flathead V-twin with four-speed transmission

43-UL Solo: 74ci high-compression flathead V-twin with four-speed transmission

43-F Solo: 74ci medium compression Knucklehead OHV V-twin with four-speed transmission

43-FL Special Sport Solo: 74ci high-compression Knucklehead OHV V-twin with four-speed transmission

43-G Servi-Car with tow bar: 45ci flathead V-twin with three-speed-and-reverse transmission

43-GA Servi-Car without tow bar: 45ci flathead V-twin with three-speed-and-reverse transmission

Specialty Notes

42-WLA: 45ci V-twin with U.S. Army

43-WLC: 45ci V-twin with Canadian Army

43-XA Solo Twin: Special model for U.S. Army

42-US Sidecar Twin: 74ci V-twin for the South African Army (to end of contract)

Sidecars and Chassis

43-LE: right-hand single-passenger sidecar

43-LEC: right-hand chassis for LE body

43-LS: right-hand single-passenger sidecar for 45ci twin

43-LSC: right-hand chassis for LS body

43-LLE: left-hand single-passenger sidecar

43-LLEC: left-hand chassis for LE body

43-LLS: left-hand single-passenger sidecar for 45ci twin

43-LLSC: left-hand chassis for LLS body

43-LLE: left-hand single-passenger sidecar for South African Army

43-M: right-hand side van with cover

43-MC: right-hand chassis for M box

43-MWC: right-hand chassis, 57-7/8in tread

43-LMC: left-hand chassis

Retail Prices

Model UL: $385

Model U: $385

Model EL: $425

Model E: $425

Model FL: $465

Model F: $465

Production

Model U: 493

Model US: 1,315

Model UL: 11

Model ES: 105

Model EL: 53

Model FS: 12

Model FL: 33

Model WLA: 24,717

Model WLC: 2,647

Model G: 22

Model GA: 113

Options

Utility Solo Group: $14.50

Standard Police Group: $42.50

Utility Group: (sidecar or Police combination) $12.00

Paint Colors

Factory optional Gray or Silver

Series W 45ci V-Twins

First Year

Tappet guides and crankcases painted Olive Drab (WLA and WLC, late year)

Tank nameplates painted Gray with Red lettering and Black speed-lines; Blue with Red lettering and Ivory speed-lines; or Black with Red lettering and Ivory speed-lines

No stainless steel fender trim

Air cleaner is Black-painted steel

Seat-post plungers are Parkerized

Front fender lamps not available

Seats use horsehair stuffing for padding

Floorboards are ribbed steel

"Winged-face" horn; horn body and cover painted gloss Black

Hand lever and bracket are painted steel

Series E and F 61ci and 74ci Knucklehead Big Twins

First Year

Tank nameplates painted Gray with Red lettering and Black speed-lines; Blue with Red lettering and Ivory speed-lines; or Black with Red lettering and Ivory speed-lines

No stainless steel fender trim

Air cleaner is Black-painted steel

Seat-post plungers are Parkerized

Front fender lamps not available

Seats use horsehair stuffing for padding

Floorboards are ribbed steel

"Winged-face" horn; horn body and cover painted gloss Black

Hand lever and bracket are painted steel

Series U 74ci Flathead Twins

First Year

Tank nameplates painted Gray with Red lettering and Black speed-lines; Blue with Red lettering and Ivory speed-lines; or Black with Red lettering and Ivory speed-lines

No stainless steel fender trim

Air cleaner is Black-painted steel

Seat-post plungers are Parkerized

Front fender lamps not available

Seats use horsehair stuffing for padding

Floorboards are ribbed steel

"Winged-face" horn; horn body and cover painted gloss Black

Hand lever and bracket are painted steel

Series G Servi-Cars

First Year

Tank nameplates painted Gray with Red lettering and Black speed-lines; Blue with Red lettering and Ivory speed-lines; or Black with Red lettering and Ivory speed-lines

No stainless steel fender trim

Air cleaner is Black-painted steel

Seat-post plungers are Parkerized

Front fender lamps not available

Seats use horsehair stuffing for padding

Floorboards are ribbed steel

"Winged-face" horn; horn body and cover painted gloss Black

Hand lever and bracket are painted steel

Motor Company Minutes, 1943

No large civilian production; only special government permits.

The federal government allows the purchase of H-D motorcycles by 137 police departments across the United States

December issue of *The Enthusiast* features ad proclaiming, "Home wouldn't be home without a H-D."

Model WLAs see action as dispatch riders and with armored units.

H-D is awarded the Army-Navy "E" award for excellence.

William S. Harley passes away.

Model Year 1944

Main Models

44-E Solo: 61ci medium-compression Knucklehead OHV V-twin with four-speed transmission

44-EL Special Sport Solo: 61ci high-compression Knucklehead OHV V-twin with four-speed transmission

44-U Solo: 74ci medium-compression flathead V-twin with four-speed transmission

44-UL Solo: 74ci high-compression flathead V-twin with four-speed transmission

44-F Solo: 74ci medium-compression Knucklehead OHV V-twin with four-speed transmission

44-FL Special Sport Solo: 74ci high-compression Knucklehead OHV V-twin with four-speed transmission

44-G Servi-Car with tow bar: 45ci flathead V-twin with three-speed-and-reverse transmission

44-GA Servi-Car without tow bar: 45ci flathead V-twin with three-speed-and-reverse transmission

Specialty Models

42-WLA: 45ci V-twin with U.S. Army

43-WLC: 45ci V-twin with Canadian Army

44-FS Sidecar Twin: 74ci V-twin with OHV

44-ES Sidecar Twin: 61ci V-twin with OHV

44-US Sidecar Twin: 74ci flathead V-twin

Sidecars and Chassis

44-LE: right-hand single-passenger sidecar

44-LEC: right-hand chassis for LE body

44-LS: right-hand single-passenger sidecar for 45ci twin

44-LSC: right-hand chassis for LS body

44-LLE: left-hand single-passenger sidecar

44-LLEC: left-hand chassis for LE body

44-LLS: left-hand single-passenger sidecar for 45ci twin

44-LLSC: left-hand chassis for LLS body

44-M: right-hand Package Truck with cover

44-MC: right-hand chassis for M box

44-LMC: left-hand chassis

44-MWC: right-hand Package Truck chassis (extra wide)

Retail Prices

Model UL: $385

Model U: $385

Model EL: $425

Model E: $425

Model FL: $465

Model F: $465

Production

Model U: 580

Model US: 206

Model UL: 366

Model ES: 180

Model EL: 116

Model FS: 67

Model FL: 172

Model WL: 57

Model WLA: 11,531

Model WLC: 5,356

Model G: 6

Model GA: 51

Options

Utility Solo Group: $14.50
Standard Police Group: $42.50
Utility Group, sidecar or package truck: $12.00

Paint Colors

Factory optional Gray or Silver

Series W 45ci V-Twins

First Year

Front fender is a simple, curved strip without a beaded edge or tip (WLA)
Keyless ignition switch (WLA)
Radio noise-suppression equipment installed

Series E and F 61ci and 74ci Knucklehead Big Twins

First Year

"S-3" synthetic rubber tires
Linkert carburetor bodies painted Black

Series U 74ci Flathead Twins

First Year

"S-3" synthetic rubber tires
Linkert carburetor bodies painted Black

Series G Servi-Cars

First Year

"S-3" synthetic rubber tire
Linkert carburetor bodies painted Black

Motor Company Minutes, 1944

February, orders for 11,331 motorcycles are canceled by the War Department
More than 500 workers are laid off, stemming from the canceled Army orders.
The work week is cut to 40 hours.
July 27, the War Production Board increases civilian production by 450 motorcycles.
September 8, the War Production Board increases civilian production by 600 motorcycles.

Model Year 1945

Main Models

45-WL: 45ci flathead V-twin with four-speed transmission
45-E Solo: 61ci medium-compression Knucklehead OHV V-twin with four-speed transmission
45-EL Special Sport Solo: 61ci high-compression Knucklehead OHV V-twin with four-speed transmission
45-ES Sidecar Twin: 61ci medium-compression Knucklehead OHV V-twin with four-speed transmission and sidecar gearing
45-U Commercial: 74ci medium-compression flathead V-twin with four-speed transmission
45-UL Solo: 74ci high-compression flathead V-twin with four-speed transmission
45-US Sidecar Twin: 74ci medium-compression flathead V-twin with four-speed transmission and sidecar gearing
45-F Solo: 74ci medium-compression Knucklehead OHV V-twin with four-speed transmission
45-FL Special Sport Solo: 74ci high-compression Knucklehead OHV V-twin with four-speed transmission
45-FS Sidecar Twin: 74ci medium-compression Knucklehead OHV V-twin with four-speed transmission and sidecar gearing
45-G Servi-Car with tow bar: 45ci flathead V-twin with three-speed-and-reverse transmission
45-GA Servi-Car without tow bar: 45ci flathead V-twin with three-speed-and-reverse transmission

Specialty Models

42-WLA: 45ci flathead V-twin for the U.S. Army
45-WSR: 45ci flathead V-twin for the Russian Army

Sidecars and Chassis

45-LE: right-hand single-passenger sidecar
45-LEC: right-hand chassis for LE body
45-LS: right-hand single-passenger sidecar for 45ci twin
45-LSC: right-hand chassis for LS body
45-LLE: left-hand single-passenger sidecar
45-LLEC: left-hand chassis for LE body
45-LLS: left-hand single-passenger sidecar for 45ci twin
45-LLSC: left-hand chassis for LLS body
45-M: right-hand Package Truck with cover
45-MC: right-hand chassis for M box
45-LMC: left-hand chassis
45-MWC: right-hand Package Truck chassis (extra wide)

Retail Prices

Model WL: $395.97
Model E: $463.67
Model EL: $463.67
Model ES: $463.67
Model F: $465.00
Model FL: $465.00
Model FS: $465.00
Model U: $427.25
Model UL: $427.25
Model US: $427.25
Model G: $580.33
Model GA: $568.43
Model XA: $500.00

Production

Model U: 513
Model US: 217
Model UL: 555
Model ES: 282
Model EL: 398
Model FS: 131
Model FL: 619
Model WL: 1,357
Model WLA: 8,317
Model G: 26
Model GA: 60

Options

Special Solo Group: $44.50
Utility Solo Group: $14.50
Standard Police Group: $42.50
Deluxe Group for Servi-Car: $44.00
Utility Group for Servi-Car: $18.50
Deluxe Group for Sport sidecar: $49.00
Utility Group for sidecar or package truck: $12.00

Paint Colors

Gray

Series W 45ci V-Twins

First Year

Aluminum heads optional on Model WL

Series U 74ci Flathead Twins

First Year

Aluminum heads optional

Motor Company Minutes, 1945

October, employees begin a 40-day strike.
Mid-October, the War Production Board increases civilian production by 6,000 motorcycles
November, civilian production resumes.
The government starts selling surplus military motorcycles to the public at a price of $450 each. All the motorcycles come fully equipped with all military equipment.

Model Year 1946

1946 WL. *Jeff Hackett*

Main Models

46-WL Solo: 45ci flathead V-twin with three-speed transmission
46-E Solo: 61ci medium-compression Knucklehead OHV V-twin with four-speed transmission
46-EL Special Sport Solo: 61ci high-compression Knucklehead OHV V-twin with four-speed transmission
46-ES Sidecar Twin: 61ci medium-compression Knucklehead OHV V-twin with four-speed transmission and sidecar gearing
46-U Solo: 74ci medium-compression flathead V-twin with four-speed transmission
46-UL Solo: 74ci high-compression flathead V-twin with four-speed transmission
46-US Sidecar Twin: 74ci medium-compression flathead V-twin with four-speed transmission and sidecar gearing
46-F Solo: 74ci medium-compression Knucklehead OHV V-twin with four-speed transmission
46-FL Special Sport Solo: 74ci high-compression Knucklehead OHV V-twin with four-speed transmission
46-FS Sidecar Twin: 74ci medium-compression Knucklehead OHV V-twin with four-speed transmission and sidecar gearing
46-G Servi-Car with tow bar: 45ci flathead V-twin with three-speed-and-reverse transmission
46-GA Servi-Car without tow bar: 45ci flathead V-twin with three-speed-and-reverse transmission

Specialty Models

46-WL-SP: 45ci flathead V-twin with aluminum heads

Sidecars and Chassis

46-LE: right-hand single-passenger sidecar
46-LEC: right-hand chassis for LE body
46-LS: right-hand single-passenger sidecar for 45ci twin
46-LSC: right-hand chassis for LS body
46-LLE: left-hand single-passenger sidecar
46-LLEC: left-hand chassis for LE body
46-LLS: left-hand single-passenger sidecar for 45ci twin
46-LLSC: left-hand chassis for LLS body
46-M: right-hand Package Truck with cover
46-MC: right-hand chassis for M box
46-LMC: left-hand chassis

Retail Prices
Model WL: $395.97
Model WL-SP: $402.97
Model UL: $427.25
Model U: $427.25
Model US: $427.25
Model EL: $463.67
Model E: $463.67
Model ES: $463.67
Model FL: $465.00
Model F: $465.00
Model FS: $465.00
Model G: $593.93
Model GA: $582.07

Production
Model U: 670
Model US: 1,052
Model UL: 1,800
Model ES: 244
Model EL: 2,098
Model FS: 418
Model FL: 3,986
Model WL: 4,410
Model WR: 100
Model G: 766
Model GA: 678

Options
Special Solo Group: $55.00
Utility Solo Group: $14.50
Standard Police Group: $57.00
Deluxe Group for Servi-Car: $44.00
Utility Group for Servi-Car: $18.50
Deluxe Group for Sport sidecar: $49.00
Utility Group for sidecar or package truck: $12.00

Paint Colors
Gray or Flight Red

Series W 45ci V-Twins

First Year
Tappet guides painted Silver (midyear)
Seat padding is spun latex rubber
Chrome plating on tank nameplates, spirals, and other parts gradually became available later in the model year

Series E and F 61ci and 74ci Knucklehead Big Twins

First Year
Seat padding is spun latex rubber
30deg-neck-angle frames
Tappet guides painted Silver (midyear)
Shock absorber for forks (optional)
Offset forks (late year)
Handlebars for offset forks (late year)
Chrome plating on tank nameplates, spirals, pushrod covers, and other parts gradually became available later in the model year

Series U 74ci Flathead Twins

First Year
Seat padding is spun latex rubber
30deg neck-angle frames
Tappet guides painted Silver (midyear)
Shock absorber for forks (optional)
Offset forks (late year)
Handlebars for offset forks (late year)
Chrome plating on tank name plates, spirals, pushrod covers, and other parts gradually became available later in the model year

Series G Servi-Cars

First Year
Seat padding is spun latex rubber
Additional terminal posts located in the rear bumper braces for the stop lamps
Tappet guides painted silver (midyear)
Chrome plating on tank nameplates, spirals, and other parts gradually became available later in the model year

Motor Company Minutes, 1946
Purchase of the A.O. Smith Propeller Plant in Wauwatosa, Wisconsin, for $1.5 million.
Production up 30 percent.
First year of hydraulic fork experimentation.
Government sales of 15,000 surplus Model WLA motorcycles to the public.

1947 EL. *Jeff Hackett*

Main Models

47-WL Solo: 45ci flathead V-twin with three-speed transmission

47-E Sport Solo: 61ci medium-compression Knucklehead OHV V-twin with four-speed transmission

47-EL Special Sport Solo: 61ci high-compression Knucklehead OHV V-twin with four-speed transmission

47-ES Sidecar Twin: 61ci medium-compression Knucklehead OHV V-twin with four-speed transmission and sidecar gearing

47-U Sport Solo: 74ci medium-compression flathead V-twin with four-speed transmission

47-UL Special Sport Solo: 74ci high-compression flathead V-twin with four-speed transmission

47-US Sidecar Twin: 74ci medium-compression flathead V-twin with four-speed transmission and sidecar gearing

47-F Sport Solo: 74ci medium-compression Knucklehead OHV V-twin with four-speed transmission

47-FL Special Sport Solo: 74ci high-compression Knucklehead OHV V-twin with four-speed transmission

47-FS Sidecar Twin: 74ci medium-compression Knucklehead OHV V-twin with four-speed transmission and sidecar gearing

47-G Servi-Car with tow bar: 45ci flathead V-twin with three-speed-and-reverse transmission

47-GA Servi-Car without tow bar: 45ci flathead V-twin with three-speed-and-reverse transmission

Specialty Models

47-WL-SP: 45ci flathead V-twin with aluminum head

Sidecars and Chassis

47-LE: right-hand single-passenger sidecar

47-LEC: right-hand chassis for LE body

47-LS: right-hand single-passenger sidecar for 45ci twin

47-LSC: right-hand chassis for LS body

47-LLE: left-hand single-passenger sidecar

47-LLEC: left-hand chassis for LE body

47-LLECC: left-hand chassis, component parts

47-LLS: left-hand single-passenger sidecar for 45ci twin

47-LLSC: left-hand chassis for LLS body

47-M: right-hand Package Truck with cover

47-MC: right-hand chassis for M box

47-LMC: left-hand chassis

47-LMCC: left-hand chassis, component parts

Retail Prices

Model WL: $490

Model UL: $545

Model U: $545

Model US: $545

Model EL: $590

Model E: $590

Model ES: $590

Model FL: $605

Model F: $605

Model FS: $605

Model G: $710

Model GA: $695

Production

Model U: 422

Model US: 1,267

Model UL: 1,243

Model ES: 237

Model EL: 4,117

Model FS: 401

Model FL: 6,893

Model WL: 3,338

Model WR: 20

Model G: 1,307

Model GA: 870

Options

Special Solo Group with hydraulic shock absorber: $100.00

Special Solo Group with ride control: $92.50

Utility Solo Group with hydraulic shock absorber: $34.00

Utility Solo Group with ride control: $26.50

Standard Police Group with hydraulic shock absorber: $75.00

Standard Police Group with ride control: $67.50

Deluxe Group for Servi-Car: $58.00

Utility Group for Servi-Car: $26.00

Utility Group for sidecar or Package Truck, with hydraulic shock absorber: $31.50

Utility Group for sidecar or Package Truck, with ride control: $24.00

Deluxe Group for Sport sidecar: $85.00

Paint Colors

Brilliant Black, Flight Red, Skyway Blue, Police Silver (police only), and Olive Green (export)

Series W 45ci V-Twins

First Year

New shifter gate pattern with first at the rear

"Tombstone" taillight, die-cast zinc alloy

Tank emblem is a small Red ball with name "Harley-Davidson" (letters in Red) stamped into the bar trailing behind; designed by Brooks Stevens

"Two-light" instrument cover, painted to match color of the tanks

Hard Black plastic handlebar grips optional

Black rubber handlebar grips standard

Black leather Solo seat standard

Taillight license bracket uses flex-lock nuts

Chrome-plated parts return after wartime shortages: air cleaner cover, front fender lamp, horn cover, and other parts

Speedometer facelift: Red pointer, larger numerals, gradual shading of dial from Black on outer ring to white in the center

Spotlight terminal post standard

Revised circuit-breaker adjustment

Series E and F 61ci and 74ci Knucklehead Big Twins

First/Only Year

New shifter gate pattern (rear to front): 1-N-2-3-4

"Tombstone" taillight, die-cast zinc alloy

Tank emblem is a small Red ball with name "Harley-Davidson" (letters in Red) stamped into the bar trailing behind; designed by Brooks Stevens

"Two-light" instrument cover, painted to match color of the tanks

Hard Black plastic handlebar grips optional

Black rubber handlebar grips standard

Black leather Solo seat standard

Taillight license bracket uses flex-lock nuts

Chrome-plated parts return after wartime shortages: air cleaner cover, front fender lamp, horn cover, and other parts

Speedometer facelift: Red pointer, larger numerals, gradual shading of dial from Black on outer ring to white in the center

Spotlight terminal post standard

Revised circuit-breaker adjustment

Series U 74ci Flathead Twins

First Year

New shifter gate pattern (rear to front): 1-N-2-3-4

"Tombstone" taillight, die-cast zinc alloy

Tank emblem is a small Red ball with name "Harley-Davidson" (letters in Red) stamped into the bar trailing behind; designed by Brooks Stevens

"Two-light" instrument cover, painted to match color of the tanks

Hard Black plastic handlebar grips optional

Black rubber handlebar grips standard

Black leather Solo seat standard

Taillight license bracket uses flex-lock nuts

Chrome-plated parts return after wartime shortages: air cleaner cover, front fender lamp, horn cover, and other parts

Speedometer facelift: Red pointer, larger numerals, gradual shading of dial from Black on outer ring to white in the center

Spotlight terminal post standard

Revised circuit-breaker adjustment

Series G Servi-Cars

First Year

Revised shifter-gate pattern for the three-speed-with-reverse transmission (front to back): 3-2-N-1-R

Servi-Car body cover is one-piece, 18-gauge steel

"Tombstone" taillight, die-cast zinc alloy

Tank emblem is a small Red ball with name "Harley-Davidson" (letters in Red) stamped into the bar trailing behind; designed by Brooks Stevens

"Two-light" instrument cover, painted to match color of the tanks

Hard Black plastic handlebar grips optional

Black rubber handlebar grips standard

Black leather Solo seat standard

Taillight license bracket uses flex-lock nuts

Chrome-plated parts return after wartime shortages: air cleaner cover, front fender lamp, horn cover, and other parts

Speedometer facelift: Red pointer, larger numerals, gradual shading of dial from Black on outer ring to white in the center; only year

Spotlight terminal post standard

Revised circuit-breaker adjustment

Motor Company Minutes, 1947

First expansion since the war. The Capitol Drive plant is purchased to accommodate a need for more manufacturing space.

Dealers Conference held November 27 at the Shroeder Hotel in Milwaukee, largest conference to date.

H-D's largest catalog printed, offering more accessory items

First year an H-D black leather motorcycle jacket is advertised in catalog.

H-D is granted the rights, along with BSA, for production of a 125cc two-stroke of DKW design.

Racing Notes

Jimmy Chann wins Grand National Championship.

Babe Tancrede wins Laconia 100-Mile Road Race.

1948 FL. *Jeff Hackett*

Main Models

48-S Lightweight: 125cc flathead single cylinder with three-speed transmission

48-WL Solo: 45ci flathead V-twin with three-speed transmission

48-E Sport Solo: 61ci medium-compression Panhead OHV V-twin with four-speed transmission

48-EL Special Sport Solo: 61ci high-compression Panhead OHV V-twin with four-speed transmission

48-ES Sidecar Twin: 61ci medium-compression Panhead OHV V-twin with four-speed transmission and sidecar gearing

48-U Sport Solo: 74ci medium-compression flathead V-twin with four-speed transmission

48-UL Special Sport Solo: 74ci high-compression flathead V-twin with four-speed transmission

48-US Sidecar Twin: 74ci medium-compression flathead V-twin with four-speed transmission and sidecar gearing

48-F Sport Solo: 74ci medium-compression Panhead OHV V-twin with four-speed transmission

48-FL Special Sport Solo: 74ci high-compression Panhead OHV V-twin with four-speed transmission

48-FS Sidecar Twin: 74ci medium-compression Panhead OHV V-twin with four-speed transmission and sidecar gearing

48-G Servi-Car with tow bar: 45ci flathead V-twin with three-speed-and-reverse transmission

48-GA Servi-Car without tow bar: 45ci flathead V-twin with three-speed-and-reverse transmission

Specialty Models

48-WL-SP: 45ci flathead V-twin with aluminum cylinder heads

48-WLS Sidecar Twin: 45ci flathead V-twin for sidecar

48-WR Racer: 45ci flathead V-twin racer

Sidecars and Chassis

48-LE: right-hand sidecar

48-M: right-hand Package Truck with cover

48-MC: right-hand chassis for M box

Retail Prices

Model WL: $535

Model UL: $590

Model U: $590

Model US: $590

Model EL: $635

Model E: $635

Model ES: $635

Model FL: $650

Model F: $650

Model FS: $650

Model G: $755

Model GA: $740

Production Totals

Model U: 401

Model US: 1,006

Model UL: 970

Model ES: 198

Model EL: 4,321

Model FS: 334

Model FL: 8,071

Model WL: 2,124

Model WR: 292

Model G: 1,050

Model GA: 728

Model S: 10,117

Paint Colors

Brilliant Black, Flight Red, Azure Blue, and Police Silver (police only)

Series S 125cc Two-Stroke Singles

First Year

Series S is a new model, powered by a 125cc two-stroke single with 2-1/6x2-9/32in bore and stroke, 6.6:1 compression ratio, and 1.7hp output

Engine serial number is stamped on the left side of the front end of the engine crankcase

3.25x19in tires

50in wheelbase

1-3/4gal tank with 1qt reserve

Rigid frame

Seat padding is latex rubber

Three-speed transmission

Girder front fork

Horn side-mounted on right side by rear chainguard

Six-volt electrical system

All enameled parts are "Bonderized" before painting

Series W 45ci V-Twins

First Year

"Edge-Lighted" speedometer dial by Stewart-Warner: mileage numerals are screened in cream-ivory on the underside of the edge-lighted face glass; greenish-gray metal ring provides a background for the numerals; lower center section has mileage hash marks around its edge and contains the odometer and tripmeter; pointer is Red

  Deluxe Solo saddle optional
  All enameled parts are "Bonderized" before painting
  Channel-shaped mounting bracket for twin lead coil body
  Wiring terminal box added below seat
  Late coded crankcase production numbers

Series E and F 61ci and 74ci Panhead Big Twins

First/Only Year

Series E and F Big Twins are updated with the new-for-1948 Panhead OHV motor—which is basically the Knucklehead lower end with a new top end featuring hydraulic valve lifters and aluminum cylinder heads—and a new frame

  Revised crankcases and cylinders feed oil internally to the heads and return it internally to the cases
  Cylinders have a lip on top of the barrel fitting into a recess in the head
  Separate steel inlet nipples that thread into the intake ports
  One-piece rockers and shafts, pivoting inside a split bearing
  Rocker covers made of chrome-plated steel (only year) that fully enclose the rockers and valves
  Aluminum tappet guides
  Wishbone frame: front downtubes "dog-leg" to each side; no horn-mount blocks on frame
  Steering head lock mounted on frame
  Revised front safety guards for the new frame are standard
  "Edge-Lighted" speedometer dial by Stewart-Warner: mileage numerals are screened in Cream-Ivory on the underside of the edge-lighted face glass; Greenish-Gray metal ring provides a background for the numerals; lower center section has mileage hash marks around its edge and contains the odometer and tripmeter; pointer is Red
  Deluxe Solo saddle optional
  All enameled parts are "Bonderized" before painting
  Wiring terminal box added below seat
  Optional tank-mounted oil filter
  Muffler painted with a special high-temperature Black paint (early year)
  Exhaust pipes painted with a special high-temperature Black paint (early-year); painted Silver late year

Series U 74ci Flathead Big Twins

First/Only Year

Wishbone frame: front downtubes "dog-leg" to each side; no horn-mount blocks on frame
  Steering head lock mounted on frame
  Revised front safety guards for the new frame are standard
  "Edge-Lighted" speedometer dial by Stewart-Warner: mileage numerals are screened in Cream-Ivory on the underside of the edge-lighted face glass; Greenish-Gray metal ring provides a background for the numerals; lower center section has mileage hash marks around its edge and contains the odometer and tripmeter; pointer is Red
  Deluxe Solo saddle optional
  All enameled parts are "Bonderized" before painting
  Wiring terminal box added below seat
  Optional tank-mounted oil filter
  Muffler painted with a special high-temperature Black paint (early year)
  Exhaust pipes painted with a special high-temperature Black paint (early-year); painted Silver late year
  (Last year of Model U production)

Series G Servi-Cars

First Year

"Edge-Lighted" speedometer dial by Stewart-Warner: mileage numerals are screened in Cream-Ivory on the underside of the edge-lighted face glass; greenish-gray metal ring provides a background for the numerals; lower center section has mileage hash marks around its edge and contains the odometer and tripmeter; pointer is Red

  Deluxe Solo saddle optional
  All enameled parts are "Bonderized" before painting
  Channel-shaped mounting bracket for twin lead coil body
  Wiring terminal box added below seat
  Late-coded crankcase production numbers
  120amp auxiliary automobile battery. Radio-equipped Models (late year)
  Automobile-style clutch pedal
  Offset tow bar
  Detachable spark plug covers, using fabric-covered cables

Motor Company Minutes, 1948

  Panhead rocker covers resemble baking pans, giving birth to the nickname "Panhead."
  November, the entire H-D dealers conference taken for surprise nighttime train ride to new 260,000sq-ft single-story plant on Capitol Drive in the Milwaukee suburb of Wauwatosa.

Racing Notes

  H-D wins 19 of 23 National Championship Races.
  Jimmy Chann wins Grand National Championship.

1949 FL. *Jeff Hackett*

Main Models

49-S Lightweight: 125cc two-stroke single with three-speed transmission

49-WL Solo: 45ci flathead V-twin with three-speed transmission

49-E Hydra-Glide Solo: 61ci medium-compression Panhead OHV V-twin with four-speed transmission

49-ES Hydra-Glide Sidecar Twin: 61ci medium-compression Panhead OHV V-twin with four-speed transmission and sidecar gearing

49-EP Sidecar Twin: 61ci medium-compression Panhead OHV V-twin with four-speed transmission, spring fork, and side-car gearing

49-EL Hydra-Glide Sport Solo: 61ci high-compression Panhead OHV V-twin with four-speed transmission

49-ELP Sport Solo: 61ci high-compression Panhead OHV V-twin with four-speed transmission and spring fork

49-F Hydra-Glide Solo: 74ci medium-compression Panhead OHV V-twin with four-speed transmission

49-F Hydra-Glide Solo: 74ci medium-compression Panhead OHV V-twin with four-speed transmission and spring fork

49-FS Hydra-Glide Sidecar Twin: 74ci medium-compression Panhead OHV V-twin with four-speed transmission and sidecar gearing

49-FP Sidecar Twin: 74ci medium-compression Panhead OHV V-twin with four-speed transmission, spring fork, and side-car gearing

49-FL Hydra-Glide Sport Solo: 74ci high-compression Panhead OHV V-twin with four-speed transmission

49-FLP Sport Solo: 74ci high-compression Panhead OHV V-twin with four-speed transmission and spring fork

49-G Servi-Car with tow bar: 45ci flathead V-twin with three-speed-and-reverse transmission

49-GA Servi-Car without tow bar: 45ci flathead V-twin with three-speed-and-reverse transmission

Specialty Models

49-WL-SP: 45ci flathead V-twin with aluminum cylinder heads

49-WLS Sidecar Twin: 45ci flathead V-twin for sidecar

49-WR Racer: 45ci flathead V-twin racer

Sidecars and Chassis

49-LE: right-hand sidecar

49-M: right-hand Package Truck with cover

49-MC: right-hand chassis for M box

Retail Prices

Model S: $325

Model WL: $590

Model EL: $735

Model E: $735

Model ES: $735

Model FL: $750

Model F: $750

Model FS: $750

Model G: $860

Model GA: $845

Production Totals

Model ES: 177

Model EL: 3,419

Model ELP: 99

Model FS: 490

Model FL: 8,014

Model FLP: 486

Model WL: 2,289

Model WLA: 436

Model WR: 121

Model G: 494

Model GA: 545

Model S: 7,291

Paint Colors

Twins and Servi-Cars: Brilliant Black, Peacock Blue, Burgundy, and Police Silver (police only); available at extra cost is Metallic Congo Green

Single: Black only

Series S 125cc Two-Stroke Singles

First Year

Flex-lock nuts used on lower motor mount bolts

Mufflers painted with a special high-temperature "siliconized" Black paint

Engine painted with high-temperature "siliconized" Silver paint

Series W 45ci V-Twins

First Year

New control spirals with shorter chrome ferrule and longer, 4.5in-long grip section

Front fender lamp is stainless steel

Mufflers painted with a special high-temperature "siliconized" Black paint

Air cleaner cover is stainless steel

Rubber-mounted bars optional

Stainless steel timer cover standard (this year only)

Stainless steel generator end cover standard (this year only)

Chrome relay cover standard (this year only)

Series E and F Hydra-Glides

First Year

Hydra-Glide hydraulic forks are standard

Hydra-Glide forks have sand-cast sliders that are painted Black (this year only)

Spring forks are optional

Hydra-Glide models have larger, 8.19in, Sealed Ray headlight

Hydra-Glide models have larger, 8in internal-expanding front brakes

Hydra-Glide models have one-piece Air-Flow front fender with spot-welded brackets (this year only) and stainless steel fender tip

Hydra-Glide models have redesigned bars and mounts for the new forks

New control spirals with shorter chrome ferrule and longer, 4.5in-long grip section

Rubber-mounted springer and Hydra-Glide bars optional

Two-piece, hinged Air-Flow rear fender with three "sergeant stripes" on each side of the taillight (all models)

Wishbone frame has horn-mount blocks, and the horn is mounted between the frame downtubes; late-year frame tubes are flattened beneath the horn mounts

Timken roller bearings used in steering head

Cylinders painted Silicon Silver

Mufflers painted with a special "siliconized" Black paint; optional stainless steel muffler cover optional

Manifold made of cast iron, cadmium-plated unpolished pipes and nuts (midyear)

Intake rocker bearings with oilers to spray the intake valves

Stainless steel air-cleaner cover

Stainless steel rocker covers

Stainless steel timer cover standard (this year only)

Stainless steel generator end cover standard (this year only)

Chrome relay cover standard (this year only)

Series G Servi-Cars

First Year

New control spirals with shorter chrome ferrule and longer, 4.5in-long grip section

Front fender lamp is stainless steel

Mufflers painted with a special high-temperature "siliconized" Black paint

Air cleaner cover is stainless steel

Rubber-mounted bars optional

Stainless steel timer cover standard (this year only)

Stainless steel generator end cover standard (this year only)

Chrome relay cover standard (this year only)

Motor Company Minutes, 1949

John E. Harley named to the board of directors.

Armando Magri buys out Frank Murray's Sacramento H-D dealership to become one of the largest and most successful H-D dealers.

Racing Notes

Jimmy Chann wins Grand National Championship.

Jimmy Chann wins 100-Mile Race, Langhorne, Pennsylvania, September 4, 87.09mph.

H-D wins 17 of 24 National Championship Races.

Model Year 1950

1950 FL Hydra-Glide. *Biker at Large MC, Tommy Freeman*

Main Models

50-S: 125cc two-stroke single with three-speed transmission

50-WL Solo: 45ci flathead V-twin with three-speed transmission

50-E Hydra-Glide Solo: 61ci medium-compression Panhead OHV V-twin with four-speed transmission

50-EL Hydra-Glide Sport Solo: 61ci high-compression Panhead OHV V-twin with four-speed transmission

50-ES Hydra-Glide Sidecar Twin: 61ci medium-compression Panhead OHV V-twin with four-speed transmission, adjustable-rake forks, and sidecar gearing

50-F Hydra-Glide Solo: 74ci medium-compression Panhead OHV V-twin with four-speed transmission

50-FL Hydra-Glide Sport Solo: 74ci high-compression Panhead OHV V-twin with four-speed transmission

50-FS Hydra-Glide Sidecar Twin: 74ci medium-compression Panhead OHV V-twin with four-speed transmission, adjustable-rake forks, and sidecar gearing

50-G Servi-Car with tow bar: 45ci flathead V-twin with three-speed-and-reverse transmission

50-GA Servi-Car without tow bar: 45ci flathead V-twin with three-speed-and-reverse transmission

Specialty Models

50-WR Racer: 45ci flathead V-twin racer

50-WL-SP: 45ci flathead V-twin with aluminum cylinder heads

50-WLS Sidecar Twin: 45ci flathead V-twin for sidecar

Sidecars and Chassis

50-LE: right-hand sidecar

50-M: right-hand Package Truck with cover

50-MC: right-hand chassis for M box

Retail Prices

Model S: $325

Model WL: $590

Model EL: $735

Model E: $735

Model ES: $735

Model FL: $750

Model F: $750

Model FS: $750

Model G: $860

Model GA: $845

Production Totals

Model ES: 268

Model EL: 2,046

Model FS: 544

Model FL: 7,407

Model WL: 1,108

Model WLA: 15

Model WR: 69

Model G: 520

Model GA: 483

Model S: 4,708

Options

Deluxe Solo Group for Hydra-Glide: $95.50

Sport Solo Group for Hydra-Glide: $53.70

Utility Solo Group for Hydra-Glide: $19.95

Standard Police Group for Hydra-Glide: $67.90

Utility Group for sidecar or Package Truck: $15.60

Deluxe Solo Group for Model WL: $81.25

Sport Solo Group for Model WL: $46.40

Utility Solo Group for Model WL: $23.50

Deluxe Servi-Car Group: $74.85

Utility Servi-Car Group: $29.75

Deluxe Sidecar Group: $102.45

Paint Colors

Single: Brilliant Black, Flight Red, Sportsman Yellow, Riviera Blue

All twins and Servi-Cars: Brilliant Black, Riviera Blue, Ruby Red, and Police Silver (police only); available at extra cost are White, Flight Red, Metallic Green, and Azure Blue

Series S 125cc Two-Stroke Singles

First Year
    Larger piston pin and bushing
    Rerouted control cables
    Redesigned jiffy stand
    "American-type" spring saddle
    Drop forged steering head
    Redesigned generator

Series W 45ci V-Twins

First Year
    Air flow front and rear fenders
    Chrome muffler optional
    Mellow-Tone "Sport" muffler. No fishtail, just a straight pipe outlet. Black or chromed
    Recalibrated carburetor with fixed jet
    Fuel filter with rubber-sleeved gas line and compression nut, feeding through the side
    Riveted front fender brackets

Series E and F Hydra-Glides

First Year
    Redesigned cylinder heads with enlarged cylinder inlet ports give 10 percent more horsepower
    Valve guides made of bronze
    Die-cast fork sliders (unpainted)
    Mellow-Tone "Sport" muffler (no fishtail, just a straight pipe outlet; Black or chrome)
    "Hydra-Glide" name stamped into fork upper front panel
    Bracket bolts to frame to hold oil filter
    3/8in brake cable tube
    Transmission covers are die-cast (midyear)
    Chrome-plated front safety guard optional

Series G Servi-Cars

First Year
    Air-flow front fender
    Fuel filter with rubber-sleeved gas line and compression nut, feeding through the side

Motor Company Minutes, 1950
    Dealers are supplied with demonstrator motorcycles.
    October advertisement in *Popular Mechanics* states, "1951 Hydra-Glide as the nearest thing to flying and modern as a spaceship."
    Arthur Davidson, the last of the four original founders, is killed in a car accident.

Model Year 1951

Main Models
    51-S Lightweight: 125cc two-stroke single with three-speed transmission
    51-WL Solo: 45ci flathead V-twin with three-speed transmission
    51-EL Hydra-Glide Sport Solo: 61ci high-compression Panhead OHV V-twin with four-speed transmission
    51-ELS Hydra-Glide Sidecar Twin: 61ci medium-compression Panhead OHV V-twin with four-speed transmission and sidecar gearing
    51-FL Hydra-Glide Sport Solo: 74ci high-compression Panhead OHV V-twin with four-speed transmission
    51-FLS Hydra-Glide Sidecar Twin: 74ci high-compression Panhead OHV V-twin with four-speed transmission
    51-G Servi-Car with tow bar: 45ci flathead V-twin with three-speed-and-reverse transmission
    51-GA Servi-Car without tow bar: 45ci flathead V-twin with three-speed-and-reverse transmission

Specialty Models
    51-WR Racer: 45ci flathead V-twin racer
    51-WLS Sidecar Twin: 45ci flathead V-twin for sidecar
    51-WL-SP: 45ci flathead V-twin with aluminum cylinder heads
    51-WRTT Racer: 45ci flathead V-twin TT racer

Sidecars and Chassis
    51-LE: right-hand sidecar
    51-M: right-hand Package Truck with cover
    51-MC: right-hand chassis for M box

Retail Prices
    Model S: $365
    Model WL: $730
    Model EL: $885
    Model ELS: $885
    Model FL: $900
    Model FLS: $900
    Model G: $1,095
    Model GA: $1,080

Production Totals
    Model ES: 76
    Model EL: 1,532
    Model FS: 135
    Model FL: 6,560
    Model WL: 1,044
    Model WLA: 1
    Model WR: 23
    Model G: 778
    Model GA: 632
    Model S: 5,101

Options

Deluxe Solo Group for Hydra-Glide: $115
Sport Solo Group for Hydra-Glide: $66.50
Utility Solo Group for Hydra-Glide: $25.50
Standard Police Group for Hydra-Glide: $78.75
Deluxe Solo Group for Model WL: $ N/A
Sport Solo Group for Model WL: $ N/A
Utility Solo Group for Model WL: $30.50
Deluxe Servi-Car Group: $60.50
Utility Servi-Car Group: $28.50
Deluxe Sidecar Group: $122

Paint Colors

Single: Persian Red, Sportsman Yellow, and Rio Blue; available at extra cost are Metallic Blue and Metallic Green

All twins and Servi-Car: Brilliant Black, Rio Blue, Persian Red, and Police Silver (police only); available at extra cost are White, Metallic Blue, and Metallic Green

Series S 125cc Two-Stroke Singles

First Year

Tank decal is the "Harley-Davidson" name in script over a thin bar running underneath
New speedometer, mounted ahead of the handlebars
Tele-Glide telescopic fork
5in-wide fenders
Streamlined taillight
Cycle-Ray 7in headlight
Waterproof front brake seal
Horn that draws less current
Coil-mount spacer
Stronger starter crank
Redesigned, freer-breathing muffler
Needle-roller-bearing on piston-pin end of connecting rod
Leak-proof fuel valve

Series W 45ci V-Twins

First Year

Heads secured to cylinders with cap screws
Stronger bypass spring in oil pump
Fixed-jet Linkert M-54 carburetor
Chrome-plated exhaust-connection pipe
Tank emblem is name "Harley-Davidson" in script with a bar underneath
Single-stripe rear fender trim
(Last year of regular Model WL 45ci Solo twin production for United States civilian market)

Series E and F Hydra-Glides

First Year

Chrome-plated piston compression rings
Two-piece cam (separate gear) with opening and closing ramps
Rocker arms with machined-in pushrod sockets
Shouldered exhaust-port clamp
Larger diameter pinion shaft (midyear)
"Sand cast" eight-rib gear cover
Neoprene cork composition pushrod seals
Handlebars with center sleeve reinforcement
Tank emblem is "Harley-Davidson" in script with a bar underneath
Generator mounting screws are Phillips-head
Chrome-plated exhaust S-pipe and Y-pipe
Rocker cover D-Ring reinforcements, made of three layers of 1/16in sheet metal spot-welded together, each fastened by nine Phillips-head screws and three Allen-head screws
Single-stripe rear fender trim
M-74B 1-1/2in Linkert carburetor on 74ci (late year)
Optional one-piece front safety guard
Optional "Hydra-Glide" front-fender emblems offered

Series G Servi-Cars

First Year

Hydraulic rear brake system
Front header pipe uses welded-on tab holding pipe tight, preventing header from dropping out exhaust port
Single-tube front safety guard
16in disc rear wheels
Five lug nuts to mount automotive-type disc rear wheel to brake drum
Front brake used as parking brake
Parking brake assembly has small lever and pivot plate attaching to front brake hand lever
Extra-large diameter automotive-type muffler with fishtail lying horizontally
Tank emblem is name "Harley-Davidson" in script with a bar underneath
Heads secured to cylinders with cap screws
Stronger bypass spring in oil pump

Motor Company Minutes, 1951

H-D starts their H-D Mileage Club for the public.
Dealers Convention held at the Milwaukee City Hall.
November 18, the Model K is shown to the dealers attending the Milwaukee dealers convention.
May 15, H-D petitions U.S. Tariff Commission for a 40 percent import tax on all imported foreign motorcycles.

Racing Notes

Jack Dale, private rider, wins Class C Race at Utah with record 123.52mph.

Model Year 1952

1952 FL Hydra-Glide. *Joe and Peggy Barber*

Main Models

52-S Lightweight: 125cc two-stroke single with three-speed transmission

52-K Sport Model: 45ci flathead V-twin with foot-shifted four-speed transmission

52-EL Hydra-Glide Sport Solo: 61ci Panhead OHV V-twin with hand-shifted four-speed transmission

52-ELS Sidecar Twin: 61ci Panhead OHV V-twin with hand-shifted four-speed transmission

52-ELF Sport Solo: 61ci Panhead OHV V-twin with foot-shifted four-speed transmission

52-FL Sport Solo: 74ci Panhead OHV V-twin with hand-shifted four-speed transmission

52-FLS Sidecar Twin: 74ci Panhead OHV V-twin with hand-shifted four-speed transmission

52-FLF Sport Solo: 74ci Panhead OHV V-twin with foot-shifted four-speed transmission

52-G Servi-Car with tow bar: 45ci flathead V-twin with three-speed-and-reverse transmission

52-GA Servi-Car without tow bar: 45ci flathead V-twin with three-speed-and-reverse transmission

Specialty Models

52-KR Racer: 45ci flathead V-twin racer

52-KRTT Competition Model: 45ci flathead V-twin TT racer

52-WLS Sidecar Twin: 45ci flathead V-twin for sidecar

Sidecars and Chassis

52-LE: right-hand sidecar

52-M: right-hand Package Truck with cover

52-MC: right-hand chassis for M box

Retail Prices

Model WL: $730
Model K: $865
Model ELF: $955
Model EL: $955
Model ELS: 955
Model FLF: $970
Model FL: $970
Model FLS: $970
Model G: $1,175
Model GA: $1,160

Production Totals

Model ES: 42
Model EL: 918
Model FS: 186
Model FL: 5,554
Model WR: 8
Model G: 515
Model GA: 532
Model K: 1,970
Model KR: 17
Model S: 4,576

Options

Deluxe Solo Group for Hydra-Glide: $73.50
Utility Solo Group for Hydra-Glide: $28.45
Standard Police Group for Hydra-Glide: $85.50
Deluxe Group for Model K: $67.50
Deluxe Servi-Car Group: $77.20
Utility Servi-Car Group: $31.00
Deluxe Sidecar Group: $77.20

Paint Colors

OHV: Brilliant Black, Rio Blue, Tropical Green, Persian Red, and Police Silver (police only); available at extra cost are Marine Blue Metallic, Bronco Bronze Metallic, and White

Single: Tropical Green, Rio Blue, and Persian Red; Marine Blue Metallic available at extra cost

Model K: Black, Rio Blue, and Persian Red; Bronco Bronze Metallic available at extra cost

Series S 125cc Two-Stroke Singles

First Year

Folding footrests
60mph speedometer
Improved jiffy stand
Improved shift lever
Redesigned shifting clutches in transmission
Low gear ratio in transmission revised from 29:1 to 26:1
Brake and clutch cables increased to 1/8in stranded cable
Waterproof rear brake
New oil seals on gearshift shaft and starter shaft
Tele-Glide fork oil lubricated instead of grease lubricated

Series K Sports Twins

First Year

Series K Sports Twin is a new 45ci V-Twin model; last year 1953

Engine: all-new 45ci flathead V-twin with 2.75x3.813in bore and stroke; 30hp

Engine and gearbox designed as an integrated unit
Cylinder heads are removable, cast of aluminum alloy
Pistons are aluminum alloy cam ground double slot
Four-cam engine—one cam per valve
Primary drive on left side
Final drive on right side
Oil pump enclosed in the crankcase
Four-speed transmission with direct-drive top gear
Combination foot shift and hand clutch
Rear swing-arm suspension
Two automotive-type rear shock absorbers
Hydraulically damped front fork
Six-volt electrical system
M-53 1-1/2in Linkert carburetor

Tank emblem is the name "Harley-Davidson" in script with one bar trailing behind and another bar curving around the front of the tank

Folding foot pegs

Mufflers are straight, without a fishtail. Black or chromed

"Jubilee Trumpet" horn (polished or unpolished stainless steel); horn by H-D and power pack by Delco-Remy; mounts on left side of the motor with power pack on the right

Headlight is a large sealed ray with prefocused 32-32 candlepower

Frame is double-loop and silver brazed tubular steel

Muffler designed with a resonating chamber producing a low note

Handlebars are rubber mounted, seamless steel tubing "buckhorn" style

Neoprene twist-grip controls

Wheel spokes cadmium-plated

Wheels are 19in with drop-center wheel rims

Tires are 3.25x19, four-ply; choice of Goodyear or Firestone

Rear brake drum cast iron; front brake drum steel

Brakes are 8in in diameter and 1in wide

Brakes have molded antiscore lining

Gas tanks have a center filling cap

Gas tank capacity of 4-1/2gal

Oil capacity of 3qt

Frame painted Black enamel

Seat is "form fitting" bucket type

Seat padding is foam rubber

Ignition and light switch designed into the top part of the front fork cowling

Series E and F Hydra-Glides

First/Only Year

Foot shift optional

Clutch lever rod 22in long and 3/16in diameter (foot-shift models)

"Mousetrap" clutch booster mounted on left downtube (foot-shift models)

"Mousetrap" clutch rod mounts to right side of the bell crank (foot-shift models)

Clutch-booster cover is painted Black (foot-shift models)

Toe lever attached to the gear shift lever (foot-shift models)

Foot-shift transmission features redesigned shifter drum, indexing cam, and a spring-loaded plunger to keep transmission in gear

New right crankcase with boss for a screen and check valve (midyear)

Screen and check valve in right case filters and regulates top-end oil flow (midyear)

"Parko-Lubricized" valves

"Rotating" exhaust valves (midyear)

Revised wishbone frame with inverted U-shaped toolbox brackets and new motor mounts

Oil pump uses stemmed check balls (late year)

Quieter, lower-toned muffler

Revised rear fender with partially cutaway chain recess with single channel stamped into its flat

Model 52 generator on civilian models; Model 51 generator on radio-equipped bikes

(The Series E 61ci Panhead model was discontinued after 1952)

Series G Servi-Cars

First Year

Bumper brought in closer to the body by 2.5in

Motor Company Minutes, 1952

The H-D Model K is only motorcycle on which Hollywood stars are insured to ride because it couldn't go as fast as others.

Model Year 1953

1953 KRM. © Harley-Davidson

Main Models

53-ST Lightweight: 165cc two-stroke single with three-speed transmission

53-K Sport Solo: 45ci flathead V-twin with four-speed transmission

53-FLF Hydra-Glide Sport Solo: 74ci Panhead OHV V-twin with foot-shifted four-speed transmission

53-FL Sport Solo: 74ci Panhead OHV V-twin with hand-shifted four-speed transmission

53-FLEF Hydra-Glide Solo: 74ci Traffic Combination Panhead OHV V-twin with foot-shifted four-speed transmission

53-FLE Hydra-Glide Solo: 74ci Traffic Combination Panhead OHV V-twin with hand-shifted four-speed transmission

53-G Servi-Car with tow bar: 45ci flathead V-twin with three-speed-and-reverse transmission

53-GA Servi-Car without tow bar: 45ci flathead V-twin with three-speed-and-reverse transmission

Specialty Models

53-KK: 45ci flathead V-twin with Model KR cams, ports, and ball bearing crank fitted to Model K frame

53-KR Racer: 45ci flathead V-twin racer

53-KRTT Track Racer: 45ci flathead V-twin racer with magneto ignition

Sidecars and Chassis

53-LE: right-hand sidecar

53-M: right-hand Package Truck with cover

53-MC: right-hand chassis for M box

Retail Prices

Model ST: $ 405

Model K: $ 875

Model FLF: $1,000

Model FL: $1,000

Model FLEF: $1,000

Model FLE: $1,000

Model G: $1,190

Model GA: $1,175

Production Totals
74 FL: 1,986
74 FLF: 3,351
Model K: 1,723
G: 1,146
ST: 4,225

Options
Deluxe Solo Group for Hydra-Glide: $83.30
Standard Solo Group for Hydra-Glide: $28.45
Standard Police Group for Hydra-Glide: $85.50
Deluxe Group for Model K: $67.50
Standard Solo Group for Model K: $22.75
Deluxe Servi-Car Group: $77.20
Standard Servi-Car Group: $31.00
Deluxe Sidecar Group: $136.60

Paint Colors
Twins: Pepper Red, Forest Green, Silver (police only), Glacier Blue, and Brilliant Black; available at extra cost are White, Cavalier Brown, and Glamour Green; Motor maids special at no extra cost is Cadillac Gray tanks with Azure Blue fenders

Single: Pepper Red, Glacier Blue, and Forest Green; available at extra cost is Glamour Green

Series ST and STU 165cc Two-Stroke Singles

First Year
Series ST 165cc replaces Series 125cc; last year 1959
New engine: 10ci (165cc) two-stroke single with bore and stroke of 2.375x2.281in
Alemite grease fittings to lube the engine main bearings after storage
Straight-section crankpin
Relocated transmission filler neck
Higher ratio between engine and transmission
Ignition coil relocated to front frame tube
Restrictor disc for carburetor throat available to make the ST conform to 5hp-and-under license restrictions
Tank decal is the name "Harley-Davidson" stamped in script over a thin bar running underneath

Series K Sports Twins

First/Only Year
Faster acting throttle
New Standard Solo Group, at no extra charge
Plastic saddlebags optional
Buddy seat optional
(Last year of Model K production)

Series F Hydra-Glides

First Year
Hydraulic lifters relocated from the top of the pushrods to the top of the tappets, below the pushrod and closer to the oil pump for more constant and reliable oil pressure
Hydraulic lifter features a cylinder with a pressed-in check-ball assembly and a plunger that fits down into the cylinder
Tappets designed with a hole in the flat on their sides helping to pick up oil from the tappet block, then feeding it to the lifter
Tappet blocks designed with an oil passage from the cases to the tappet
Pushrods designed with the ball end at the top, pressed-in bottom fitting threaded for a screw-in adjuster
Cast-iron tappet blocks

Right crankcase redesigned to incorporate an oil passage for oil to feed to the tappet blocks and to eliminate the return oil channel on the rear cylinder base
Left case redesigned to delete the return oil channel on the rear cylinder base and the oil passage on the front cylinder base
Cylinders designed with a smaller rocker-feed passage on the right side featuring a new style oil return passage going to a hole in the cylinder wall
New, heat-treated-steel oil-scraper rings
Traffic Combination FLE 74ci motor is introduced to replace the 61ci motor for slow-speed and escort work and features the milder cam and smaller carburetor (M-61 Linkert) from the discontinued 61ci motor
Four-rib gear-case cover
Revised pinion-shaft bearing with twice as many rollers (late year)
New-style "Edge-Lighted" speedometer dial by Stewart-Warner: the mile numbers are 1 through 12 in large block type in yellow-silver; the 2mph hash marks are screened on the underside of the glass, in yellow-silver; the raised ring that is the background for the numbers is painted Black; the lower, center disc is painted Gray-Black; the pointer is white; tenth numbers on the odometer are Black over a white background
Lower front engine mount made stronger
Optional Deluxe Buddy seat now has vinyl covering
Sidecar or Police gearing optional on all models

Series G Servi-Cars

First Year
New-style "Edge-Lighted" speedometer dial by Stewart-Warner: the mile numbers are 1 through 12 in large block type in Yellow-Silver; the 2mph hash marks are screened on the underside of the glass, in Yellow-Silver; the raised ring that is the background for the numbers is painted Black; the lower, center disc is painted Gray-Black; the pointer is White; tenth numbers on the odometer are Black over a White background

Motor Company Minutes, 1953
H-D experiments with prototype Model KL 45ci flathead V-twin built with the cylinders angled at 60deg. Because of patent restrictions with the Vincent Motorcycle Company, the idea is scrapped.
Sales down 20 percent.
The main competitor, Indian, closes its doors.

Racing Notes
Paul Goldsmith on Model KR Sport Racer wins Daytona 200-Mile Expert Championship.
Don Pink on Model KH wins the Jack Pine endurance run.

Model Year 1954

1954 KH. *Tom Wien*

Main Models

54-ST Lightweight: 165cc two-stroke single with three-speed transmission

54-STU Lightweight: 165cc two-stroke single with restricted intake and three-speed transmission

54-KH Sport Solo: 55ci flathead V-twin with four-speed transmission

54-FLF Hydra-Glide Sport Solo: 74ci Panhead OHV V-twin with foot-shifted four-speed transmission

54-FL Hydra-Glide Sport Solo: 74ci Panhead OHV V-twin with hand-shifted four-speed transmission

54-FLEF Hydra-Glide Solo: 74ci Traffic Combination Panhead OHV V-twin with foot-shifted four-speed transmission

54-FLE Hydra-Glide Solo: 74ci Traffic Combination Panhead OHV V-twin with hand-shifted four-speed transmission

54-G Servi-Car with tow bar: 45ci flathead V-twin with three-speed-and-reverse transmission

54-GA Servi-Car without tow bar: 45ci flathead V-twin with three-speed-and-reverse transmission

Specialty Models

54-KR Racer: 45ci flathead V-twin racer

54-KRTT Racer: 45ci flathead V-twin TT racer

54-KHRM: 55ci flathead V-twin

Sidecars and Chassis

54-LE: right-hand sidecar

54-M: right-hand Package Truck with cover

54-MC: right-hand chassis for M box

54-LMC: left-hand chassis

Retail Prices

Model ST: $405

Model STU: $405

Model KH: $925

Model FLF: $1,015

Model FL: $1,015

Model FLEF: $1,015

Model FLE: $1,015

Model G: $1,240

Model GA: $1,225

Production Totals

FL: 4,757

KH: 1,579

G: 1,397

ST: 2,835

Paint Colors

Standard solid colors: Pepper Red, Daytona Ivory, Glacier Blue, Anniversary Yellow, Forest Green, Black, White (police only), and Silver (police only)

Available at no extra cost are Daytona Ivory tanks with Forest Green fenders, Pepper Red tanks with Daytona Ivory fenders, Daytona Ivory tanks with Glacier Blue fenders, Glacier Blue tanks with Daytona Ivory fenders, Daytona Ivory tanks with Pepper Red fenders, Forest Green tanks with Daytona Ivory fenders

Motor Maids Special at no extra cost is Cadillac Gray tanks with Azure Blue fenders

Series ST and STU 165cc Two-Stroke Singles

First Year

Series STU: the ST with a restricted intake

Piston has a slot at rear of its skirt

Non-serrated gear-shift shaft and gear-shift lever

Gear-shift lever strengthened

Thicker insulating bushing on intake boss of carburetor

Ball-bearing-type clutch thrust bearing

Exhaust boss lengthened and fitted with a piston ring on outer surface; a new, longer flange on the exhaust pipe fits over the lengthened boss and ring and is fastened by a clamp

70mph speedometer with light Gray face and Black numerals

Golden Anniversary brass medallion mounted on the front fender, 2-1/2in diameter

Series KH Sports Twins

First Year

55ci Series KH Sports Twin replaced 45ci Series K; last year 1956

Engine: 55ci (883cc) flathead OHV V-twin with 2.745x4.562in bore and stroke, 6.8:1 compression ratio, and 38hp output

Power increase of 12 percent over Series K

Longer cylinders to accommodate the KH's longer stroke

Cam-ground aluminum pistons with eight holes drilled around the piston's circumference below the oil-control ring

Intake valve diameter increased 7/64in

Inlet and exhaust ports reshaped

New cast-iron flywheels with taper-fit shafts

Big-end bearing features 34 rollers

Redesigned retainer on big end bearing

KR-type valve springs

Primary-drive chain cover

Transmission/crankcases redesigned for greater strength

Redesigned clutch has seven plates instead of five

Front chain cover lengthened, widened, and strengthened to accommodate the new clutch and attaches with three screws and four dowels

Transmission oil-level plug moved to the side of the front chain cover

One-way valve to drain primary case

Front chain tensioner is strengthened

Front chain cover is polished

Nonserrated gear-shifter shaft and lever

Revised rake and trail on frame constructed from chrome-moly steel; rake is 29.75 degrees and trail is 3.22in

Pressed-steel brake shoes

Revised brake lining

Redesigned oil-pressure switch

Rubber fork boots replace steel fork covers

Redesigned saddle is similar to the ST saddle

Redesigned compensating sprocket is optional

Golden Anniversary brass medallion mounted on the front fender, 2-1/2in diameter (only year)

Series F Hydra-Glides

First Year

Tapered pinion shaft and revise pinion gear and oil-pump worm gear (this year only)

Three frame types: Wishbone frame with flattened front downtubes but no horn-mount blocks (early year), wishbone frame without horn-mount blocks or downtubes flattened for horn mounts (midyear), and new straight-leg frame (late year)

New one-piece tubular safety guard with an inverted T-shaped mounting bracket with four holes (for straight-leg frame)

"Jubilee" trumpet horn (polished or unpolished stainless steel); horn mounts on right side of motor; power pack on left side

Faster acting throttle and spark control spirals like those introduced for the 1953 Model K; spirals affixed by a screw that threads into the handlebar end

New handlebars threaded for new spirals

Oil pump uses round check balls

New-style cast aluminum D-rings using six mounting holes (late year)

Nonsplined shifter shaft and shift lever

New foot-shift lever and optional heel lever

Front brake fitted with the same pressed-steel shoes and revised linings used on the Model KH

Golden Anniversary medallion on front fender, 2-1/2in in diameter

Minor speedometer facelift: the pointer is Red and the tenth-mile numerals are Red on a Black background

Dual exhaust system optional

Series G Servi-Cars

First Year

Pinion-shaft-seal rings

Golden Anniversary medallion on front fender, 2-1/2in in diameter (this year only)

Motor Company Minutes, 1954

It is publicized that 73 members of the H-D Mileage Club topped the 100,000-mile mark.

The Cincinnati Police Department begins a motorcycle training exercise called "Police Training Road Run."

The movie *The Wild One* premiers. It continues the outlaw bad guy/rebel on a H-D image. Condemned and picketed by the AMA.

Racing Notes

Joe Leonard on Model KR wins AMA Grand National Championship and receives AMA Number 1 plate.

Paul Goldsmith on Model KR wins second place AMA Grand National Championship.

Charlie West on Model KR wins third place AMA Grand National Championship.

Model Year 1955

1955 FLF Hydra-Glide. *Greg Field*

Main Models

55-B Hummer Lightweight: 125cc two-stroke single with three-speed transmission

55-ST Lightweight: 165cc two-stroke single with three-speed transmission

55-STU Lightweight: 165cc two-stroke single with restricted intake and three-speed transmission

55-KH Sport Solo: 55ci flathead V-twin with four-speed transmission

55-FLF Hydra-Glide Sport Solo: 74ci Panhead OHV V-twin with foot-shifted four-speed transmission

55-FL Hydra-Glide Sport Solo: 74ci Panhead OHV V-twin with hand-shifted four-speed transmission

55-FLEF Hydra-Glide Solo: 74ci Traffic Combination Panhead OHV V-twin with foot-shifted four-speed transmission

55-FLE Hydra-Glide Solo: 74ci Traffic Combination Panhead OHV V-twin with hand-shifted four-speed transmission

55-FLHF Hydra-Glide Super Sport Solo: 74ci Super Sport Panhead OHV V-twin with foot-shifted four-speed transmission

55-FLH Hydra-Glide Super Sport Solo: 74ci Super Sport Panhead OHV V-twin with hand-shifted four-speed transmission

55-G Servi-Car with tow bar: 45ci flathead V-twin with three-speed-and-reverse transmission

55-GA Servi-Car without tow bar: 45ci flathead V-twin with three-speed-and-reverse transmission

Specialty Models

55-KHK Super Sport Solo: 55ci Super Sport flathead V-twin with special speed kit, racer cams, and polished cylinder heads

55-KHRM: 55ci flathead V-twin for scrambles and trials

55-KR Track Racer: 45ci flathead V-twin flat-track racer

55-KRTT Tourist Trophy Racer: 45ci flathead V-twin racer

55-KHRTT Tourist Trophy Racer: 55ci flathead V-twin racer

Sidecars and Chassis

55-LE: right-hand sidecar

55-M: Package Truck with cover

55-MC: chassis for M box

Retail Prices

Model ST: $405

Model STU: $405

Model KH: $925

Model KHK: $993
Model FL: $1,015
Model FLE: $1,015
Model FLF: $1,015
Model FLEF: $1,015
Model FLHF: $1,083
Model FLH: $1,083
Model G: $1,240
Model GA: $1,225

Production Totals
Model FL: 953
Model FLE: 853
Model FLH: 63
Model FLF: 2,013
Model FLEF: 220
Model FLHF: 1,040
Model G: 394
Model GA: 647
Model KHK: 449
Model KH: 616
Model KHRM: 77
Model KR: 37
Model KRTT: 14
Model KHR: 1
Model KHRTT: 6
Model ST: 2,263
Model B: 1,040

Paint Colors

Black, Pepper Red, Aztec Brown, Anniversary Yellow, Atomic Blue, Silver (police only), and White (police only); available at extra cost are Hollywood Green or any combination of colors other than Hollywood Green

Series B Hummer 125cc Two-Stroke Singles
First Year

Model B Hummer is a new model, introduced in March 1955; last year 1957

Engine: 125cc two-stroke single with 6.6:1 compression ratio, 2-1/16x2-9/32in bore and stroke, and output of 1.7hp
Black enamel handlebars
Manually operated chrome-plated bulb horn on the left fork
Multiple-disc-type clutch
American-type form-fitting saddle filled with soft foam rubber
Black neoprene grips
Clutch lever on left handlebar
Three-speed constant mesh transmission
No ignition switch on fuel tank
Black, waterproof vinyl saddle covering
Tubular steel, single loop frame with silver brazed steering head
Fenders 5in wide
Sweeping design exhaust pipe
Aluminum, silicon resin-based paint baked onto the exhaust pipe
Spark plugs are air-cooled and can be disassembled
Tank emblem features the name "Harley-Davidson" designed with a long letter "H" that begins the name "Hummer" placed directly beneath; both names are in a long bar winged at both ends

Series ST and STU 165cc Two-Stroke Singles
Sweeping, streamlined exhaust pipe
Shorter muffler bracket
Kickstart gear 58 percent wider
Clutch key ring cyanide hardened
Tank emblem is a large letter "V" with the name "Harley-Davidson" in script trailing behind

Series KH Sports Twins

First Year
Tank emblem is a large letter "V" with the name "Harley-Davidson" in script trailing behind
M-53A1 1-1/2in Linkert carburetor
Steering geometry designed with trail increased 1in to 4.22in
Front fork legs redesigned 1in shorter
Bottom of front fender is streamlined
Speedometer is rubber-mounted
Stronger rear-wheel hub flanges
Larger-diameter spokes
Stamped steel taillight
Red glass lens in taillight
Oiler hole added to clutch cable
Rubber-mounted speedometer
Transmission sprocket increased to 22 teeth
Hexagonal steering-damper stem
Frames made of chrome-moly steel
Synthetic lip-type seal on rear-wheel bearing
Polished cylinder heads
Access cover added to transmission case
KH front fender medallion
Redesigned buddy seat

Series F Hydra-Glides

First Year
Model FLH Super Sport added; FLH has 8:1 compression and polished and flowed intake ports
"H" in "FLH" stamped as part of serial number on the engine
Cast-iron "O-Ring" manifold (painted silver); O-ring placed between both the end of each nipple and the end of each manifold tube
Cylinder heads designed with a cast-in inlet nipple to connect with O-ring intake manifold
Heads drilled for six valve-cover mounting holes (late 1954 and 1955 only)
New bottom end with larger cases and Timken main bearings
Left flywheel designed with a thick shoulder allowing the Timken bearing to seat against it (this year only)
Left case redesigned with a smooth surface inside the primary-chain mounting ring
Flywheels redesigned to eliminate thrust washers
Right crankcase and pinion shaft "crowned" and redesigned to use new larger size bearing
Smooth rounded outer primary cover; painted Black
Inner primary chain cover designed with a larger sprocket-shaft hole and redesigned mounting perch
Tank emblem is a large letter "V" with the name "Harley-Davidson" in script trailing behind
Rubber-mounted headlight bracket
Oval-shaped taillight with stamped steel; body is painted the color of fender and rim piece is chromed
Separate license plate bracket, painted Black, is standard, mounted ahead of the light
New rear fender with redesigned mounting holes for the new taillight
Cadmium-plated clutch booster cover
Front fork cover featuring three diagonal stripes on each side of headlight
Wing nut replaces lock on the toolbox
M-74B Linkert carburetor on Traffic Combination FLE motor (FLE still has the cam from the 61ci motor)
Speedometer facelift: tenth-mile numerals are Black on a White background

1955-only stamped V-shaped front-fender medallion with "Harley-Davidson" stamped in relief out of the bar of a superimposed bar and shield; stamped in relief at top of shield is "1955" and stamped at the bottom of the shield either a "FL" or "FLH"

Series G Servi-Cars

First Year
Two chrome-plated compression rings
Tank emblem displaying a large letter "V" with the name "Harley-Davidson" in script trailing behind
Oval taillight

Motor Company Minutes, 1955
National Drill Team Competition is won by the H-D riding Miami Beach Police Department.

Racing Notes
Dan Richards wins Daytona 100-Mile Junior Championship with record 92.43mph.
Brad Andres wins the Daytona 200-Mile Expert Championship with record 94.57mph.
Brad Andres wins AMA Grand National Championship.
Everett Brashear wins second place Grand National Championship.
Joe Leonard places third Grand National Championship.

Model Year 1956

1956 KHK. *Doug Mitchel*

Main Models
56-B Hummer Lightweight: 125cc two-stroke single with three-speed transmission
56-ST Lightweight: 165cc two-stroke single with three-speed transmission
56-STU Lightweight: 165cc two-stroke single with restricted intake and three-speed transmission
56-KH Sport: 55ci flathead V-twin with four-speed transmission
56-KHK Sport: 55ci flathead V-twin with racer cams, polished heads, and four-speed transmission
56-FLHF Hydra-Glide Super Sport Solo: 74ci Super Sport Panhead OHV V-twin with foot-shifted four-speed transmission
56-FLH Hydra-Glide Super Sport Solo: 74ci Super Sport Panhead OHV V-twin with hand-shifted four-speed transmission
56-FLF Hydra-Glide Sport Solo: 74ci Panhead OHV V-twin with foot-shifted four-speed transmission
56-FL Hydra-Glide Sport Solo: 74ci Panhead OHV V-twin with hand-shifted four-speed transmission
56-FLEF Hydra-Glide Solo: 74ci Traffic Combination Panhead OHV V-twin with foot-shifted four-speed transmission
56-FLE Hydra-Glide Solo: 74ci Traffic Combination Panhead OHV V-twin with hand-shifted four-speed transmission
56-G Servi-Car with tow bar: 45ci flathead V-twin with three-speed-and-reverse transmission
56-GA Servi-Car without tow bar: 45ci flathead V-twin with three-speed-and-reverse transmission

Specialty Models
56-KR Track Racer: 45ci flathead V-twin racers
56-KRTT Tourist Trophy Racer: 45ci flathead V-twin TT racer
56-KHRTT Tourist Trophy Racer: 55ci flathead V-twin TT racer

Sidecars and Chassis
56-LE: right-hand sidecar
56-M: right-hand Package Truck with cover
56-MC: right-hand chassis for M box

Retail Prices
Model ST: $405
Model STU: $405
Model B: $320
Model KH: $935
Model KHK: $1,003
Model FLHF: $1,123
Model FLH: $1,123

Model FLF: $1,055
Model FL: $1,055
Model FLEF: $1,055
Model FLE: $1,055
Model G: $1,240
Model GA: $1,225

Production Totals

Model FL: 856
Model FLE: 671
Model FLH: 224
Model FLF: 1,578
Model FLEF: 162
Model FLHF: 2,315
Model G: 467
Model GA: 736
Model KHK: 714
Model KH: 539
Model KR: 29
Model KRTT: 18
Model XL: 1
Model KHRTT: 13
Model ST: 2,219
Model B: 1,384

Paint Colors

Twins: Pepper Red with White tank panels and Red fenders, Black with Champion Yellow tank panels and Black fenders, Atomic Blue with Champion Yellow tank panels and Blue fenders, Champion Yellow with Black tank panels and Yellow fenders, Silver (police only), and White (police only); available at extra cost are Flamboyant Metallic Green with White tank panels and Flamboyant Metallic Green fenders

Hummer: Pepper Red or Atomic Blue (no tank panels)

ST: Pepper Red, Atomic Blue, Champion Yellow, and Tangerine

Servi-Cars: Pepper Red, Atomic Blue, Champion Yellow, Black, Silver (police only), and White (police only)

Series ST Two-Stroke Singles

First Year

Round taillight like the Hummer's taillight
18in wheels

Series KH Sports Twins

First/Only Year

Saddle height lowered
Frame modified to lower the bike
New-style air cleaner
Shocks shortened 9/16in
Shocks redesigned with an increase in outer diameter and oil capacity
Redesigned rear chain guard
Redesigned and reinforced oil tank
Oil pump redesigned eliminating relief valve
Oil pump shaft uses a Woodruff key
Rear wheel uses new roller-type wheel bearings
Thicker kickstarter crank gear
Spring-steel guides for the clutch and brake cables
Carburetor support bracket
Oval-shaped taillight with stamped steel body; body painted the color of the fender and rim piece is chromed
Redesigned gears in transmission
Carburetor-support bracket added
(Last year of Model KH street-bike production)

Series F Hydra-Glides

First Year

Redesigned right crankcase routes oil to the top and through the oil-pump check valve
Left flywheel designed without the bearing shoulder
Sprocket-shaft designed with bearing shoulder and deeper key slot
FLH motors are fitted with the "Victory" camshaft, featuring a higher lift of 1.342in (standard is 1.334in) and narrower lobes of 1.075in (standard is 1.10in)
Models with the FLH motor feature the "FLH" decal—a large Red "V" on a Silver shield with Black FLH letters over both—on each side of the oil tank
Cylinder heads with nine fins on the pushrod side, twelve valve-cover mounting screws, and the casting mark at top of the head
Cast aluminum D-rings with twelve mounting holes
Oil pump fitted with a new check-valve spring
Patent decal placed on the front of the oil tank, behind the seat post
Chromed instrument cover optional
Frames designed with coil-mounting block holes measuring 3/8in
Frames have stainless steel cover added to the steering head lock
Stainless steel air cleaner cover, 7in diameter, featuring a center screw mounting hole using a large head Phillips-head screw
Restyled "Edge-Lighted" speedometer dial by Stewart-Warner: lower level painted light Gold; numbers 1, 2, 3, and so on and hash marks silk screened in bright "Day-Glo" Green on the glass; pointer painted bright Red
Redesigned air-cleaner cover that fastens with a center screw
Data-plate information stamped into air cleaner cover
Replaceable corrugated paper air filter backed with wire mesh
(Last year of the FLE Traffic Combination motor)

Series G Servi-Cars

First Year

Five spring mounts on the rear chain guard
Battery box deleted
Iron heads with 7/16in head bolt holes and designed for 14mm spark plugs
Restyled "Edge-Lighted" speedometer dial by Stewart-Warner: lower level painted light Gold; numbers 1, 2, 3, and so on and hash marks silk screened in bright "Day-Glo" Green on the glass; pointer painted bright Red
Air cleaner information stamped into the cover
Redesigned stainless steel air cleaner cover fastened by a center screw
Replaceable corrugated paper air filter backed with wire mesh

Motor Company Minutes, 1956

May issue of The Enthusiast features cover picture of new singing sensation Elvis Presley astride a 1956 Model KH.

Racing Notes

Joe Leonard wins AMA Grand National Championship.
Brad Andres places second Grand National Championship.
John Gibson on Model KR wins Daytona 200-Mile Expert Championship with record 94.21mph.
Bates Molyneaux on Model KR wins Daytona 100-Mile Junior Championship with record 93.58mph.

1957 FLHF Hydra-Glide. *Greg Field*

Main Models

57-B Hummer Lightweight: 125cc two-stroke single with three-speed transmission

57-ST Lightweight: 165cc two-stroke single with three-speed transmission

57-STU Lightweight: 165cc two-stroke single with restricted intake and three-speed transmission

57-XL Sportster: 883cc medium-compression Sportster OHV V-twin with four-speed transmission

57-FLHF Hydra-Glide Super Sport Solo: 74ci Super Sport Panhead OHV V-twin with foot-shifted four-speed transmission

57-FLH Hydra-Glide Super Sport Solo: 74ci Super Sport Panhead OHV V-twin with hand-shifted four-speed transmission

57-FLF Hydra-Glide Sport Solo: 74ci Panhead OHV V-twin with foot-shifted four-speed transmission

57-FL Hydra-Glide Sport Solo: 74ci Panhead OHV V-twin with hand-shifted four-speed transmission

57-G Servi-Car with tow bar: 45ci flathead V-twin with three-speed-and-reverse transmission

57-GA Servi-Car without tow bar: 45ci flathead V-twin with three-speed-and-reverse transmission

Specialty Models

57-KR Track Racer: 45ci flathead V-twin flat-track racer

57-KRT T Tourist Trophy Racer: 45ci flathead V-twin TT racer

57-KHRTT Tourist Trophy Racer: 55ci flathead V-twin TT racer

Sidecars and Chassis

57-LE: right-hand sidecar

57-M: right-hand Package Truck with cover

57-MC: right-hand chassis for M box

Retail Prices

Model B: $356

Model ST: $445

Model STU: $445

Model XL: $1,103

Model FLHF: $1,243

Model FLH: $1,243

Model FLF: $1,167

Model FL: $1,167

Model G: $1,367

Model GA: $1,352

Production Totals

Model FL: 1,579

Model FLH: 164

Model FLF: 1,259

Model FLHF: 2,614

Model G: 518

Model GA: 674

Model KH: 90

Model XL: 1,983

Model XLA: 418

Model KR: 16

Model KRTT: 9

Model KHRTT: 4

Model ST: 2,401

Model B: 1,350

Paint Colors

Twins: Pepper Red with Black tank panels and Pepper Red fenders, Black with Pepper Red tank panels and Black fenders, Skyline Blue and Birch White panels and Blue fenders, Birch White with Black tank panels and Birch White fenders, and Silver (police only); available at no extra cost are Birch White (solid or with Black panels), fenders to match tank panel, Metallic Midnight Blue with Birch White tank panels and Midnight Blue fenders

Singles: Pepper Red, High Fire, Skyline Blue, Birch White

Servi-Car: Pepper Red, Black, Skyline Blue, and Silver (police only); available at extra cost is Metallic Midnight Blue

Series B Hummer 125cc Two-Stroke Singles

First Year

Painted with "H-D 100" enamel

Front brake added to Hummer

Front-brake lever added to right handlebar

Sturdier muffler mounting

Tank decal is a round disc divided by split name "Harley-Davidson" with name "Hummer" in bar trailing behind (this year only)

Series ST and STU 165cc Two-Stroke Singles

First Year

Needle bearings on front wheel

Painted with "H-D 100" enamel

Sturdier muffler brackets

Sturdier horn mounting

Redesigned speedometer face: Black numbers on a White background; odometer tenths figure is White on a Black background

Tank emblem is a round disc divided by split name "Harley-Davidson" with number "165" in bar trailing behind (this year only)

Series XL Sportsters

First Year
Series XL Sportster is a new model

Engine: 55ci OHV V-twin with 7.5:1 compression ratio and 3x3.812in bore and stroke

Single-unit construction of engine and transmission

Recirculating oil system for engine oil

Engine oil tank below seat on right side; holds 3qt

Primary chain and transmission are lubricated by an oil bath separate from the engine oil

Cast iron barrels and heads

Hemispherical combustion chambers

Aluminum rocker boxes enclose valves and rockers

Cam-ground aluminum pistons featuring a chrome-plated top compression ring, nonplated center compression ring, and lower U-Flex oil-control ring

Stellite-faced exhaust valves

Cams ramped on both closing and opening side; one camshaft per valve

Aluminum-alloy pushrods extend up through the covers to reach rocker

Roller valve lifters called "High Speed Racing Tappets"

Double-tapered Timken roller bearings on sprocket shaft

Straight, retained roller bearings on gear shaft

Spark plugs are air-cooled and can be disassembled

Engine I.D. numbers on pad located on left side between the cylinders

Compact, short-barrel Linkert carburetor

Four-speed transmission with foot shift on right side

Seven-plate clutch operated by lever on left handlebar

Two-brush generator with two-unit voltage regulator; six-volt system

"Jubilee" trumpet horn; horn mounts on right side of motor, power pack on left side

18in wheels standard

Speedometer designed into the sheet metal of the fork shroud

Telescopic front forks

Rear swingarm frame with Timken bearings at swingarm pivot

Coil-over rear shocks

Front drum brakes operated by lever on left handlebar

Rear brakes operated by foot pedal on left side

Solo seat (dual seat optional)

Tank capacity is 4.4gal

Painted with "H-D 100" enamel

Windshield optional

Saddlebags optional

Painted with "H-D 100" enamel

Only Year
Woodruff keys for camshaft gears

Six splines on shaft that supports the drive gear and second gear

Choke control operated by a left-side lever

Tank emblem is round plastic disc featuring two silver and two Red quadrants with Red "Harley-Davidson" name over it, press-riveted to the tank

Series F Hydra-Glides

First/Only Year
Motors have special steel alloy valve guides for both intake and exhaust (midyear)

Rocker covers are polished stamped aluminum

Motors have special steel alloy valve guides for both intake and exhaust

Shorter pushrods with longer adjusters

Exhaust-valve guides threaded on the inside helping to trap more oil

Stronger valve springs on FLH motors (midyear)

Thinner speedometer cable

Minor facelift to speedometer: tenth-mile numerals are Red on a Black background

Tank emblem is a round Lucite plastic disc featuring two Silver and two Red quadrants with Red "Harley-Davidson" name over it, press-riveted to the tank (this year only)

Fender tip is also cast of Lucite; features the H-D bar-and-shield logo over a "V"

Series G Servi-Cars

First Year
Tank emblem is a round Lucite plastic disc featuring two Silver and two Red quadrants with Red "Harley-Davidson" over it, press-riveted to the tank (this year only)

Fender tip is also cast of Lucite; features the H-D bar-and-shield logo over a "V"

Motor Company Minutes, 1957
New tank logo is designed by Willie G. Davidson before actually joining the company.

Dick O'Brien named racing director.

The Royal Canadian Mounted Police receives a new Model FLH.

Racing Notes
Joe Leonard wins AMA Grand National Championship.

Joe Leonard wins Daytona 200-Mile Expert Championship with record 98.52mph.

Gerald McGovern on Sportster wins Jack Pine endurance run.

Model Year 1958

1958 FL Duo-Glide. *Jeff Hackett*

Main Models

58-B Hummer Lightweight: 125cc two-stroke single with three-speed transmission

58-ST Lightweight: 165cc two-stroke single with three-speed transmission

58-STU Lightweight: 165cc two-stroke single with restricted intake and three-speed transmission

58-XL Sportster: 55ci (883cc) medium-compression Sportster OHV V-twin with four-speed transmission

58-XLH Sportster Sport: 55ci (883cc) high-compression Sportster OHV V-twin with four-speed transmission

58-XLC Sportster Racing: 55ci (883cc) medium-compression Sportster OHV V-twin with four-speed transmission, no lighting, and bobbed fenders

58-XLCH Sportster Super Sport: 55ci (883cc) high-compression Sportster OHV V-twin with four-speed transmission, no lighting, and bobbed fenders

58-FLHF Duo-Glide Super Sport Solo: 74ci high-compression Panhead OHV V-twin with foot-shifted four-speed transmission

58-FLH Duo-Glide Super Sport Solo: 74ci high-compression Panhead OHV V-twin with hand-shifted four-speed transmission

58-FLF Duo-Glide Sport Solo: 74ci Panhead OHV V-twin with foot-shifted four-speed transmission

58-FL Duo-Glide Sport Solo: 74ci Panhead OHV V-twin with hand-shifted four-speed transmission

58-G Servi-Car with tow bar: 45ci flathead V-twin with three-speed-and-reverse transmission

58-GA Servi-Car without tow bar: 45ci flathead V-twin with three-speed-and-reverse transmission

Specialty Models

58-KR Track Racer: 45ci flathead V-twin flat-track racer

58-KRTT Tourist Trophy Racer: 45ci flathead V-twin TT racer

58-XLRTT Tourist Trophy Racer: 55ci (883cc) Sportster OHV V-twin TT racer

Sidecars and Chassis

58-LE: right-hand sidecar

58-LEC: right-hand chassis

Retail Prices

Model FLHF: $1,320

Model FLH: $1,320

Model FLF: $1,255

Model FL: $1,255

Model XL: $1,155

Model B: $375

Model ST: $465

Model STU: $465

Model G: $1,465

Model GA: $1,450

Production Totals

Model FL: 1,591

Model FLH: 195

Model FLF: 1,299

Model FLHF: 2,953

Model G: 283

Model GA: 643

Model XL: 579

Model XLH: 711

Model XLCH: 239

Model KRTT: 26

Model KR: 9

Model XLRTT: 26

Model ST: 2,445

Model B: 1,677

Options

Chrome Finish Group #F-1 for Duo-Glide

Road Cruiser Group #F-2 for Duo-Glide

Road Cruiser Group #F-3 for Duo-Glide

Road Cruiser Group #F-4 for Duo-Glide

King of the Highway Group #F-5 for Duo-Glide

King of the Highway Group #F-6 for Duo-Glide

King of the Highway Group #F-7 for Duo-Glide

Standard Police Group #FP-1 for Duo-Glide

Standard Police Group #FP-2 for Duo-Glide

Deluxe Equipment Group #SP-1 for Sportster

Deluxe Equipment Group #SP-2 for Sportster

Deluxe Equipment Group #SP-3 for Sportster

Standard Servi-Car Group #G-1

Deluxe Servi-Car Group #G-2

Deluxe Servi-Car Group #G-3

Police Servi-Car Group #G-4

Police Servi-Car Group #G-5

Police Servi-Car Group #G-6

Police Servi-Car Group #G-7

Deluxe Sport Sidecar Group #SC-1

Paint Colors

Big Twins: Calypso Red tank top and fender sides with Birch White tank sides and fender top; Black tank top and fender sides with Birch White tank sides and fender top; Skyline Blue tank top and fender sides with Birch White tank sides and fender top; Sabre Gray Metallic tank top and fender sides with Birch White tank sides and fender top; solid Police Silver (police only); solid Birch White (police only); and any solid standard color without tank panels

Sportster: Skyline Blue tank top with Birch White sides, Sabre Gray Metallic tank top with Birch White sides, Calypso Red tank top with Birch White sides, Black tank top with Birch White sides; mudguards any standard color

Lightweights: Skyline Blue tank top with Birch White sides, Tropical Coral tank top with Birch White sides, Calypso Red tank top with Birch White sides, and Black tank top with Birch White sides and fenders

Servi-Car: Calypso Red, Black, Skyline Blue, Birch White, Police Silver (police only)

Series B Hummer 125cc Two-Stroke Singles

Only Year

Tank decal is a large circular disc with name "Hummer" in the center, flanked at top and bottom by "wings," the top one with "Harley" and bottom one with "Davidson" in it

Series ST and STU 165cc Two-Stroke Singles

Only Year

Tank emblem is a large circular disc with number "165" in the center, flanked at top and bottom by "wings," the top one with "Harley" and bottom one with "Davidson" in it

Series XL Sportsters

First Year

New oil-tank cap gasket

Camshaft gears integrated with the shafts

Eight splines on shaft that supports the drive gear and second gear

Choke control lever on the air cleaner

Heavier-duty clutch cover

New clutch cover gasket

New oil-resistant clutch hub seal

New gear-shaft O-ring

Drive gear-shaft diameter enlarged 0.125in

Nonvalanced front fender

Optional shock absorbers extended 1in

Tank emblem is a round plastic disc featuring two Gold and two Black quadrants with a Red "Harley-Davidson" over it (this year only)

Series XLH Sportsters

First Year

Series XLH Sportster is a new high-compression Sportster model; has all the new features of the XL

Letter "H" designates "High Compression"

Series XLC Sportsters

First/Only Year

Model XLC Sportster is an off-road version of the XL Sportster

"C" designates Competition

Peanut gas tank with 2.25gal capacity

Tank emblem is a large V with the checkered flag in between and the name "Harley-Davidson" in the area behind

Magneto ignition

Eight splines on shaft that support the drive gear and second gear

Choke control lever on the air cleaner

Stamped-steel primary cover

Lightened tappets

No headlight or taillight

No speedometer

Wide-ratio gearing

Short dual pipes without mufflers

Bobbed front and rear fenders

(Model XLC discontinued after the 1958 model year)

Series XLCH Sportsters

First Year

Model XLCH Sportster is an off-road version of the XLH Sportster

Peanut gas tank with 2.25gal capacity

Tank emblem is a large V with the checkered flag in between and the name "Harley-Davidson" in the area behind

Letters "CH" designate "Competition High-Compression"

Larger-than-standard XL ports and valves

No headlight or taillight

High-domed pistons

Light rod tappets

Shortened rear fender

Stamped-metal primary cover

Small section semi-knobby off-road tires

Magneto ignition

Short dual pipes without mufflers

1in extended shock suspension unit optional

Roller valve lifters

Choke control lever on the air cleaner

Sprung Solo seat

Alloy wheel rims optional

Only Year

No speedometer

No headlight

No battery

Staggered dual exhaust without mufflers

Series FL and FLH Duo-Glides

First Year

Series F Duo-Glide is a new model based on the Hydra-Glide; last year 1964

Hydraulic-rear-shock suspension system

Shock absorber and spring protected in a chrome cover

Redesigned frame for rear suspension

Redesigned fork stem and triple tree for new frame

New one-piece front safety guard mounts at top with one bolt

Redesigned horseshoe oil tank to fit new frame

Vertically mounted toolbox with smooth cover

Rear chain guard redesigned to work with rear suspension

Twin alloy rear-fender supports

Rear fender skirt redesigned with a ridge stamped in relief following curvature of fender and each side dimpled for the fender braces for the alloy rear-fender supports

Two-piece rear safety guard for Duo-Glide frame

Rear hydraulic braking system consisting of a new foot pedal, hydraulic lines, new rear hub, master cylinder mounted by the right footboard, backing plate with attached hydraulic cylinder

Hydraulic brake stoplight switch, using a harness with eyelet terminals

New Model 58 brush generator with two-unit voltage regulator, six-volt system

Single exhaust system standard; dual exhaust optional

Y-pipe is 16-1/2in long on single exhaust systems

Stellite-faced valves (midyear) for Model FLH

Chrome-plated "Duo-Glide" front fender emblems standard

Transmission covers are die-cast

3/8in brake cable tube

Black-painted inner primary chain housing redesigned to reposition the breather pipe hole to where breather pipe exits the crankcase

Model 58 two-brush generator, current output limited with an external voltage regulator

Cast aluminum O-ring intake manifolds

Left crankcase has redesigned rear motor mount, allowing voltage regulator mounting

Right crankcase redesigned for a larger-diameter pinion race and a new roller bearing for the cam gear

Cylinder heads with fins redesigned thicker and wider

New gear cover with 5/16in generator-mounting holes

Streamline teardrop-shaped toolbox, with plain cover, mounted vertically

Black-painted rear chain guard moves up and down with the wheel

Rear fender designed with new mounts keeping the fender rigid against upper part of frame, free of the swingarm

Oil filter assembly features new frame bracket and oil return line

Oil tank designed with two battery tie-down tabs at the back of the battery well

"Step-down" straight-leg cradle frame with twin downtubes, larger diameter backbone tube, vertical seat post behind motor, left and right lower tubes reach a swing-arm pivot forging

Redesigned rear fender for swingarm frame

Tank emblem is a round plastic disc featuring two Gold and Black quadrants with a Red "Harley-Davidson" over it (this year only)

Series G Servi-Cars

First Year

Hydra-Glide front fork standard

Glide fork brake

Glide front axles

Two-brush generator with two-unit voltage regulator, six-volt system

Hydra-Glide fork headlight

Headlight bracket rubber mounted

Tank emblem is a round plastic disc featuring two Gold and two Black quadrants with a Red "Harley-Davidson" over it (this year only)

Motor Company Minutes, 1958

Gross sales for year total $16,390,000.

Racing Notes

Carroll Resweber wins AMA Grand National Championship.

Joe Leonard places second Grand National Championship.

Everett Brashear ties third Grand National Championship.

Joe Leonard wins Daytona 200-Mile Expert Championship with record 99.86mph on Model KR.

Jack Heller, private rider, sets Salt Flats record of 134.881mph on a Sportster.

1959 FL Duo-Glide. *Jeff Hackett*

Main Models

59-B Hummer Lightweight: 125cc two-stroke single with three-speed transmission

59-ST Lightweight: 165cc two-stroke single with three-speed transmission

59-STU Lightweight: 165cc two-stroke single with restricted intake and three-speed transmission

59-XL Standard Sportster: 55ci (883cc) medium-compression Sportster OHV V-twin with four-speed transmission

59-XLH Sportster Super H: 55ci (883cc) high-compression Sportster OHV V-twin with four-speed transmission

59-XLCH Sportster Super CH: 55ci (883cc) high-compression Sportster OHV V-twin with four-speed transmission

59-FLHF Duo-Glide Super Sport Solo: 74ci high-compression Panhead OHV V-twin with foot-shifted four-speed transmission

59-FLH Duo-Glide Super Sport Solo: 74ci high-compression Panhead OHV V-twin hand-shifted four-speed transmission

59-FLF Duo-Glide Sport Solo: 74ci medium-compression Panhead OHV V-twin with foot-shifted four-speed transmission

59-FL Duo-Glide Sport Solo: 74ci Panhead OHV V-twin with hand-shifted four-speed transmission

59-G Servi-Car with tow bar: 45ci flathead V-twin with three-speed-and-reverse transmission

59-GA Servi-Car without tow bar: 45ci flathead V-twin with three-speed-and-reverse transmission

Specialty Models

59-KR Track Racer: 45ci flathead V-twin flat-track racer

59-KRTT Tourist Trophy Racer: 45ci flathead V-twin TT racer

59-XLRTT Tourist Trophy Racer: 55ci Sportster OHV V-twin TT racer

Sidecars and Chassis

59-LE: right-hand sidecar

Retail Prices

Model FLHF: $1,345
Model FLH: $1,345
Model FLF: $1,280
Model FL: $1,280
Model XL: $1,175
Model XLH: $1,200
Model XLCH: $1,285
Model B: $385
Model ST: $475
Model STU: $475
Model G: $1,500
Model GA: $1,470

Production Totals

Model FL: 1,201
Model FLH: 121
Model FLF: 1,222
Model FLHF: 3,223
Model G: 288
Model GA: 524
Model XL: 42
Model XLH: 947
Model XLCH: 1,059
Model XLR: 5
Model XLRTT: 13
Model KR: 10
Model KRTT: 23
Model ST: 2,311
Model B: 1,285
Model A: 73

Options

Chrome Finish Group #F-1 for Duo-Glide
Road Cruiser Group #F-2 for Duo-Glide
Road Cruiser Group #F-2A for Duo-Glide
Road Cruiser Group #F-3 for Duo-Glide
Road Cruiser Group #F-3A for Duo-Glide
Road Cruiser Group #F-4 for Duo-Glide
Road Cruiser Group #F-4A for Duo-Glide
King of the Highway Group #F-5 for Duo-Glide
King of the Highway Group #F-5A for Duo-Glide
King of the Highway Group #F-6 for Duo-Glide
King of the Highway Group #F-6A for Duo-Glide
King of the Highway Group #F-7 for Duo-Glide
King of the Highway Group #F-7A for Duo-Glide
Police Group #FP-1 for Duo-Glide
Police Group #FP-2 for Duo-Glide
Deluxe Equipment Group #SP-1 for Models XL and XLH
Deluxe Equipment Group #SP-1A for Models XL and XLH
Deluxe Equipment Group #SP-1B for Models XL and XLH
Deluxe Equipment Group #SP-2 for Models XL and XLH
Deluxe Equipment Group #SP-3 for Models XL and XLH
Standard Servi-Car Group #G-1
Deluxe Servi-Car Group #G-2
Deluxe Servi-Car Group #G-3
Police Servi-Car Group #G-4
Police Servi-Car Group #G-5
Police Servi-Car Group #G-6
Police Servi-Car Group #G-7
Deluxe Sport Sidecar Group #SC-1

Paint Colors

Big Twins

Calypso Red: Tank top is Calypso Red with Birch White side panels; mudguards are Calypso Red
Skyline Blue: Tank top is Skyline Blue with Birch White side panels; mudguards are Skyline Blue
Black: Tank top is Black with Birch White side panels; mudguards are Black
Hi-Fi Red: Tank top is Hi-Fi Red with Birch White side panels; mudguards are Hi-Fi Red
Hi-Fi Turquoise: Tank top is Hi-Fi Turquoise with Birch White sides; mudguards are Hi-Fi Turquoise
Police Silver (police only)
Birch White (police only)
Any standard color-solid without panels

Sportster

Skyline Blue: tank top is Blue with Birch White side panels
Black: tank top is Black with Birch White side panels
Calypso Red: tank top is Red with Birch White side panels
Any standard color solid, no cost
Hi-Fi Turquoise: tank top is Turquoise with Birch White side panels
Hi-Fi Red: tank top is Red with Birch White side panels

Lightweights

Skyline Blue: tank top is Blue with Birch White side panels
Calypso Red: tank top is Red with Birch White side panels
Hi-Fi Turquoise: tank top is Turquoise with Birch White side panels
Hi-Fi Red: tank top is Red with Birch White side panels

Servi-Car

Black, Skyline Blue, Birch White, Calypso Red, and Police Silver (police only)

Series B Hummer 125cc Two-Stroke Singles

First/Only Year

Arrow-Flite tank decal designed as a graphic oval Red ball pierced by an arrow with name "Harley-Davidson" on arrow shaft
Optional Buddy seat
(Last year of Model B production)

Series ST and STU 165cc Two-Stroke Singles

First/Only Year

Arrow-Flite tank decal designed as a graphic oval Red ball pierced by an arrow with name "Harley-Davidson" on arrow shaft
Headlight 5-3/4in
New Trip-O-Meter speedometer mounted on redesigned Tele-Glide fork panel
Optional Buddy seat
(Last year of Models ST and STU production)

Series XL Sportsters

First Year

    Sheet-metal nacelle housing headlight
    Speedometer mounted in the headlight nacelle
    Trip-O-Meter speedometer
    Single-switch ignition on back of left fork
    Valanced front fender
    Nylon chain tensioner
    End-relieved connecting-rod bearings
    Arrow-Flite tank emblem designed with an oval Red ball behind a chromed arrow with name "Harley-Davidson" in Red on arrow shaft
    Redesigned buddy seat optional
    Optional exhaust with dual, stacked mufflers
    (Last year of Model XL Standard Sportster)

Series XLH Sportsters

First Year

    High-lift intake cams and recontoured exhaust cams
    Sheet-metal nacelle housing headlight
    Speedometer mounted in the headlight nacelle
    Trip-O-Meter speedometer
    Single-switch ignition on back of left fork
    Valanced front fender
    Nylon chain tensioner
    End-relieved connecting-rod bearings
    Arrow-Flite tank emblem designed with an oval Red ball behind a chromed arrow with name "Harley-Davidson" in Red on arrow shaft
    Redesigned buddy seat optional
    Optional exhaust with dual, stacked mufflers

Series XLCH Sportsters

First Year

    Model XLCH is now street legal
    Headlight 5-3/4in diameter, hung below an eyebrow mount
    Electrical system including a generator, headlight, and stop/taillight
    Horn mounted on left side of engine
    Tripmeter speedometer mounted behind handlebars
    High-lift intake cam and recontoured exhaust cam
    High mounted two-into-one exhaust system; unmuffled dual exhaust optional
    Laconia chrome rubber mounted handlebars, standard
    Handlebar for clamp cover, standard
    Steering damper adjusted from bottom side of fork bracket
    Nylon chain tensioner
    End-relieved connecting-rod bearings

Series FL Duo-Glides

First Year

    Arrow-Flite tank emblem designed with an oval Red ball behind a chrome arrow with the name "Harley-Davidson" stamped in Red on arrow shaft
    Dash on foot-shift models features neutral-indicator light covered with a green domed lens
    Chrome-plated front and rear fender tips designed with a "mountain peak" rising above a large "V"
    Footboards painted Black over Parkerized finish
    Chrome-plated clutch-booster cover optional
    Chrome-plated toolbox cover optional

Series G Servi-Cars

First Year

    Arrow-Flite tank emblem designed with an oval Red ball behind a chrome arrow, the name "Harley-Davidson" in Red stamped on arrow shaft
    Diaphram-type gas petcock below tank
    Aluminum-bodied carburetor and modified manifold and gas lines

Motor Company Minutes, 1959

    John Davidson joins the company.
    Honda comes to America to "meet the nicest people" and become a stiff competitor.

Racing Notes

    Brad Andres on Model KR wins Daytona 200-Mile Expert Championship with record 98.70mph.
    Carroll Resweber wins AMA Grand National Championship and the Number 1 plates.

CHAPTER 7

1960-1969

Model Year 1960

1960 FL Duo-Glide. *Jeff Hackett*

Main Models

60-A Topper Scooter: 165cc two-stroke single with automatic transmission

60-AU Topper Scooter: 165cc two-stroke single with restricted intake (for under-5hp limits) and automatic transmission

60-BT Super 10 Lightweight: 165cc two-stroke single with three-speed transmission

60-BTU Super 10 Lightweight: 165cc two-stroke single with restricted intake (for under-5hp limits) and three-speed transmission

60-XLH Sportster Super H: 55ci (883cc) Sportster OHV V-twin with four-speed transmission

60-XLCH Sportster Super CH: 55ci (883cc) Sportster OHV V-twin with four-speed transmission

60-FLHF Duo-Glide Super Sport Solo: 74ci Super Sport Panhead OHV V-twin with foot-shifted four-speed transmission

60-FLH Duo-Glide Super Sport Solo: 74ci Super Sport Panhead OHV V-twin with hand-shifted four-speed transmission

60-FLF Duo-Glide Sport Solo: 74ci medium-compression Panhead OHV V-twin with foot-shifted four-speed transmission

60-FL Duo-Glide Sport Solo: 74ci Panhead OHV V-twin with hand-shifted four-speed transmission

60-G Servi-Car with tow bar: 45ci flathead V-twin with three-speed-and-reverse transmission

60-GA Servi-Car without tow bar: 45ci flathead V-twin with three-speed-and-reverse transmission

Specialty Models

60-KR Track Racer: 45ci flathead V-twin flat-track racer

60-KRTT Tourist Trophy Racer: 45ci flathead V-twin TT racer

60-XLRTT Tourist Trophy Racer: 55ci Sportster OHV V-twin TT racer

Sidecars and Chassis

60-LE: Sport Sidecar

Retail Prices

Model FLHF: $1,375
Model FLH: $1,375
Model FLF: $1,310
Model FL: $1,310
Model XLH: $1,225
Model XLCH: $1,310
Model BT: $455
Model BTU: $465
Model A: $430
Model AU: $430
Model G: $1,530
Model GA: $1,500

Production Totals

Topper: 3,801
Duo-Glide: 5,967
Servi-Car: 707
Sportster: 2,765
Lightweight: 2,488

Options

Chrome Finish Group #F-1 for Duo-Glide
Road Cruiser Group #F-2 for Duo-Glide
Road Cruiser Group #F-2A for Duo-Glide
Road Cruiser Group #F-3 for Duo-Glide
Road Cruiser Group #F-3A for Duo-Glide
Road Cruiser Group #F-4 for Duo-Glide
Road Cruiser Group #F-4A for Duo-Glide
King of the Highway Group #F-5 for Duo-Glide
King of the Highway Group #F-5A for Duo-Glide
King of the Highway Group #F-6 for Duo-Glide
King of the Highway Group #F-6A for Duo-Glide
King of the Highway Group #F-7 for Duo-Glide
King of the Highway Group #F-7A for Duo-Glide
Police Group #FP-1 for Duo-Glide
Police Group #FP-2 for Duo-Glide
Police Group #FP-3 for Duo-Glide
Deluxe Equipment Group #SP-1 for Sportster
Deluxe Equipment Group #SP-1A for Sportster
Deluxe Equipment Group #SP-2 for Sportster
Deluxe Equipment Group #SP-2A for Sportster
Deluxe Equipment Group #SP-3 for Sportster
Standard Servi-Car Group #G-1
Deluxe Servi-Car Group #G-2

Deluxe Servi-Car Group #G-3
Police Servi-Car Group #G-4
Police Servi-Car Group #G-5
Police Servi-Car Group #G-6
Police Servi-Car Group #G-7
Deluxe Sport Sidecar Group #SC-1

Paint Colors

Big Twins: Black with Birch White tank panels, Skyline Blue with Birch White tank panels, Police Silver (police only), and Birch White (police only); available at no extra cost is any standard color without panels; optional at extra cost are Hi-Fi Red with Birch White tank panels, Hi-Fi Green with Birch White tank panels, and Hi-Fi Blue with Birch White tank panels

Sportster: Skyline Blue with Birch White tank panels or Black with Birch White tank panels; available at no extra cost is any standard color without side panels; available at extra cost are Hi-Fi Blue with Birch White tank panels, Hi-Fi Red with Birch White tank panels, and Hi-Fi Green with Birch White tank panels

Lightweights: Skyline Blue with Birch White tank panels; available at extra cost are Hi-Fi Red with Birch White tank panels, Hi-Fi Blue with Birch White tank panels, Hi-Fi Green with Birch White tank panels

Topper: Two-toned Strato Blue

Servi-Car: Birch White, Skyline Blue, Black, Police Silver (police only)

Series A Topper Scooters

First Year

Models A and AU Topper Scooters are all-new models

Engine: 165cc horizontal two-stroke single cylinder with 2.375x2.281in bore and stroke and 6.6:1 compression ratio; AU engine has a restricted intake to meet 5hp licensing restrictions

Reed-valve intake

"Scootaway" automatic transmission automatically changes the drive ratio by changing the diameter of both the front and rear driving flanges on which the belt drive ran

Belt drive, from engine to automatic clutch; chain final drive

Serial number stamped on the engine crankcase

5in brakes at each wheel

1.7gal tank with .5 pint reserve

Fiberglass body with steel frame and front fender

Leading link front suspension

Pivoted-fork rear suspension with two adjustable extension springs

Rubber-mounted engine

Two-tone paint scheme

Body emblem is stamped out name "Topper" with the name "Harley-Davidson" stamped into the crossbar of the letter T

Front brake lever on left handlebar that when a cam is locked works as a parking brake

Hand-pulled recoil starting method

Storage compartment under the buddy seat

(1960 is the only year of reproduction for the Model A Topper)

Series BT Super 10 Singles

First Year

Model BT Super 10 is an update of the discontinued ST model; last year 1961

New engine: 165cc two-stroke single with a bore and stroke of 2.375x2.281in, compression ratio of 6.6:1, and an output of 6hp (BT) or 5hp (BTU)

Aluminum cylinder head

Waterproof electrical system with two low-tension output coils

Arrow-Flite tank decal designed with an oval Red ball behind a chrome arrow with name "Harley-Davidson" in Red stamped on arrow shaft (this year only)

Series XLH Sportster

First Year

Recalibrated damping on shock absorbers, similar to Big Twin 74s

Series XLCH Sportster

First Year

Recalibrated damping in shock absorbers

Standard from rim is now 19in; rear is still 18in

Series FL Duo-Glides

First Year

Two-piece stamped aluminum fork nacelle that shrouds headlight; polished or painted Black

Two-piece handlebars with a bar for each side and center handlebar clamp that bolts to the revised fork top bracket

Large aluminum (polished or unpolished) handlebar clamp cover

Windshield assembly brackets and lower panels redesigned, accommodating the new nacelle

FLH-type Stellite-faced exhaust valves fitted to FL model

Spotlight mounts redesigned, accommodating the new nacelle

Rear brake drum drive sprocket is riveted with 3/16in rivets

More powerful rear brakes

Recalibrated damping in rear shock absorbers

Rail-type oil-control piston rings

Extra-heavy valve springs

Revised ration on kickstarter gear

Crowned rollers on gear side of main bearing

Rear brake drum with 3/16in rivets used to attach the sprocket

Series G Servi-Cars

First Year

Two-piece stamped aluminum fork nacelle that shrouds headlight; painted Black

Two-piece handlebars with a bar for each side and center handlebar clamp that bolts to the revised fork top bracket

Large aluminum handlebar clamp cover; painted Black

Adjusting space between nacelle and headlight

Redesigned summer and winter windshields

Motor Company Minutes, 1960

H-D purchases half the bike division of Italian Aermacchi company.

H-D International is established to provide better control in the overseas marketing of their motorcycles and accessories. Overseas expansion of company becomes focal point.

Racing Notes

Brad Andres wins Daytona 200-Mile Expert Championship with record 98.06mph.

Tom Seagraves wins Daytona 100-Mile Junior Championship with record 97.05mph.

Carroll Resweber wins AMA Grand National Championship.

Joe Leonard places second Grand National Championship.

Bart Markel places third Grand National Championship.

Last year Daytona motorcycle races held on beach sand.

1961 FLHF Duo-Glide. *Greg Field*

Main Models

61-BT Super 10 Lightweight: 165cc two-stroke single with three-speed transmission

61-BTU Super 10 Lightweight: 165cc two-stroke single with restricted intake and three-speed transmission

61-AH Topper Scooter: 165cc high-compression two-stroke single with automatic transmission

61-AU Topper Scooter: 165cc two-stroke single with restricted intake and automatic transmission

61-XLH Sportster Super H: 55ci (883cc) Sportster OHV V-twin with four-speed transmission

61-XLCH Sportster Super CH: 55ci (883cc) Sportster V-twin with four-speed transmission

61-FLHF Duo-Glide Super Sport: 74ci Panhead OHV V-twin with foot-shifted four-speed transmission

61-FLH Duo-Glide Super Sport: 74ci Panhead OHV V-twin with hand-shifted four-speed transmission

61-FLF Duo-Glide Sport: 74ci Panhead OHV V-twin with foot-shifted four-speed transmission

61-FL Duo-Glide Sport: 74ci Panhead OHV V-twin with hand-shifted four-speed transmission

61-G Servi-Car with tow bar: 45ci flathead V-twin with three-speed-and-reverse transmission

61-GA Servi-Car without tow bar: 45ci flathead V-twin with three-speed-and-reverse transmission

Specialty Models

61-KR Track Racer: 45ci flathead V-twin flat-track racer

61-KRTT Tourist Trophy Racer: 45ci flathead V-twin TT racer

61-XLRTT Tourist Trophy Racer: 55ci Sportster OHV V-twin TT racer

Sidecars and Chassis

61-LE: Sport sidecar

61-LA: Topper sidecar

61-LM: Topper utility box

Retail Prices

Model FLHF: $1,400

Model FLH: $1,400

Model FLF: $1,335

Model FL: $1,335

Model XLH: $1,250

Model XLCH: $1,335

Model BT: $465

Model BTU: $465

Model AH: $445

Model AU: $445

Model G: $1,555

Model GA: $1,525

Production Totals

Topper: 1,341

Duo-Glide: 4,927

Servi-Car: 628

Sportster: 2,014

Lightweight: 1,587

Options

Chrome Finish Group #F-1

Road Cruiser Group #F-2

Road Cruiser Group #F-2A

Road Cruiser Group #F-3

Road Cruiser Group #F-4

King of the Highway Group #F-5

King of the Highway Group #F-5A

King of the Highway Group #F-6

King of the Highway Group #F-7

Standard Police Group #FP-1

Standard Police Group #FP-2

Standard Police Group #FP-3

Deluxe Sidecar Group #SC-1

Paint Colors

Big Twin: Black with Birch White tank panels, Pepper Red with Birch White tank panels, Police Silver (police only), and Birch White (police only); available at no extra cost is any standard color solid without panels; available at extra cost are Hi-Fi Green with Birch White panels, Hi-Fi Red with Birch White panels, and Hi-Fi Blue with Birch White panels

Sportster XLH: Solid Pepper Red or Solid Black; Hi-Fi Blue, Hi-Fi Red, and Hi-Fi Green available at extra cost

Sportster XLCH: Pepper Red with White or Black with White; available at extra cost are Hi-Fi Blue with White, Hi-Fi Red with White, and Hi-Fi Green with White

Lightweight: Pepper Red with White; available at extra cost are Hi-Fi Red with White, Hi-Fi Blue with White, and Hi-Fi Green with White

Scooter: Pepper Red and White, Strato Blue and White, and Granada Green and White

Servi-Car: Black, Skyline Blue, Birch White, Pepper Red, and Silver (police only)

Series AU and AH Topper Scooters

First Year

Model AH Topper scooter replaces the Model A; Model AU returns with updates for 1961

Higher compression engine with 9hp output on Model AH

Jiffy stand on right side

Sidecar optional (White body and fenders with a Black frame)

Utility box optional (White body and fenders with a Black frame)

Series BT Super 10 Singles

First Year

16in wheels

Tank emblem is a circle crossed over by a four-point "star" with the name "Harley-Davidson" stamped in a bar trailing from the lower rear quadrant of the star

Series XLH Sportster

First Year

Tank emblem is a long oval circle containing a long pointed star divided into four quadrants with name "Harley-Davidson" across top

"Double-duty" seat

Series XLCH Sportster

First Year

"Double-duty" seat

Tank emblem is a long oval circle containing a long pointed star divided into four quadrants with name "Harley-Davidson" across top

Series FL Duo-Glides

First Year

"Single-fire" ignition (each cylinder using separate set of points and coil)

Manual-advance dual-point timer using two sets of contact points and a single-lobe points cam; each set of points has its own condenser

Twin round-section, single-lead coils

Left flywheel with timing mark for rear cylinder (midyear)

FLH decal designed as a "lightning bolt H" in Red against a white background with checkered stripes at both the top and the bottom, placed on both sides of the oil tank on FLH models

Pushrods redesigned with a longer main body section and a shorter pressed-in bottom section

Model 61 generator using an external voltage regulator mounted at the left side of the rear cylinder

Tank emblem is a circle crossed over by a four-point "star" with the name "Harley-Davidson" stamped in a bar trailing from the lower rear quadrant of the star

Optional dual exhaust system with interconnected pipes (midyear)

Series G Servi-Cars

First Year

Tank emblem is a circle crossed over by a four-point "star" with the name "Harley-Davidson" stamped in a bar trailing from the lower rear quadrant of the star

Racing Notes

Carroll Resweber wins 50-Mile National Race, August 20.

Roger Reiman on Model KR wins Daytona 200-Mile Expert Championship with record 69.25mph.

Carroll Resweber wins AMA Grand National Championship.

Joe Leonard places second Grand National Championship.

Motor Company Minutes, 1961

John A. Davidson joins the Dealer Relations Department.

William H. Davidson is named the chairman of Aermacchi.

Model Year 1962

1962 FLHF Duo-Glide. *Greg Field*

Main Models

62-AH Topper Scooter: 165cc two-stroke single with automatic transmission

62-AU Topper Scooter: 165cc two-stroke single with restricted intake (for under-5hp regulations) and automatic transmission

62-BTU Pacer Lightweight: 165cc flathead two-stroke single with restricted intake (for under-5hp regulations) and three-speed transmission

62-BTF Ranger Off-Road Trail: 165cc two-stroke single with three-speed transmission

62-BT Pacer Lightweight: 175cc two-stroke single with three-speed transmission

62-BTH Scat On/Off Road Lightweight: 175cc two-stroke single with three-speed transmission

62-XLH Sportster Super H: 55ci (883cc) Sportster OHV V-twin with four-speed transmission

62-XLCH Sportster Super CH: 55ci (883cc) Sportster OHV V-twin with four-speed transmission

62-FLHF Duo-Glide Super Sport: 74ci Panhead OHV V-twin with foot-shifted four-speed transmission

62-FLH Duo-Glide Super Sport: 74ci Panhead OHV V-twin with hand-shifted four-speed transmission

62-FLF Duo-Glide Sport: 74ci Panhead OHV V-twin with foot-shifted four-speed transmission

62-FL Duo-Glide Sport: 74ci Panhead OHV V-twin with hand-shifted four-speed transmission

62-G Servi-Car with tow bar: 45ci flathead V-twin with three-speed-and-reverse transmission

62-GA Servi-Car without tow bar: 45ci flathead V-twin with three-speed-and-reverse transmission

Specialty Models

62-KR Track Racer: 45ci flathead V-twin flat-track racer

62-KRTT Tourist Trophy Racer: 45ci flathead V-twin TT racer

Sidecars and Chassis

62-LE: Sport Sidecar for Duo-Glides

62-LEC: sidecar chassis with wheel and fender

62-LA: Topper sidecar

62-LM: Topper utility box

Retail Prices

Model FLHF: $1,400
Model FLH: $1,400
Model FLF: $1,335
Model FL: $1,335
Model XLH: $1,250
Model XLCH: $1,335
Model BT: $465
Model BTH: $475
Model BTF: $440
Model BTU: $465
Model AH: $445
Model AU: $445
Model G: $1,555
Model GA: $1,525

Production Totals

Duo-Glide: 5,184
Sportster: 1,998
Servi-Car: 703
Lightweight: 1,983

Options

Chrome Finish Group #F-1
Road Cruiser Group #F-2
Road Cruiser Group #F-3
Road Cruiser Group #F-4
King of the Highway Group #F-5
King of the Highway Group #F-6
King of the Highway Group #F-7
Standard Police Group #FP-3

Paint Colors

Big Twin: Tango Red with Birch White tank panels, Black with Birch White tank panels, Police Silver (police only), and Birch White (police only); available at extra cost are Hi-Fi Purple with Birch White tank panels, Hi-Fi Blue with Birch White tank panels, and Hi-Fi Red with Birch White tank panels

Sportsters: Black and White, Tango Red and White; available at extra cost are Hi-Fi Blue and White, Hi-Fi Red and White, Hi-Fi Purple and White

Lightweights: Tango Red with White panels or Skyline Blue with White panels; available at extra cost are Hi-Fi Red with White panels or Hi-Fi Purple with White panels (except Model BTF)

Topper: Birch White with Skyline Blue, Tango Red, or Granada Green

Servi-Car: Black, Birch White, Tango Red, Skyline Blue, and Silver (police only)

Series AH and AU Topper Scooters

First Year

Streamlined handlebars with fingertip ignition and new grips
Positive neutral lockout mechanism

Series BTF Ranger Singles

First/Only Year

Model BTF Ranger is a new off-road-only model based on the 165cc Model BT of 1961, with differences as listed below
No lights
Buckhorn handlebars
No front fender
Shortened rear fender
High-mounted off-road exhaust system

Muffler painted Black
Shortened folding foot pegs
18x3.50in rims
Grasshopper front tire
Continental rear tire
(Model BTF Ranger was built only during the 1962 model year)

Series BTU Pacer Singles

First Year

The Model BTU Pacer is a carryover of the Model BTU Super 10 of 1961, with revised paint scheme

Series BT Pacer Singles

First Year

The 175cc Model BT Pacer is a new model, based on the 165cc Model BT Super 10 of 1961
Longer stroke for displacement of 175cc
Higher compression ratio of 7.63:1
Revised intake-port timing
Beefed-up lower end
Buddy seat optional (Black and White, Red and White, or all White)
Black saddlebags optional
White saddlebags optional

Series BTH Scat Singles

First Year

Model BTH Scat is a new model that is an on/off-road version of the 175cc Model BT Pacer and differs from the Pacer in the following details
High-mounted, off-road-type front fender
Shortened rear fender
Upswept tuned exhaust
Buckhorn handlebars
Grasshopper tires both front and rear
Buddy seat optional (Black and White, Red and White, or all White)
Black saddlebags optional
White saddlebags optional

Only Year

Rigid rear suspension

Series XLH and XLCH Sportsters

First Year

Aluminum upper fork bracket
Oval-shaped tank badges

Series FL Duo-Glides

First Year

New instrument cover for foot-shift models, designed with three individual round indicator-lens covers: left red lens covers the generator light, center green lens covers the neutral indicator, and the right red lens covers the oil-pressure indicator light; covers painted the color of the motorcycle, but chrome instrument cover is optional

New two-lens instrument cover for hand-shift bikes, designed with two individual, round indicator-lens covers: left red lens covers the generator light, and the right red lens covers the oil-pressure indicator light; covers painted the color of the motorcycle, but chrome instrument cover is optional

"Tombstone" speedometer featuring a flat, single-level face with brushed-aluminum center panel in a tombstone shape, brushed-aluminum 2mph dots, brushed-aluminum hash marks for the tens, and brushed-aluminum numerals 1 to 12 against a Black-painted face; White odometer and trip-meter mile numbers against a Black background; Black tenth-mile tripmeter numbers against a White background; Red pointer; and light that illuminates the outer edge of face

Optional front spot lights, redesigned with a shallower, rounder back

Spot lamp brackets redesigned to mount redesigned lights

Series G Servi-Cars

First Year

New two-lens instrument cover, designed with two individual, round indicator-lens covers: left red lens covers the generator light, and the right red lens covers the oil-pressure indicator light; covers painted the color of the motorcycle, but chrome instrument cover is optional

"Tombstone" speedometer featuring a flat, single-level face with brushed-aluminum center panel in a tombstone shape, brushed-aluminum 2mph dots, brushed-aluminum hash marks for the tens, and brushed-aluminum numerals 1 to 12 against a Black-painted face; white odometer and tripmeter mile numbers against a Black background; Black tenth-mile tripmeter numbers against a White background; Red pointer; and light that illuminates the outer edge of face

Horn with cover having large center hole circled with six smaller holes

Motor Company Minutes, 1962

H-D acquires 60 percent stock in Tomahawk Boat Company, and established Tomahawk Division in Tomahawk, Wisconsin, covering 35,300sq-ft of manufacturing space, responsible for all golf cart bodies, saddlebags, windshields, and miscellaneous motorcycle components.

The Milwaukee Police Department receives a new H-D Duo-Glide and Servi-Car.

Racing Notes

Bart Markel wins AMA Grand National Championship.
Carroll Resweber places second Grand National Championship.

1963 FL Duo-Glide. *Doug Mitchel*

Main Models

63-AH Topper Scooter: 165cc two-stroke single with automatic transmission

63-AU Topper Scooter: 165cc two-stroke single with restricted intake (for under-5hp restrictions) and automatic transmission

63-BT Pacer Street Model: 175cc two-stroke single with three-speed transmission

63-BTH Scat Trail Model: 175cc two-stroke single with three-speed transmission

63-BTU Pacer: 175cc two-stroke single with restricted intake (for under-5hp restrictions) and three-speed transmission

63-XLH Sportster Super H: 55ci (883cc) Sportster OHV V-twin with four-speed transmission

63-XLCH Sportster Super CH: 55ci (883cc) Sportster OHV V-twin with four-speed transmission

63-FLHF Duo-Glide Super Sport: 74ci Panhead OHV V-twin with foot-shifted four-speed transmission

63-FLH Duo-Glide Super Sport: 74ci Panhead OHV V-twin with hand-shifted four-speed transmission

63-FLF Duo-Glide Sport Solo: 74ci Panhead OHV V-twin with foot-shifted four-speed transmission

63-FL Duo-Glide Sport Solo: 74ci Panhead OHV V-twin with hand-shifted four-speed transmission

63-G Servi-Car with tow bar: 45ci flathead V-twin with three-speed-and-reverse transmission

63-GA Servi-Car without tow bar: 45ci flathead V-twin with three-speed-and-reverse transmission

Specialty Models

63-KR Flat Track Racer: 45ci flathead V-twin flat-track racer
63-KRTT TT Racer: 45ci flathead V-twin
63-KR Track Racer: 45ci flathead V-twin flat-track racer
63-KRTT Tourist Trophy Racer: 45ci flathead V-twin TT racer
63-XLRTT Racer: 55ci Sportster OHV V-twin TT racer

Sidecars and Chassis

63-LE: Sport Sidecar for Duo-Glides
63-LEC: sidecar chassis with wheel and fender
63-LA: Topper sidecar
63-LM: Topper utility box

Retail Prices
Model FLH: $1,425
Model FLHF: $1,425
Model FLF: $1,360
Model FL: $1,360
Model XLH: $1,270
Model XLCH: $1,355
Model BT: $485
Model BTH: $495
Model FTU: $485
Model AH: $460
Model AU: $460
Model G: $1,590
Model GA: $1,550

Production Totals
Model BT: 824
Model BTU: 39
Model BTH: 877
Model AH: 972
Model AU: 6
Model XLH: 432
Model XLCH: 1,001
Model KR: 80
Model FL: 1,096
Model FLF: 950
Model FLH: 100
Model FLHF: 2,100

Options
Chrome Finish Group #F-1 for Duo-Glide
King of the Highway Group #F-5 for Duo-Glide
King of the Highway Group #F-6
King of the Highway Group #F-7
Standard Police Group #FP-1
Standard Police Group #FP-2
Optional Group #F-6 for Duo-Glide
Optional Group #F-7 for Duo-Glide
Standard Police Group #FP-1
Police Group #FP-2
Deluxe Equipment Group #SP-1 for XLH
Highway Cruiser Group #SP-2 for XLH
Optional Group #SP-2A for XLH
Optional Group #SP-3H (Low Road Clearance Kit) for XLCH

Paint Colors
Big Twin: Tango Red with Birch White tank panels, Horizon Metallic Blue with Birch White tank panels, Black with Birch White tank panels, Police Silver (police only), and Birch White (police only); available at extra cost are Hi-Fi Purple with Birch White tank panels, Hi-Fi Turquoise with Birch White tank panels, and Hi-Fi Red with Birch White tank panels

Servi-Car: Black Birch White, Tango Red, Horizon Metallic Blue, and Police Silver (police only)

Topper: Black and White, Tango Red and White, and solid White

Sportster: Black and White, Tango Red and White, and Horizon Metallic Blue and White; available at extra cost are Hi-Fi Turquoise and White, Hi-Fi Red and White, and Hi-Fi Purple and White

Lightweights: Tango Red and White or Black and White; available at extra cost are Hi-Fi Turquoise and White or Hi-Fi Red and White

Series AH and AU Topper Scooters

First Year

Body emblem is stylized version of H-D bar-and-shield with the bar part stretched out to the rear
Hypalon seat

Series BT and BTU Pacer Singles

First Year

Model BTU is now a restricted carburetor version of 175cc Model BT Pacer
Tank emblem is stylized version of H-D bar-and-shield with the bar part stretched out
Swingarm rear suspension
Rear-suspension springs under frame, similar to the way they were later mounted on the Big Twin Softtail models
Sport-style bars from the BTH Scat

Series BTH Scat Singles

First Year

Tank emblem is stylized version of H-D bar-and-shield with the bar part stretched out
Swingarm rear suspension
Rear-suspension springs under frame, similar to the way they were later mounted on the Big Twin Softtail models
Upswept rear fender

Series XLH Sportsters

First Year

Revised third-gear ratio of 5.56:1
Restyled starter pedal
Tank emblem is stylized version of H-D Bar-and-Shield with the bar part stretched out to the rear

Series XLCH Sportsters

First Year

Revised third-gear ratio of 5.85:1
Restyled starter pedal
Rubber-mounted sealed beam headlight
Headlight dimmer switch mounted on handlebar
Improved magneto with ignition-key lock on magneto
Tank emblem is stylized version of H-D Bar-and-Shield with the bar part stretched out to the rear

Series FL Duo-Glides

First Year

Outside-oiler heads and external oil lines featuring a boss designed near the intake port for the outside oil line

Cylinders redesigned without the oil passages on the right side

Right crankcase redesigned with external-oil-line boss

Right gear cover redesigned to fit redesigned crankcase

Tank emblem is stylized version of H-D Bar-and Shield with the bar part stretched out to the rear

Wider rear brake hub and shoes

Revised rear brake backing plate and cylinder

Valanced rear chain guard

Round-back front and rear turn-signal lights

Mounting redesigned for front and rear/turn signal lights

Black rubber one-piece kickstarter pedal

Series G Servi-Cars

First Year

Tank emblem is stylized version of H-D Bar-and-Shield with the bar part stretched out to the rear

Motor Company Minutes, 1963

William G. Davidson, the founder's grandson, joins the company.

The California Highway Patrol now has 433 H-D motorcycles in its fleet.

Racing Notes

Ralph White wins Daytona 200-Mile Expert Championship with record 77.678mph.

Buddy Stubbs wins Daytona 100-Mile Junior Championship with record 73.224mph.

Dick Hammer wins Daytona 100-Mile Combined Junior and Expert Race Title with record 71.490mph.

1964 XLCH. *Paul Patten*

Main Models

64-AH Topper Scooter: 165cc two-stroke single with automatic transmission

64-AU Topper Scooter: 165cc two-stroke single with restricted intake (for under-5hp restrictions) and automatic transmission

64-BT Pacer Street Model: 175cc two-stroke single with three-speed transmission

64-BTH Scat Trail Model: 175cc two-stroke single with three-speed transmission

64-BTU Pacer: 175cc two-stroke single with restricted intake (for under-5hp restrictions) and three-speed transmission

64-XLH Sportster Super H: 55ci (883cc) Sportster OHV V-twin with four-speed transmission

64-XLCH Sportster Super CH: 55ci (883cc) Sportster OHV V-twin with four-speed transmission

64-FL Duo-Glide Sport Solo: 74ci Panhead OHV V-twin with hand-shifted four-speed transmission

64-FLH Duo-Glide Super Sport Solo: 74ci Super Sport Panhead OHV V-twin with hand-shifted four-speed transmission

64-FLHF Duo-Glide Super Sport Solo: 74ci Super Sport Panhead OHV V-twin with foot-shifted four-speed transmission

64-FLF Duo-Glide Sport Solo: 74ci medium-compression Panhead OHV V-twin with foot-shifted four-speed transmission

64-GE Servi-Car without tow bar: 45ci flathead V-twin with electric start and three-speed with reverse transmission

Specialty Models

64-KR Track Racer: 45ci flathead V-twin flat-track racer

64-KRTT Tourist Trophy Racer: 45ci flathead V-twin TT racer

64-XLRTT Racer: 55ci Sportster V-twin TT racer

Sidecars and Chassis

LE: Sport Sidecar for Duo-Glides

LEC: sidecar chassis with wheel and fender

Retail Prices
Model FLHF: $1,450
Model FLH: $1,450
Model FLF: $1,385
Model FL: $1,385
Model XLH: $1,295
Model XLCH: $1,360
Model BT: $495
Model BTH: $505
Model BTU: $495
Model AH: $470
Model AU: $470
Model GE: $1,628

Production Totals
Model BT: 600
Model BTH: 800
Model BTU: 50
Model AH: 800
Model AU: 25
Model XLH: 810
Model XLCH: 1,950
Model XLA: 100
Model GE: 725
Model XLRTT: 30
Model KRTT: 30
Model KR: 20
Model CR: 50

Options
Chrome Finish Group #F-1 for Duo-Glide
Optional Group #F-6 for Duo-Glide
Optional Group #F-7 for Duo-Glide
King of the Highway Group #F-5 for Duo-Glide
King of the Highway Group #F-6
King of the Highway Group #F-7
Deluxe Equipment Group #SP-1 for XLH
Highway Cruiser Group #SP-2 for XLH
Optional Group #SP-2A for XLH
Equipment Group #SP-3H for XLCH
Standard Police Group #FP-1
Police Group #FP-2
Standard Police Group #FP-3

Paint Colors
Big Twin: Fiesta Red with Birch White tank panels, Black with Birch White tank panels, Police Silver (police only), and Birch White (police only); available at extra cost are Hi-Fi Blue with Birch White tank panels or Hi-Fi Red with Birch White tank panels
Sportster: Fiesta Red with Birch White tank panels or Black with Birch White tank panels; available at extra cost are Hi-Fi Blue with Birch White tank panels or Hi-Fi Red with Birch White tank panels
Servi-Car: Fiesta Red, Birch White, Black, and Silver (police only)
Topper: Black and White or Fiesta Red and White
Lightweights: Black and White or Fiesta Red and White

Series AU and AH Topper Scooters

First Year
Rear nameplate
Redesigned flywheel compression plate
Magneto chamber shield
(Model AU discontinued after the 1964 model year)

Series BT and BTU Pacer Singles

First/Only Year
New-style tank panels
(Model BTU discontinued after the 1964 model year)

Series BTH Scat Singles

First/Only Year
New-style tank panels

Series XLH Sportsters

First Year
Full-width die-cast aluminum front brake drum
Aluminum tappet guides

Only Year
Wide white tank paneling

Series XLCH Sportsters

First Year
Full-width die-cast aluminum front brake drum
Chrome panel for lower fork bracket
Aluminum tappet guides
Chrome-plated primary chain guard

Only Year
Wide white tank panels

Series FL Duo-Glides

First/Only Year
Two keys, one for ignition and one for steering head lock; last year 1968
Inner primary-chain housing redesigned with a new breather-hole position
Two-part chrome-plated rear chainguard optional (late year)
Wider jiffy stand
New oil-pressure switch
Hollow hex-head timer adjusting unit

Series GE Servi-Cars
First Year
Electric starter
Transmission is designed for electric starter
Automatic advance single-point timers
12-volt electrical system
Battery box recessed into the floor
Two-brush generator with voltage regulator
Primary chain uses adjusting shoe with a hard plastic pad placed under chain

Racing Notes
Roger Reiman on Model Sprint Streamliner sets new Kilometer Speed Record at Bonneville Salt Flats.
Roger Reiman wins AMA Grand National Championship.
Roger Reiman wins Daytona 200-Mile Expert Championship with record 94.833mph.

Model Year 1965

1965 FLHF Electra Glide. *Greg Field*

Main Models

65-BT Pacer Street Model: 175cc two-stroke single with three-speed transmission

65-BTH Scat: 175cc two-stroke single with three-speed transmission

65-AH Topper Scooter: 165cc two-stroke single with automatic transmission

65-XLH Sportster Super H: 55ci (883cc) Sportster OHV V-twin with four-speed transmission

65-XLCH Sportster Super CH: 55ci (883cc) Sportster OHV V-twin with four-speed transmission

65-FLHFB Electra Glide Super Sport: 74ci Panhead OHV V-twin with foot-shifted four-speed transmission

65-FLHB Electra Glide Super Sport: 74ci Panhead OHV V-twin with hand-shifted four-speed transmission

65-FLFB Electra Glide: 74ci Panhead OHV V-twin with foot-shifted four-speed transmission

65-FLB Electra Glide: 74ci Panhead OHV V-twin with hand-shifted four-speed transmission

65-GE Servi-Car without tow bar: 45ci flathead V-twin with electric start and three-speed with reverse transmission

Sidecars and Chassis

LE: Sport Sidecar for Electra Glide
LEC: sidecar chassis with wheel and fender

Production Totals

Model BT: 500
Model BTH: 750
Model AH: 500
Model XLH: 955
Model XLCH: 2,815
Model GE: 625
Model XLRTT: 25
Model KRTT: 10
Model KR: 8
Model CR: 35
Model CRS: 175

Options

Chrome Finish Group #F-1 for Electra Glide
King of the Highway Group #F-5 for Electra Glide
King of the Highway Group #F-6 for Electra Glide
King of the Highway Group #F-7 for Electra Glide
Standard Police Group #FP-1
Police Group #FP-2
Deluxe Equipment Group #SPH-1 for XLH
Highway Cruiser Group #SPH-2 for XLH
Group #SPH-3 for XLH
Deluxe Equipment Group #SPCH-1 for XLCH

Paint Colors

OHV: Black with White tank bottom panels and pinstripes along the panel edge, Holiday Red with White tank bottom panels and pinstripes along the panel edge, Police Silver (police only), and Birch White (police only); available at extra cost are Hi-Fi Red with White tank panel bottoms and pinstripes along the panel edge or Hi-Fi Blue with White tank panel bottoms and pinstripes along the panel edge

Sportster: Black with White tank bottom panels and pinstripes along the panel edge or Holiday Red with White tank bottom panels and pinstripes along the panel edge; available at extra cost are Hi-Fi Red with White tank panel bottoms and pinstripes along the panel edge or Hi-Fi Blue with White tank panel bottoms and pinstripes along the panel edge

Topper: Pacific Blue and White or Holiday Red and White

Lightweights: Black and White, Holiday Red and White, and Pacific Blue and White

Servi-Car: Birch White, Black, Holiday Red, and Silver (police only)

Series AH Topper Scooters

First/Only Year

Carryover model from 1964
(Model AH discontinued after the 1965 model year)

Series BT Pacer Singles

First/Only Year

New-style tank panels
(The Model BT was discontinued at the end of the 1965 model year)

Series BTH Scat Singles

First/Only Year

New-style tank panels

Series XLH Sportsters

First Year

12-volt electrical system
Twin six-volt batteries
3.7gal gas tank
Two-brush generator with two-unit voltage regulator, 12-volt system
"Ball-tip" hand levers
"High fidelity" horn (without the Jubilee trumpet) mounted on the left side of the engine
Adjusting cam for setting shock preload
Automatic-advance timer

Only Year
New-style tank panels

Series XLCH Sportsters

First Year
12-volt electrical system
Twin six-volt batteries
"Ball-tip" hand levers
"High-fidelity" horn mounted on the left side of the engine

Only Year
New-style tank panels

Series FL Electra Glides

First/Only Year
Series Electra Glide 74ci Panhead
Electric starter
Unpolished cast-aluminum primary cases rigidly connect the motor to the transmission
Straight-leg swingarm frame designed without "step-down" in front of top shock mounts
Oil tank redesigned square, mounting on the left with the battery on the right
Clutch sprocket has electric-start ring
Two-brush generator with voltage regulator
Gear cover is fin-less with additional oil passage
"Turnpike" five-gallon gas tank for nonstop riding
Letter "B" designates electric start model
Automatic-advance single-point timer
12-volt electrical system
"Ball-tip" hand levers
One-piece heel-toe shifter lever optional (foot-shift models)
No toolbox (space now taken by the battery box of the Electra Glide)
12v headlight, taillight, signal lights
Two-piece handlebars now redesigned: left bar designed without a control spiral; right bar designed with a starter button
Chrome oil tank strips optional
Optional rear safety guard attaches to upper shock-mount stud
(Panhead engine production ceases at end of 1965 model year)

Series GE Servi-Cars

First Year
"Ball-tip" hand levers

Motor Company Minutes, 1965
Gross sales for year total $30,560,000.

Racing Notes
Bart Markel wins Grand National Championship.

Model Year 1966

1966 FLH Electra Glide. *Jeff Hackett*

Main Models
66-BTH Bobcat: 175cc two-stroke single with three-speed transmission
66-XLH Sportster Super H: 55ci (883cc) Sportster OHV V-twin with four-speed transmission
66-XLCH Sportster Super CH: 55ci (883cc) Sportster OHV V-twin with four-speed transmission
66-FLHFB Electra Glide Super Sport: 74ci Shovelhead OHV V-twin with foot-shifted four-speed transmission
66-FLHB Electra Glide Super Sport: 74ci Shovelhead OHV V-twin with hand-shifted four-speed transmission
66-FLFB Electra Glide: 74ci Shovelhead OHV V-twin with foot-shifted four-speed transmission
66-FLB Electra Glide: 74ci Shovelhead OHV V-twin with hand-shifted four-speed transmission

Specialty Models
66-KR Track Racer: 45ci flathead V-twin flat-track racer
66-KRTT Tourist Trophy Racer: 45ci flathead V-twin TT racer
66-XLRTT Tourist Trophy Racer: 55ci Sportster OHV TT racer

Sidecars and Chassis
LE: Sport Sidecar
LEC: sidecar chassis with wheel and fender

Retail Prices
Model FLHB: $1,610
Model FLHFB: $1,610
Model FLB: $1,545
Model FLFB: $1,545
Model XLCH Sportster: $1,411
Model XLH Sportster: $1,415
Model BTH Bobcat: $515

Production Totals

Model BTH: 1,150
Model XLH: 900
Model XLCH: 3,900
Model FLB: 2,175
Model FLHB: 5,625
Model GE: 625
Model KR: 10
Model KRTT: 10
Model XLRTT: 25

Options

Chrome Finish Group #F-1 for Electra Glide
King of the Highway Group #F-5 for Electra Glide
Group #F-6 for Electra Glide
Group #F-7 for Electra Glide
Deluxe Group #SPH-1 for XLH
Group #SPH-2 for XLH
Group #SPH-3 for XLH
Group #SPH-4 for XLH
Highway Cruiser Group #SPH-5 for XLH
Group #SPH-6 for XLH
Group #SPH-7 for XLH
Deluxe Equipment Group #SPCH-1 for XLCH
Group #SPCH-2 for XLCH
Group #SPCH-3 for XLCH
Group #SPCH-4 for XLCH

Paint Colors

Big Twin: Black with White tank panels, Indigo Metallic with White tank panels, or Birch White (police only); available at extra cost are Hi-Fi Blue with White tank panels or Sparkling Burgundy with White tank panels
Servi-Car: Birch White, Holiday Red, or Black
Bobcat: Holiday Red or Indigo Metallic; available at extra cost is Sparkling Burgundy

Series BTH Bobcat Singles

First/Only Year

Model BTH Bobcat is a new model that is a restyle of the 175cc Model BT Pacer
One-piece molded Cycolac resin body molded as seat base and covering gas tank and rear wheel
Tank capacity of 1.87gal
Off-the-road continental rear optional
Hexagonal tank decal
(The Model BTH Bobcat was discontinued at the end of the 1966 model year)

Series XLH and XLCH Sportsters

First Year

"P" cams
Advertised increase of 15 percent power
Tillotson diaphragm carburetor
"Ham-can" air-cleaner cover
Patented insulator isolating the carburetor from engine heat
Hexagonal tank badge

Series FL Electra Glides

First Year

Update of the Electra Glide motorcycle with the new 74ci Shovelhead OHV engine
New cylinders
Rocker boxes similar to those used on the Sportster engine enclose new rockers, rocker shafts, and exhaust valves
Redesigned aluminum cylinder heads
Redesigned pushrods
Redesigned right crankcase
Linkert DC carburetor
Tillotson carburetor (late year)
"Ham-can" air cleaner
Revised ignition timer
Gear covers are finless and without overhead oil line passage bolt hole
Two keys, one for ignition and one for steering head lock
Seven-tooth speedometer drive gear
Transmission shifter fork width of 13/32in and a diameter of 9/32in
Two spacers used between backing plate and the swingarm
Shift gear is notched at neutral position in the rim
Rectangular footboards
Fuel petcock below left tank
New left tank without the old-style fuel valve on top
Rubber fuel line
Hexagonal tank badge

Series GE Servi-Cars

First Year

Air cleaner backing plate with a three-bolt mounting and fitted for a Tillotson carburetor
Delco alternator with rectifier
Alternator drive gear
Hexagonal tank badge

Racing Notes

Bart Markel wins AMA Grand National Championship, 434 points, Model KR.
Renzo Pasolini places third in 350cc World Class Championship on a Sprint.
Kenneth Ridder wins Daytona Motorcycle Classic 100-Mile Junior Championship with record 91.350mph.

1967 FLH Electra Glide. *Bill Koup*

Main Models

67-XLH Sportster Super H: 55ci (883cc) Sportster OHV V-twin with four-speed transmission and electric start

67-XLCH Sportster Super CH: 55ci (883cc) Sportster OHV V-twin with four-speed transmission

67-FLHFB Electra Glide Super Sport: 74ci Shovelhead OHV V-twin with foot-shifted four-speed transmission

67-FLHB Electra Glide Super Sport: 74ci Shovelhead OHV V-twin with hand-shifted four-speed transmission

67-FLFB Electra Glide: 74ci Shovelhead OHV V-twin with foot-shifted four-speed transmission

67-FLB Electra Glide: 74ci Shovelhead OHV V-twin with hand-shifted four-speed transmission

67-GE Servi-Car without tow bar: 45ci flathead V-twin with three-speed-and-reverse transmission

Sidecars and Chassis

LE: Sport Sidecar and chassis
LEC: sidecar chassis only

Retail Prices

Model FLHFB: $1,800
Model FLHB: $1,800
Model FLFB: $1,735
Model FLB: $1,735
Model XLH Sportster: $1,650
Model XLCH Sportster: $1,600
Model GE: $1,930

Production Totals

Model XLH: 2,000
Model XLCH: 2,500
Model FL: 2,150
Model FLH: 5,600
Model GE: 600
Model CRTT: 35
Model CRS: 50

Options

Chrome Finish Group for Electra Glide
King of the Highway Group for Electra Glide
Police Equipment Group
Deluxe Equipment Group for XLH
Highway Cruiser Group for XLH
Standard equipment Group for XLCH
Deluxe Equipment Group for XLCH

Paint Colors

Big Twin: Black with White tank panels or Crystal Blue with White tank panels; available at extra cost are Sparkling Burgundy with White tank panels or Hi-Fi Blue with White tank panels

Servi-Car: Holiday Red or Birch White

Series XLH Sportsters

First Year

Electric start
Cases redesigned to allow an electric starter
Revised shock absorbers

Series XLCH Sportsters

First Year

Revised shock absorbers

Series FL Electra Glides

First Year

Revised rear brake drum, rear axle, and axle spacer
Wheel hubs with two sealed ball bearing units
Rectangular fender tips
Optional "turnout" mufflers

Series GE Servi-Cars

First Year

Fiberglass boxes (late year)

Motor Company Minutes, 1967

John Harley becomes active in the Parts and Accessories Division.

March 6, Gordon Davidson passes away.

New York-based Bangor Punta attempts H-D stock buyout.

Racing Notes

Walter Fulton wins Daytona 100-Mile Junior Championship with record 94mph.

George Roeder wins Sacramento Mile in September.

Model Year 1968

1968 Sportster XLCH. *Jim Roberto*

Main Models

68-XLH Sportster Super H: 55ci (883cc) Sportster OHV V-twin with four-speed transmission

68-XLCH Sportster Super CH: 55ci (883cc) Sportster OHV V-twin with four-speed transmission

68-FLHFB Super Sport: 74ci Shovelhead OHV V-twin with foot-shifted four-speed transmission

68-FLHB Super Sport: 74ci Shovelhead OHV V-twin with hand-shifted four-speed transmission

68-FLFB Super Sport: 74ci Shovelhead OHV V-twin with foot-shifted four-speed transmission

68-FLB Super Sport: 74ci Shovelhead OHV V-twin with hand-shifted four-speed transmission

68-GE Servi-Car without tow bar: 45ci flathead V-twin with three-speed-and-reverse transmission

Sidecars and Chassis

68-LE: Sport Sidecar and chassis

68-LEC: sidecar chassis

Retail Prices

Model FLHFB: $1,800

Model FLHB: $1,800

Model FLFB: $1,735

Model FLB: $1,735

Model XLH Sportster: $1,650

Model XLCH Sportster: $1,600

Model GE: $1,930

Production Totals

Model XLH: 1,975

Model XLCH: 4,900

Model FL: 1,650

Model FLH: 5,300

Model GE: 600

Options

Chrome Finish Group for Electra Glide

King of the Highway Group for Electra Glide

Police Equipment Group

Deluxe Equipment Group for XLH

Highway Cruiser Group for XLH

Deluxe Equipment Group for XLCH

Paint Colors

Big Twin: Black with Black Wrinkle panel and White strip or Jet Fire Orange with Black Wrinkle panel and White strip; available at extra cost are Sparkling Burgundy with Black Wrinkle panel and White strip or Hi-Fi Sparkling Blue with Black Wrinkle panel and White strip

Servi-Car: Birch White

Series XLH Sportsters

First Year

Front fork internals featuring revised damping

Front fork features 1in additional travel

No kickstarter

Peanut tank optional

Series XLCH Sportsters

First Year

Front fork internals featuring revised damping

Front fork features 1in additional travel

Series FL Electra Glides

First Year

Aluminum-bodied oil pump

Restyled tank-top instrument console with rectangular indicator lights in a strip

Larger switch keyhole cover with same components

Wet clutch plates and redesigned clutch spring

Fiberglass body on sidecar

Motor Company Minutes, 1968

H-D Motor Company faces financial crisis. Negotiations and meetings with American Machine and Foundry Company (AMF) to negotiate a merger.

December 18 H-D votes to merge with AMF.

First year of *Easyrider* magazine, furthering the chopper trend.

Racing Notes

Calvin Rayborn wins Daytona 200-Mile Expert Championship on Model KRTT with record 101.290mph.

Calvin Rayborn wins Daytona 200-Mile Championship with record 100.882mph.

Roger Reiman sets a record at the Daytona time trials of 150 mph.

Model Year 1969

Main Models

69-XLH Sportster Super H: 55ci (883cc) Sportster OHV V-twin with four-speed transmission

69-XLCH Sportster Super CH: 55ci (883cc) Sportster OHV V-twin with four-speed transmission

69-FLHFB Super Sport: 74ci Shovelhead OHV V-twin with foot-shifted four-speed transmission

69-FLHB Super Sport: 74ci Shovelhead OHV V-twin with hand-shifted four-speed transmission

69-FLFB Super Sport: 74ci Shovelhead OHV V-twin with foot-shifted four-speed transmission

69-FLB Super Sport: 74ci Shovelhead OHV V-twin with hand-shifted four-speed transmission

69-GE Servi-Car without tow bar: 45ci flathead V-twin with three-speed-and-reverse transmission

Sidecars and Chassis

69-LE: Sport Sidecar and chassis

69-LEC: sidecar chassis only

Retail Prices

Model FLHFB: $1,900

Model FLHB: $1,900

Model FLFB: $1,885

Model FLB: $1,885

Model XLH Sportster: $1,765

Model XLCH Sportster: $1,698

Model GE: $2,065

Production Totals

Model XLH: 2,700

Model XLCH: 5,100

Model FL: 1,800

Model FLH: 5,500

Model GE: 475

Options

Chrome Finish Group for Electra Glide

King of the Highway Group for Electra Glide

Police Equipment Group

Deluxe Equipment Group for XLH

Highway Cruiser Group for XLH

Deluxe Equipment Group for XLCH

Paint Colors

Big Twin and XLH: Black with Black Wrinkle panel and White strip, Jet Fire Orange with Black Wrinkle panel and White strip, or Birch White with Black Wrinkle panel; available at extra cost are Sparkling Burgundy with Black Wrinkle panel and White strip, Sparkling Blue with Black Wrinkle panel and White strip, or Sparkling Gold with Black Wrinkle panel and White strip

XLCH: Black with White strip, Jet Fire Orange with White strip, or Birch White; optional colors are Sparkling Burgundy with White strip, Sparkling Blue with White strip, or Sparkling Gold with White strip

Servi-Car: Birch White

Series XLH and XLCH Sportsters

First Year

Standard exhaust: stacked dual mufflers and separate head pipes with interconnecting balance pipe

Redesigned plastic lens on taillight

Series FL Electra Glides

First Year

Front brake relocated to right side

Brake operating cam for right-mounted brake

Seven-tooth speedometer drive gear

Spade-tip terminals on harness for hydraulic brake stoplight switch

Redesigned plastic lens on taillight

Series GE Servi-Cars

First Year

Redesigned plastic lens on taillight

Hydraulic brake stoplight switch uses spade-tip terminals.

Motor Company Minutes, 1969

January 7, AMF shareholders approve purchase of major portion of H-D Motor Company, for $21 million.

Rodney C. Gott becomes chairman of AMF/H-D.

October, H-D petitions the AMA Competition Committee to sanction a new Class C Race, allowing OHV engines.

Racing Notes

Mert Lawwill wins Daytona 200.

Mert Lawwill wins AMA Grand National Championship.

CHAPTER 8
1970-1979

Model Year 1970

1970 XR-750. *Credit Harley-Davidson*

Main Models

70-XLH Sportster Super H: 55ci (883cc) Sportster OHV V-twin with four-speed transmission

70-XLCH Sportster Super CH: 55ci (883cc) Sportster OHV V-twin with four-speed transmission

70-FLHF Super Sport: 74ci Shovelhead OHV V-twin with foot-shifted four-speed transmission

70-FLH Super Sport: 74ci Shovelhead OHV V-twin with hand-shifted four-speed transmission

70-FLPF Super Sport: 74ci Shovelhead OHV V-twin with foot-shifted four-speed transmission

70-FLP Super Sport: 74ci Shovelhead OHV V-twin with hand-shifted four-speed transmission

70-GE Servi-Car without tow bar: 45ci flathead V-twin with three-speed-and-reverse transmission

Specialty Models

70-XR-750 Racer: 45ci OHV racing V-twin

Sidecars and Chassis

70-LE

Production Totals

Model XLH: 3,033
Model XLCH: 5,527
Model FL: 1,706
Model FLH: 5,909
Model GE: 494

Paint Colors

Birch White or Hi-Fi Sparkling Blue

Series XLH and XLCH Sportsters

First Year

Magneto ignition on the XLCH replaced by the XLH's points-and-coil ignition

Optional "boattail" fiberglass seat-fender combination

Frame numbers

Series FL Electra Glides

First Year

Alternator with rectifier replaces generator

Mechanical breaker points and advance in the gear case replaces the external timer

Timing case cover cone-shaped because the alternator and ignition are now located in the timing case

Timer gear connected directly to cam; separate gear for timer deleted

Redesigned crankcases

Redesigned inner and outer primary covers for the alternator, which is mounted in the primary case

Redesigned oil tank with filler hole near the front left edge of the tank top and a pull-out dipstick

Exhaust header pipes are chrome plated; chrome-plated flex covers no longer offered

Saddlebags with a tumbler lock, locking hook and heavy duty hinge

Racing Notes

Calvin Rayborn on Model KR wins three first-place positions and three second-place positions out of six races at Anglo-American Races in England.

Motor Company Minutes, 1970

Production of H-D snowmobiles, limited availability.

H-D "number 1" logo is designed to celebrate Mert Lawwill's win as the AMA Grand National champion.

Model Year 1971

1971 Sportster with boat-tail option.
Credit Harley-Davidson

Main Models

71-XLH Sportster Super H: 55ci (883cc) Sportster OHV V-twin with four-speed transmission

71-XLCH Sportster Super CH: 55ci (883cc) Sportster OHV V-twin with four-speed transmission

71-FLHF Super Sport: 74ci Shovelhead OHV V-twin with foot-shifted four-speed transmission

71-FLH Super Sport: 74ci Shovelhead OHV V-twin with hand-shifted four-speed transmission

71-FLPF Super Sport: 74ci Shovelhead OHV V-twin with foot-shifted four-speed transmission

71-FLP Super Sport: 74ci Shovelhead OHV V-twin with hand-shifted four-speed transmission

71-FX Super Glide: 74ci Shovelhead OHV V-twin with foot-shifted four-speed transmission

71-GE Servi-Car without tow bar: 45ci flathead V-twin with three-speed-and-reverse transmission

Sidecars and Chassis

71-LE

Production Totals

Model FL: 1,200
Model FLH: 5,475
Model XLH: 3,950
Model XLCH: 6,825
Model GE: 500
Model FX: 4,700

Paint Colors

Birch White or Sparkling Blue

Series XLH and XLCH Sportsters

First Year

Wet clutch with single spring
Points and condenser now behind plate on timing case cover

Series FL Electra Glides

First Year

10in front disc brake
Bendix/Zenith carburetor
Modern twist-grip throttle

Series FX Super Glides

First Year

The Model FX Super Glide was a new model with radical styling, combining Model FLH frame, engine (without electric start), and running gear with the Model XLH front end and an optional boattail rear end like the one on the Sportster

Foot pegs instead of footboards

Shift lever is reversed on the shaft so that it extends back toward the left foot peg

Rear brake pedal revised for use with foot pegs; new linkage to connect it to the master cylinder

Four-speed transmission with foot shift

Kickstarter with XL-style kickstarter pedal

Two low pipes feeding into one muffler on the right side

16in rear wheel

19in front wheel

3.5gal dual gas tanks with center-mounted instrument console holding the speedometer

Sportster horn mounted to left frame downtube

Only Year

One-piece fiberglass rear fender and seat base

Motor Company Minutes, 1971

The first year of the AMF/H-D logo.
William J. Harley, engineering vice president, passes away.
John Davidson named executive vice president
William H. Davidson named chairman.
AMF moves assembly operations to York Plant.
Engines and transmissions now built at the Capitol Drive Plant.
Full swing production of snowmobiles.
Business partnership with Evel Knievel.

Racing Notes

Joe Smith on H-D crashes the 9sec time barrier for motorcycle drag racing.

Model Year 1972

1972 XR-750. *Jim Roberto*

Main Models

72-XLH Sportster Super H: 1,000cc Sportster OHV V-twin with four-speed transmission

72-XLCH Sportster Super CH: 1,000cc Sportster OHV V-twin with four-speed transmission

72-FLHF Super Sport: 74ci Shovelhead OHV V-twin with foot-shifted four-speed transmission

72-FLH Super Sport: 74ci Shovelhead OHV V-twin with hand-shifted four-speed transmission

72-FLPF Super Sport: 74ci Shovelhead OHV V-twin with foot-shifted four-speed transmission

72-FLP Super Sport: 74ci Shovelhead OHV V-twin with hand-shifted four-speed transmission

72-FX Super Glide: 74ci Shovelhead OHV V-twin with foot-shifted four-speed transmission

71-GE Servi-Car without tow bar: 45ci flathead V-twin with three-speed-and-reverse transmission

Sidecars and Chassis

72-LE

Production Totals

Model FL: 1,600
Model FLH: 8,100
Model XLH: 7,500
Model XLCH: 10,650
Model GE: 400
Model FX: 6,500

Paint Colors

Birch White or Sparkling Blue

Series XLH and XLCH Sportsters

First Year

Engine bore increased to 3.18in, bumping displacement up to a nominal 1,000cc
Oil tank placed near chain
Seat is thinner with less padding

Series FX Super Glides
First Year

Sportster-style rear fender
Scalloped dual seat
Oil pump updated with new drive and driven gears
Rectangular "AMF Harley-Davidson" tank badge

Series FL Electra Glides

First Year

10in front disc brake
Rectangular "AMF Harley-Davidson" tank badge
Plastic switch housings for handlebars

Racing Notes

Mark Brelsford on Model XR-750 wins Grand National Championship.

Model Year 1973

1973 FL Electra Glide. *Doug Mitchel*

Main Models

73-XLH Sportster Super H: 1,000cc Sportster OHV V-twin with four-speed transmission

73-XLCH Sportster Super CH: 1,000cc Sportster OHV V-twin with four-speed transmission

73-FL: 74ci Shovelhead OHV V-twin with four-speed transmission

73-FLH: 74ci Shovelhead OHV V-twin with four-speed transmission

73-FX Super Glide: 74ci Shovelhead OHV V-twin with four-speed transmission

Sidecars and Chassis

73-LE

Production Totals

Model XLH: 9,875
Model XLCH: 10,825
Model FL: 1,025
Model FLH: 7,750
Model GE: 425
Model FX: 7,625

Paint Colors

Birch White

Series XLH and XLCH Sportsters

Single front disc brake
Japanese Kayaba-brand front forks
Plastic switch housings for handlebars
Front and rear hydraulic disc brakes

Series FL Electra Glides

First Year

Rear hydraulic disc brakes
Kickstarter deleted
Updated cone gear cover
Redesigned taillight

Series FX Super Glides

First Year

Front and rear hydraulic disc brakes
Improved, firmer suspension
Single teardrop-style gas tank
Handlebar-mounted speedometer
Ignition switch moved to left side, below the gas tank
Master cylinder repositioned to a new location in front of the right foot peg
Revised foot-brake lever for new master cylinder
Front and rear hydraulic disc brakes
Plastic switch housings for handlebars

Series GE Servi-Cars

First Year

Six lug nuts to mount rear wheel to brake drum
Six lug bolt wheels
Rear disc brakes (late year)

Motor Company Minutes, 1973

William H. Davidson, chairman, retires from the company.

John O'Brien is named chairman. O'Brien was an AMF production expert.

John Davidson named president.

The Juneau Avenue plant is turned into a huge combination warehouse and office complex.

1974 Superglide FXE. *Credit Harley-Davidson*

Main Models

74-XLH Sportster Super H: 1,000cc Sportster OHV V-twin with four-speed transmission

74-XLCH Sportster Super CH: 1,000cc Sportster OHV V-twin with four-speed transmission

74-FLH-1200: 1,200cc (74ci) Shovelhead V-twin with OHV and four-speed transmission

74-FLHF: 1,200cc (74ci) Shovelhead OHV V-twin with four-speed transmission

74-FL-Police: 1,200cc (74ci) Shovelhead OHV V-twin for with four-speed transmission

74-FX Super Glide: 1,200cc (74ci) Shovelhead OHV V-twin with four-speed transmission

74-FXE Super Glide: 1,200cc (74ci) Shovelhead OHV V-twin with four-speed transmission and electric start

Sidecars and Chassis

74-LE

Production Totals

Model XLH: 13,295

Model XLCH: 10,535

Model FX: 3,034

Model FXE: 6,199

Model FLH-1200: 5,166

Model XR: 100

Model FLHF: 1,310

Model FL-Police: 791

Paint Colors

Birch White, Vivid Black, Sunburst Burgundy, or Sunburst Blue

Series XLH and XLCH Sportsters

First Year

Throttles now given return springs

Series FL Electra Glides

First Year

Keihin brand carburetors

Redesigned saddle

Alarm system

Series FX Super Glide

Two-cable throttle with return springs

Chain-inspection cover with mount for left foot peg and hole for the shifter shaft

New shift lever that extends forward

Revised inner primary cover with hole for shifter shaft

Higher first gear; new mainshaft for low/second gear and countershaft for low gear

Series FXE Super Glides

First Year

Model FXE Super Glide is an electric-start version of the FX Super Glide

Electric starter from the FLH

Battery from the XLH Sportster

Two-cable throttle with return springs

Chain-inspection cover with mount for left foot peg and hole for the shifter shaft

New shift lever that extends forward

Revised inner primary cover with hole for shifter shaft

Higher first gear; new mainshaft for low/second gear and countershaft for low gear

Motor Company Minutes, 1974

The union goes on strike for 101 days over the cost-of-living wage increase.

This year plant security tightens. Much stricter security procedures are followed after the conviction of then-current employee, John Buschman, for major theft.

The last year of business partnership with Evel Knievel after failed Snake River Jump on Flash Gordon rocket.

Racing Notes

Walter Villa on Model RR-250 wins 250cc Class World Championship.

Gary Scott wins 250cc Road Race at Loudon, New Hampshire.

Gary Scott places second Grand National Championship.

1975 Sportster XL. *Doug Mitchel*

Main Models

75-XLH Sportster Super H: 1,000cc Sportster OHV V-twin with four-speed transmission

75-XLCH Sportster Super CH: 1,000cc Sportster OHV V-twin with four-speed transmission

75-FLH-1200: 1,200cc Shovelhead OHV V-twin with four-speed transmission

75-FLHF: 1,200cc Shovelhead OHV V-twin with four-speed transmission

75-FL-Police: 1,200cc Shovelhead OHV V-twin for with four-speed transmission

75-FX Super Glide: 1,200cc Shovelhead OHV V-twin with four-speed transmission

75-FXE Super Glide: 1,200cc Shovelhead OHV V-twin with four-speed transmission and electric start

Sidecars and Chassis

75-LE

Production Totals

Model XLH: 13,515
Model XLCH: 5,895
Model FX: 3,060
Model FXE: 9,350
Model FLHF: 1,535
Model FL-Police: 900

Paint Colors

Birch White, Vivid Black, Sunburst Burgundy, Sunburst Blue, or Sunburst/Vivid Orange

Series XLH and XLCH Sportsters

First Year

New shifter linkage to put foot shift on left side
New rear-brake linkage to put brake pedal on right side

Series FL Electra Glides

First Year

Two-cable throttle with return springs
(Last year Models FLHF and FL-Police are listed)

Racing Notes

Gary Scott wins Grand National Championship.
Jay Springsteen places third Grand National Championship.
Walter Villa on Model RR-250 wins the 250cc Class World Championship.

Main Models

76-XLH Sportster Super H: 1,000cc Sportster OHV V-twin with four-speed transmission

76-XLCH Sportster Super CH: 1,000cc Sportster OHV V-twin with four-speed transmission

76-FLH-1200: 1,200cc Shovelhead OHV V-twin with four-speed transmission

76-FX Super Glide: 1,200cc Shovelhead OHV V-twin with four-speed transmission

76-FXE Super Glide: 1,200cc Shovelhead OHV V-twin with four-speed transmission and electric start

Specialty Models

76-XLH Sportster Super H Liberty Edition featuring Black metal-flake paint with Red, White, and Blue decorations

76-XLCH Sportster Super CH Liberty Edition featuring Black metal-flake paint with Red, White, and Blue decorations

76-FLH-1200 Liberty Edition featuring Black metal-flake paint with Red, White, and Blue decorations

76-FX Super Glide Liberty Edition featuring Black metal-flake paint with Red, White, and Blue decorations

76-FXE Super Glide Liberty Edition featuring Black metal-flake paint with Red, White, and Blue decorations

Sidecars and Chassis

76-LE

Production Totals

Model XLH: 12,844
Model XLCH: 5,238
Model FX: 3,857
Model FXE: 13,838
Model FLH-1200: 11,891

Paint Colors

Birch White, Vivid Black, Sunburst/Vivid Orange, Vivid Blue, Vivid Red, Vivid Brown, or Champagne Silver

Motor Company Minutes, 1976

John Harley, son of founder William S. Harley, passes away.

1977 XLCR. *Randy Leffingwell*

Main Models

77-XLH Sportster Super H: 1,000cc Sportster OHV V-twin with four-speed transmission

77-XLCH Sportster Super CH: 1,000cc Sportster OHV V-twin with four-speed transmission

77-XLT: 1,000cc Sportster OHV V-twin with four-speed transmission

77-XLCR Cafe Racer: 1,000cc Sportster OHV V-twin with four-speed transmission

77-FLH-1200: 1,200cc Shovelhead OHV V-twin with four-speed transmission

77-FLHS Electra Glide: 1,200cc Shovelhead OHV V-twin with four-speed transmission

77-FX Super Glide: 1,200cc Shovelhead OHV V-twin with four-speed transmission

77-FXE Super Glide: 1,200cc Shovelhead OHV V-twin with four-speed transmission and electric start

77-FXS Low Rider: 1,200cc Shovelhead OHV V-twin with four-speed transmission

Sidecars and Chassis

77-LE

Production Totals

Model XLH: 12,742
Model XLCH: 4,074
Model FX: 2,049
Model FXE: 9,400
Model FXS: 3,742
Model FLH-1200: 8,691
Model FLHS: 535
Model XLT: 1,099
Model XLCR: 1,923

Paint Colors

Birch White, Vivid Black, Vivid Blue, Charcoal Silver, Vivid Brown, Midnight Blue Metallic, Arctic White, or Bright Blue

Series XLH and XLCH Sportsters

First Year

New cases designed to allow the gearshift shaft to emerge direct to the lever on the left side

Frame designed allowing oil pump removal with engine in the frame

Series XLT Touring Sportster

First Year

The Model XLT is a touring version of the XLH Sportster
Thicker seat
3.5gal tank like the one on the FX Super Glide
Touring handlebars
Saddlebags from FLH Electra Glide
Higher geared final drive
Windshield

Series XLCR Sportster Cafe Racers

First Year

Model XLCR Cafe Racer is a new model based powered by the Sportster engine
Redesigned frame with rear frame rails extended so the shock absorbers could be repositioned more vertically, with the lower shock mount more near the rear axle for better handling
Morris cast aluminum wheels
Fiberglass tail section and solo seat
New oil tank
Wrinkle-finish Black paint on engine
Bikini fairing
Siamese exhaust system
Dual-disc front brakes
Low bars
Wheelbase measures 58.5in
Glossy Black-on-Black paint scheme
Four-speed transmission
Rear-set foot pegs
Exhaust pipes painted flat Black
Unique, restyled gas tank (4gal capacity)

Series FLH-1200 Electra Glides

First Year

Revised transmission with caged bearing for the main drive gear, new main drive gear, and caged needle bearings for the countershaft
Updated engine scavenge-breather valve
Longer dual-bucket sprung saddle

Series FLHS Electra Glide Sports

First/Only Year

Model FLHS is a limited-edition, one-year-only version of the FLH
Super sprung seat
Revised transmission with caged bearing for the main drive gear, new main drive gear, and caged needle bearings for the countershaft
Updated engine scavenge-breather valve
Brown with tan trim paint scheme

Series FX and FXE Super Glides

First Year

Cast rear wheel optional
Showa fork
Revised kickstarter lever with the swing-out pivot at the bottom of the lever

Series FXS Low Riders

First Year

Model FXS Low Rider is a new model based on the FXE Super Glide
Gun-metal-Gray paint
3.5gal dual tanks with a smaller tachometer and speedometer mounted in tandem on the tank console
Cast-aluminum Morris wheels: 19in front and 16in rear (painted Gray, with polished edges)
Showa fork
Raked frame
Shorter, rear shocks with stiffer springs
Thin, deeply dished king-and-queen seat with separate front and rear sections
Flat drag bars on curved-back risers
Dual front disc brakes
Highway pegs
Oil cooler
Black crinkle-finish crankcases, barrels, and cylinder heads with polished primary cover, gear cover, and rocker boxes
Air cleaner has Black-painted center and number "1200"
Separate head pipes sweep back to separate connections on a single muffler
Revised kickstarter lever with the swing-out pivot at the bottom of the lever

Motor Company Minutes, 1977

Vaughn Beals named president.
The Rodney C. Gott H-D Museum opens its doors to the public. On June 8, a dedication is held in York, Pennsylvania.
First year of HDOA, H-D Owners Association, organized by Carl T. Wicks.
H-D controls 21 percent of the 750cc and larger motorcycle market.

Racing Notes

Jay Springsteen on Model XR-750 wins Grand National Championship and Number 1 Plate.
Ted Boody places second Grand National Championship.
Gary Scott places third Grand National Championship.
Walter Villa wins 350cc World Class Championship.

Model Year 1978

Main Models

78-XLH Sportster Super H: 1,000cc Sportster OHV V-twin with four-speed transmission

78-XLCH Sportster Super CH: 1,000cc Sportster OHV V-twin with four-speed transmission

78-XLT: 1,000cc Sportster OHV V-twin with four-speed transmission

78-XLCR Cafe Racer: 1,000cc Sportster OHV V-twin with four-speed transmission

78-FX Super Glide: 1,200cc Shovelhead OHV V-twin with four-speed transmission

78-FXE Super Glide: 1,200cc Shovelhead OHV V-twin with four-speed transmission and electric start

78-FXS Low Rider: 1,200cc Shovelhead OHV V-twin with four-speed transmission

78-FLH-1200: 1,200cc Shovelhead OHV V-twin with four-speed transmission

78-FLH-80: 80ci Shovelhead OHV V-twin with four-speed transmission

Specialty Models

78-XLH Sportster Anniversary: 75th Anniversary edition featuring a Midnight Black with Gold trim paint scheme, limited-edition anniversary graphics, and aluminum wheels finished in Gold

78-FLH-1200 Anniversary: 75th Anniversary edition featuring a Midnight Black with Gold trim paint scheme, limited-edition anniversary graphics, real leather on seat, and Gold anodized cast eagle on clutch cover

Sidecars and Chassis

78-LE

Retail Prices

75th Anniversary Sportster XLH: $3,127
75th Anniversary FLH-1200: $4,852
Model FLH-80: $4,905
Model XLCH: $3,370

Production Totals

Model XLH: 11,271
Model XLH Anniversary: 2,323
Model XLCH: 2,758
Model XLCR: 1,201
Model XLS: 2
Model XLT: 6
Model FX: 1,774
Model FXE: 8,314
Model FXS: 9,787
Model FLH-1200: 4,761
Model FLH-1200 Anniversary: 2,120
Model FLH-80: 2,525

Paint Colors

Birch White, Vivid Black, Brilliant Red, Charcoal Silver, Arctic White, Concord Blue, Chestnut Brown, or Black Cherry

Series XLH, XLCH, and XLT Sportsters

First Year

Dual disc front brakes
Electronic ignition
Siamese exhaust system
Battery and oil tank moved inboard
Revised frame with the XLCR rear section
Cast wheels optional
(Last year for the Model XLT)

Series XLCR Sportster Cafe Racers

First/Only Year

Dual seat optional
(Last year for the Model XLCR)

Series FXS Low Riders

First/Only Year

Optional paint: Silver with Black tank panels and Red pinstriping and Black stripe and Red pinstriping on front fender
Electronic ignition
Cast-iron valve guides (midyear)
Updated valves with harder stems (midyear)
Revised intake manifold and flat manifold O-rings (midyear)

Series FX and FXE Super Glides

First/Only Year

Electronic ignition
Cast-iron valve guides (midyear)
Updated valves with harder stems (midyear)
Revised intake manifold and flat manifold O-rings (midyear)
(Last year of the Model FX)

Series FLH-1200 and FLH-80 Electra Glides

First Year

The FLH-80 motor is a bored and stroked version of the FLH-1200 (74ci), for a displacement of 80ci

Larger, squarer air cleaner with the number "80" (FLH-80) or "1200" (FLH-1200)

Cast-iron valve guides (midyear)

Updated valves with harder stems (midyear)

Revised intake manifold and flat manifold O-rings (midyear)

Electronic ignition

Revised cam

Optional cast-aluminum wheels

Motor Company Minutes, 1978

The 75th Anniversary is celebrated.

The last year business connection between the Aermacchi Company of Italy and H-D. H-D closes the factory down in June.

Racing Notes

Jay Springsteen wins Grand National Championship and Number 1 Plate.

Hank Scott places third Grand National Championships.

Jay Springsteen places sixth 250cc Daytona 100-Mile Race.

Main Models

79-XLH Sportster Super H: 1,000cc Sportster OHV V-twin with four-speed transmission

79-XLCH Sportster Super CH: 1,000cc Sportster OHV V-twin with four-speed transmission

79-XLS Roadster: 1,000cc Sportster OHV V-twin with four-speed transmission

79-FLH-1200 Electra Glide: 1,200cc Shovelhead OHV V-twin with four-speed transmission

79-FLH-80 Electra Glide: 80ci Shovelhead OHV V-twin with four-speed transmission

79-FLH-1200 Police Electra Glide: 1,200cc Shovelhead OHV V-twin with four-speed transmission

79-FLH-80 Police Electra Glide: 80ci Shovelhead OHV V-twin with four-speed transmission

79-FLHC Electra Glide Classic: 80ci Shovelhead OHV V-twin with four-speed transmission

79-FXS-1200 Low Rider: 1,200cc Shovelhead OHV V-twin with four-speed transmission

79-FXS-80 Low Rider: 80ci Shovelhead OHV V-twin with four-speed transmission

79-FXE-1200 Super-Glide: 1,200cc Shovelhead OHV V-twin with four-speed transmission

79-FXEF-1200 Fat Bob: 1,200cc Shovelhead OHV V-twin with four-speed transmission

79-FXEF-80 Fat Bob: 80ci Shovelhead OHV V-twin with four-speed transmission

Sidecars and Chassis

79-LE

Production Totals

Model XLH: 6,525

Model XLS: 5,123

Model XLCR: 9

Model XLCH: 141

Model FXE-1200: 3,117

Model FXEF-80: 5,264

Model FXEF-1200: 4,678

Model FXS-80: 9,433

Model FXS-1200: 3,827

Model FLT: 19

Model FLHC: 4,368

Model FLHC and sidecar: 353

Model FLH-80: 3,429

Model FLH-1200: 2,612

Model FLH-80 Police: 84

Model FLH-1200 Police: 596

Paint Colors

Birch White, Vivid Black, Brilliant Red, Concord Blue, Chestnut Brown, Classic Tan, Classic Creme, FXS Silver, and Charcoal Gray

Series XLH and XLCH Sportsters

First Year

New rear brake master cylinder
Brake system placed where kickstart was
Kickstarter optional
(Last year of the XLCH)

Series XLS Sportsters

First Year

Model XLS (later named Roadster) is a new model based on the Sportster that is billed as a Sportster version of the FXS Low Riders
Extended forks
16in rear wheel
Siamese exhaust system
Drag bars on 3.5in risers
Sissy bar with leather pouch
Highway pegs
Two-piece seat
Rear sprocket chromed

Series FXEF-1200 and FXEF-80 Fat Bobs

First/Only Year

The 1,200cc and 80ci FXEF Fat Bobs are new models based on the FXE Super Glide
Dual gas tanks with tach and speedo on the center console, like those on the FXS Low Riders
Bobbed rear fender
Buckhorn bars

Series FXS-1200 Low Riders

First Year

Sissy bar
Leather pouch

Series FXE-1200 Super Glides

First Year

Twin front disc brakes

Series FLH-1200 and FLH-80 Electra Glides

First Year

FLHC Classic with special Tan and Cream paint job, cast wheels, and Tour Pak, in addition to all the FLH equipment
Frame-mounted seats standard
Standard equipment includes fairing, saddlebags, safety guards, and luggage rack

Motor Company Minutes, 1979

The heavyweight models receive the highest priority.
Sales in United States fall to less than 4 percent of motorcycle market.

Racing Notes

Jay Springsteen places second Grand National Championship.
Randy Goss places third Grand National Championship.
Scott Parker wins two Nationals.

CHAPTER 9

1980-1989

1980

1980 Sturgis FXB. *Randy Leffingwell*

Main Models

80-XLH: 1,000cc Sportster OHV V-twin with four-speed transmission

80-XLS Roadster: 1,000cc Sportster OHV V-twin with four-speed transmission

80-FLH-80 Electra Glide: 80ci Shovelhead OHV V-twin with four-speed transmission

80-FLH-1200 Electra Glide: 1,200cc Shovelhead OHV V-twin with four-speed transmission

80-FLHS Electra Glide: 80ci Shovelhead OHV V-twin with four-speed transmission

80-FLHC Electra Glide Classic: 80ci Shovelhead OHV V-twin with four-speed transmission

80-FLT Tour Glide: 80ci Shovelhead OHV V-twin with five-speed transmission

80-FXE-1200 Super Glide: 1,200cc Shovelhead OHV V-twin with four-speed transmission

80-FXEF-80 Fat Bob: 80ci Shovelhead OHV V-twin with four-speed transmission

80-FXS-80 Low Rider: 80ci Shovelhead OHV V-twin with four-speed transmission

80-FXS-1200 Low Rider: 1,200cc Shovelhead OHV V-twin with four-speed transmission

80-FXWG Wide Glide: 80ci Shovelhead OHV V-twin with four-speed transmission

80-FXB Sturgis: 80ci Shovelhead OHV V-twin with four-speed transmission

Sidecars and Chassis

80-LE

Retail Prices

Model XLH: $ 5,867
Model FXWG: $ 5,683
Model FLH-80 Electra Glide: $ 5,867
Model FLH-1200 Electra Glide: $ 5,867
Model FLT: $ 6,013
Model FXB Sturgis: $ 5,687

Production Totals

Model XLH: 11,841
Model XLS: 2,926
Model FXE-1200: 3,169
Model FXEF-80: 4,773
Model FXS-80: 5,922
Model FXS-1200: 3
Model FXWG: 6,085
Model FXB: 1,470
Model FLT-80: 4,480
Model FLHC: 2,480
Model FLHC and Sidecar Twin: 463
Model FLH-80: 1,625
Model FLH-1200: 1,111
Model FLHS: 914
Model FLH-80 Police: 391
Model FLH-1200 Police: 528

Paint Colors

Birch White, Vivid Black, FXS Silver, Charcoal Gray, Rich Red, Bright Blue, Saddle Brown, or Candy Red

Series XH Sportsters

First Year

Optional Hugger package with shorter shock absorbers and thinner seat

Series FXS-80 and FXS-1200 Low Riders

First Year

Motorola electronic ignition featuring an electronic advance mechanism
Two-into-one exhaust system
Stash pouch
Sissy bar

Series FXB Sturgis

First Year

The Model FXB Sturgis is a new model based on the FXS-80 Low Riders
- Belt primary drive
- Belt final drive
- 2in extended forks
- Motorola electronic ignition featuring an electronic advance mechanism
- Drag-style handlebars
- Kickstarter
- "Sturgis" lettered badge on forks
- Widened swingarm designed to compensate for wide belt final drive
- Rubber block compensator sprocket
- Rubber-mounted instruments on tank
- Oil cooler, featuring a vinyl cover
- Short sissy bar
- Leather stash pouch on sissy bar
- Closed breather from crankcase to breather
- Highway pegs
- Black chrome and paint engine scheme
- Nine-spoke cast wheels

Series FXEF-80 Fat Bobs

First Year

- Electronic ignition featuring electronic advance mechanism
- Optional cast or spoke wheels
- Dual gas tank

Series FLT-80 Tour Glides

First Year

The Model FLT-80 Tour Glide is an all-new model powered by the 80ci motor
- Engine, primary case and transmission bolted into one unit
- Three-point rubber-mounted vibration isolated engine
- Five-speed transmission
- Oil-bath enclosed rear chain
- "Sport bike" steering geometry
- New frame of welded tubes and stampings
- Frame extending in front of the steering head
- Frame featuring a rectangular steel backbone, no center post, two downtubes, and shocks in position to allow more rear wheel travel
- Cone cover shape to oil tank
- Wheelbase measures 62.5in
- 16in wheels
- Weight (tank half-full) is 781lb
- "Classic" logo on front fender
- Instruments mounted on the forks
- Improved exhaust system
- Frame-mounted fairing with dual headlights
- Spin-on oil filter
- Motorola electronic ignition featuring an electronic advance mechanism

- Larger than standard saddlebags and top box
- Frame-mounted seat
- Dual 10in disc front brakes
- Rear brake is single 12in disc
- Storage compartments in fairing
- Tank without mounted speedometer
- Footboards not spring-mounted
- Ignition switch includes a integral fork lock
- Two-piece heel-and-toe shifter

Series FLHC Electra Glide Classics

First Year

- "Classic" logo on front fender
- Motorola electronic ignition featuring an electronic advance mechanism

Series FXWG Wide Glides

First Year

Model FXWG Wide Glide is a new model powered by the 80ci engine and four-speed transmission
- Blacked-out engine with polished fin edges
- Special Black paint with orange flames on tank
- Extended front forks
- Wider triple clamps to space the forks out wide
- Small front fender
- Wider front axle
- 21in front wheel
- Dual gas tanks (5gal) and center console with large speedometer (like the tank and console on the FLH)
- Bobbed rear fender
- Rigid mount engine
- Stepped seat
- Forward controls
- Stash pouch
- Padded sissy bar
- Kickstarter
- Seat height is 26-1/4in
- Spoke wheels
- Motorola electronic ignition featuring an electronic advance mechanism
- Buckhorn handlebars on risers
- Tiny headlight
- Staggered shorty dual exhaust system

Motor Company Minutes, 1980

The federal government asked the motorcycle industry to complicate their ID system, due to the high rate of motorcycle theft.

April, Charles K. Thompson named to position of president and deputy group executive of H-D.

Racing Notes

Randy Goss wins AMA Grand National Championship.

Model Year 1981

1981 FLT. *Doug Mitchel*

Main Models

81-XLH: 1,000cc Sportster OHV V-twin with four-speed transmission

81-XLS Roadster: 1,000cc Sportster OHV V-twin with four-speed transmission

81-FXB Sturgis: 80ci Shovelhead OHV V-twin with four-speed transmission

81-FXWG Wide Glide: 80ci Shovelhead OHV V-twin with four-speed transmission

81-FXS Low Rider: 80ci Shovelhead OHV V-twin with four-speed transmission

81-FXE Super Glide: 80ci Shovelhead OHV V-twin with four-speed transmission

81-FXEF Fat Bob: 80ci Shovelhead OHV V-twin with four-speed transmission

81-FLH Electra Glide: 80ci Shovelhead OHV V-twin with four-speed transmission

81-FLHS Electra Glide: 80ci Shovelhead OHV V-twin with four-speed transmission

81-FLHC Electra Glide Classic: 80ci Shovelhead OHV V-twin with four-speed transmission

81-FLH Electra Glide Heritage: 80ci Shovelhead OHV V-twin with four-speed transmission

81-FLT Tour-Glide: 80ci Shovelhead OHV V-twin with five-speed transmission

81-FLTC Tour-Glide Classic: 80ci Shovelhead OHV V-twin with five-speed transmission

Sidecars and Chassis

81-LE

Production Totals

Model XLH: 8,442

Model XLS: 1,660

Model FXE: 3,085

Model FXEF: 3,691

Model FXS: 7,223

Model FXWG: 5,166

Model FXB: 3,543

Model FLT: 1,636

Model FLTC: 1,157

Model FLHC: 1,472

Model FLHC and Sidecar Twin: 152

Model FLH: 2,131

Model FLHS: 1,062

FLH Heritage: 784

Model FLH-80 Police: 402

Paint Colors

Birch White, Vivid Black, Classic Tan, Classic Creme, Candy Root Beer, Metallic Blue, Light Red, Dark Carmine, Orange, Olive, Light Charcoal Metallic, or Dark Silver

Series XLS Roadsters

First/Only Year

Buckhorn handlebars

Shorty dual exhaust

3.3gal tank

Wire or cast wheels optional

16in or 18in rear wheel optional

2.2gal tank optional

Series XLH Sportsters

First Year

Shorter front forks

Wire or cast wheels optional

16in or 18in rear wheel optional

3.3gal tank optional

All 80ci Models

First Year

V-Fire II electronic ignition

Reduced compression ratio to 7.4:1

Longer valve guides

Redesigned valve-guide seals

Additional drain lines from rocker boxes

Girling rear-brake caliper

Series FLH Heritage Electra Glide

First Year

The Heritage is a retro-restyle of the FLH

Suspended seat

Fringed leather saddlebags

Windshield

Case guards

Paint scheme is Orange and Olive Drab

Series FLT Tour Glides

First Year

Revised exhaust system

Model FLTC has special paint and decals

Motor Company Minutes, 1981

February 26, Vaughn Beals heads up a group including Charlie Thompson and Willie G. Davidson, along with other H-D executives, who sign a letter of intent to buy H-D back from AMF.

June 16, H-D history is made when Vaughn Beals and Willie G. Davidson, along with their backers, buy H-D back from AMF.

H-D shareholders celebrate with York-to-Milwaukee ride.

Close to 200 clerical positions are eliminated.

"The Eagle Soars Alone" slogan is born.

A gold dipstick was inserted by Vaughn Beals into the first non-AMF motorcycle to roll off the assembly line at York, Pennsylvania.

Racing Notes
Mike Kidd wins Grand National Championship.
Gary Scott places second Grand National Championship.
Randy Goss places third Grand National Championship.

Model Year 1982

1982 FLT. *Larry Brotzman*

Main Models
82-XLH: 1,000cc Sportster OHV V-twin with four-speed transmission

82-XLS Roadster Custom Sport: 1,000cc Sportster OHV V-twin with four-speed transmission

82-FLH Electra Glide: 80ci Shovelhead OHV V-twin with four-speed transmission

82-FLT Tour-Glide: 80ci Shovelhead OHV V-twin with five-speed transmission

82-FLTC Tour-Glide Classic: 80ci Shovelhead OHV V-twin with five-speed transmission

82-FXE Super-Glide: 80ci Shovelhead OHV V-twin with five-speed transmission

82-FXS Low Rider: 80ci Shovelhead OHV V-twin with four-speed transmission

82-FXWG Wide Glide: 80ci Shovelhead OHV V-twin with four-speed transmission

82-FXB Sturgis: 80ci Shovelhead OHV V-twin with four-speed transmission

82-FXR Super-Glide II: 80ci Shovelhead OHV V-twin with five-speed transmission

82-FXRS Super-Glide II: 80ci Shovelhead OHV V-twin with five-speed transmission

Specialty Models
82-XLSA Anniversary Roadster: 25th Anniversary graphics and special paperwork about bike's history signed by Chairman Vaughn Beals, President Charlie Thompson, and Styling Vice President Willie G. Davidson

82-XLHA Anniversary Sportster: 25th Anniversary graphics and special paperwork about bike's history signed by Chairman Vaughn Beals, President Charlie Thompson, and Styling Vice President Willie G. Davidson

Sidecars and Chassis
82-LE

Production Totals
Model XLH: 5,015
Model XLS Roadster Custom Sport: 1,261
Model FXR: 3,065
Model FXRS: 3,190
Model FXE: 1,617
Model FXS: 1,816
Model FXB: 1,833
Model FXWG: 2,348
Model FLT: 1,196
Model FLTC Tour Glide Classic: 833
Model FLH: 1,491
Model FLC FLH Classic: 1,284
Model FLHF Heritage: 313
Model FLHS Electra Glide Sport: 948
Model XLHA Anniversary: 932
Model XLSA Anniversary: 778
Model FLHP Police 80: 161
Model FLHP Police 80: 156
Model FLHP 80: 1,261
Model FLHP Deluxe: 270
Model FLHP Shrine: 19
Model FLHP: 282

Paint Colors
Birch White, Vivid Black, Classic Tan, Classic Creme, Metallic Blue, Light Red, Dark Carmine, Orange, Brown, Emerald Green, Red, Pewter, or Maroon

Series XLH Sportsters

First Year
New lighter frame designed without iron junctions
Oil tank repositioned
Battery repositioned
Thicker head gasket producing lower 8:1 compression ratio
larger rear disc
Thicker head gasket to reduce compression ratio

Series XLS Roadster Custom Sports

First Year
New lighter frame designed without iron junctions
Oil tank repositioned
Battery repositioned
Thicker head gasket producing lower 8:1 compression ratio
larger rear disc
Thicker head gasket to reduce compression ratio

All 80ci Models

First Year
Revised valves and valve springs in motor

All FX Series

First Year
New plastic switch housings for handlebars

Series FXB Sturgis

First Year
Higher bars
Gold cast wheels
(Last year of FXB production)

Series FXR Super Glide IIs

First Year

The Model FXR Super Glide II was a new model powered by the 80ci engine
- New-style frame with rubber engine mounts
- Ignition switch placed under the gas tank
- Instruments mounted on handlebars
- Electronic tachometer
- 5.5in headlight featuring 43,000 candlepower halogen light
- Weight (with half-tank) is 605lb
- Oil Consumption Control Package
- Tank capacity is 4.2gal
- Wheelbase measures 64.7in
- 19in front wheel
- 16in rear wheel
- Dual 10in disc front brakes
- Push-button turn signals
- Wire wheels
- Single-color paint scheme

Series FXRS Super Glide IIs

First Year

The Model FXRS Super Glide II was a new model powered by the 80ci engine
- New-style frame with rubber engine mounts
- Ignition switch placed under the gas tank
- Instruments mounted on handlebars
- Electronic tachometer
- 5.5in headlight featuring 43,000 candlepower halogen light
- Weight (with half-tank) is 605lb
- Oil Consumption Control Package
- Tank capacity is 4.2gal
- Wheelbase measures 64.7in
- 19in front wheel
- 16in rear wheel
- Dual 10in disc front brakes
- Push-button turn signals
- Wire wheels
- Single-color paint scheme
- Polished covers
- Small sissy bar
- Stepped seat
- Highway pegs
- Contrasting tank panels
- Nine-spoke cast wheels

Series FLT Tour Glides

First Year

- Lowered footboards
- New-style handlebars
- New seat
- Improved seals on saddlebags
- Locks for top box
- Locks for saddlebags
- New primary chain oiler
- Higher-output alternator

Motor Company Minutes, 1982

The first year application of MAN (Materials-As-Needed) or just-in-time production.

This is the Sportster's 25th Anniversary.

The first year of the new custom-paint program.

H-D petitions International Trade Commission for tariff relief from Japan motorcycles.

President Ronald Reagan imposes five-year additional tariffs on all Japanese 700cc-or-larger imports.

Layoffs total 1,600 out of 3,800 employees.

Aggressive program initiated to clean up all bootleg H-D merchandise.

In May, more than 100 riders leave the Capitol Drive plant on protest ride to Madison in response to Wisconsin State Police using Kawasaki motorcycles.

Advertising budget is estimated at about $3 million.

Racing Notes

Ricky Graham wins Grand National Championship.

Ricky Graham wins Winston Pro Series National Championship.

Jay Springsteen places second Grand National Championship.

Jay Springsteen wins 32 National races.

Randy Goss places third Grand National Championship.

Model Year 1983

1983 FLT. *Tom Wien*

Main Models

83-XLX-61: 1,000cc Sportster OHV V-twin with four-speed transmission

83-XLH: 1,000cc Sportster OHV V-twin with four-speed transmission

83-XLS Roadster Custom Sport: 1,000cc Sportster OHV V-twin with four-speed transmission

83-XR-1000: 1,000cc Sportster OHV V-twin with four-speed transmission

83-FLHT Electra Glide: 80ci Shovelhead OHV V-twin with five-speed transmission

83-FLHTC Electra Glide Classic: 80ci Shovelhead OHV V-twin with five-speed transmission

83-FLH: 80ci Shovelhead OHV V-twin with four-speed transmission

83-FLHS Electra Glide Sport: 80ci Shovelhead OHV V-twin with four-speed transmission

83-FLT Tour-Glide: 80ci Shovelhead OHV V-twin with five-speed transmission

83-FLTC Tour-Glide Classic: 80ci Shovelhead OHV V-twin with five-speed transmission

83-FXDG Disc Glide: 80ci Shovelhead OHV V-twin with four-speed transmission

83-FXE Super Glide: 80ci Shovelhead OHV V-twin with four-speed transmission

83-FXSB Low Rider: 80ci Shovelhead OHV V-twin with four-speed transmission

83-FXWG Wide Glide: 80ci Shovelhead OHV V-twin with four-speed transmission

83-FXR Super Glide II: 80ci Shovelhead OHV V-twin with five-speed transmission

83-FXRS Super Glide II: 80ci Shovelhead OHV V-twin with five-speed transmission

83-FXRT Sport Glide: 80ci Shovelhead OHV V-twin with five-speed transmission

Sidecars and Chassis

83-LE

Production Totals

Model XLH: 2,230
Model XLS: 1,616
Model XLX: 4,892
Model XR-1000: 1,018
Model FXR: 60
Model FXR: 1,069
Model FXRS: 1,413
Model FXRT: 1,458
Model FXE: 1,215
Model FXWG: 2,873
Model FXSB: 3,277
Model FXDG: 810
Model FLT: 1
Model FLT: 565
Model FLTC: 475
Model FLTC and sidecar: 37
Model FLH: 1,272
Model FLHT: 1,426
Model FLHTC: 1,302
Model FLHTC: 2
Model FLHTC and sidecar: 75
Model FLHS: 985
Model FLHP Police Standard: 334
Model FLHP Deluxe (Birch White): 414
Model FLHTP (chain): 341
Model FLHP Shrine: 11
Model FLHP (belt): 112
Model FLHTC (chain): 211

Paint Colors

Birch White, Vivid Black, Classic Tan, Classic Creme, Pewter, Maroon, Indigo Blue, Claret Red, or Slate Gray Metallic

Series XLH Sportsters

First Year

High bars
Vacuum-advance ignition
Tank capacity is 3.3gal
New seat
Less restrictive exhaust system

Series XLS Roadsters

First Year

Vacuum-advance ignition
New, FXRS-style tank with center console

Series XLX-61 Sportsters

First Year

The Model XLX-61 Sportster is a new, stripped-down version of the Sportster, built to sell for $3,995

Solo seat
Peanut gas tank
Staggered shorty dual exhaust system
Low handlebars
Speedometer only; no tachometer
Wheels are nine-spoke cast aluminum
Vacuum-advance ignition
Satin-finished cases

Only Year
> Clutch uses six coil springs
> 156 watt generator mounted at front of the crankcases
> Transmission output shaft features loose rollers
> Output shaft oil seal secured by a bolt-on cover
> Three generator drive gears
> 10in dual front disc brakes

Series XR-1000 Sportsters

First Year
> The Model XR-1000 is a new model based on the XLX chassis
> Aluminum, XR-style heads with intake ports on the right and exhaust ports on the left; heads ported and polished by Jerry Branch
> > Helicoil inserts where rocker boxes bolt to the head
> > High compression, 9:1, aluminum XR pistons
> > Light aluminum pushrods
> > Eccentric rocker shafts adjust valve lash
> > Iron cylinders with through-bolts
> > Vacuum-advance V-Fire III electronic breaker-less ignition
> > Twin 36mm Dell'Orto dual carburetors with accelerator pump
> > Satin-textured engine cases
> > Left-side, high megaphone dual mufflers
> > Nine-spoke cast aluminum wheels
> > Oiled felt air filter
> > New design calipers

Series FXRT Sport Glides

First Year
> The Model FXRT Sport Glide is a new sport-touring machine based on the FXRS chassis
> > Aerodynamic frame-mounted fairing
> > Antidive front suspension
> > Enclosed rear chain
> > Adjustable air suspension
> > Frame-mounted streamlined hard saddlebags
> > Saddlebags come with removable liners
> > Weight (with half tank) is 668lb
> > Tank capacity is 4.2gal
> > Wheelbase measures 64.7in
> > Seat height is 28.9in
> > Adjustable passenger pegs
> > Low-rise touring handlebars
> > Improved wider seat with thicker foam
> > Luggage rack/sissy bar optional
> > Touring box optional
> > Touring gauge kit optional
> > AM-FM stereo cassette optional

Only Year
> Shovelhead engine

Series FXDG Disc Glides

First Year
> The FXDG Disc Glide is a new model based on the FXWG Wide Glide
> > Aluminum disc rear wheel
> > Belt final drive
> > Black shorty dual exhaust
> > Leather stash pouches, front and rear

Series FXSB Low Riders

First Year
> The FXSB Low Rider is a new model based on the FXS Low Riders
> > Gates polychain belt final drive
> > 21in front tire

Series FLT and FLTC Tour Glides

First Year
> Improved seat shape to lower seat height 1.5in
> Stiffer suspension

Series FLH Electra Glides

First Year
> Belt final drive

Series FLHT Electra Glides

First/Only Year
> Models FLHT and FLHTC were new models that combined and FLH-style frame-mounted fairing with the chassis of the FLT
> > 16in rear wheels
> > Battery placement under the seat
> > Saddlebags 15 percent larger
> > Saddlebag lids hinged and attached permanently

Motor Company Minutes, 1983
> Factory-sponsored Harley Owners Group (H.O.G.) is founded.
> International Trade Commission levies a five-year tariff on Japanese motorcycles 700 cc and larger.
> Dick O'Brien, long-time manager of H-D's factory race team, retires.

Racing Notes, 1983
> Randy Goss wins the AMA Grand National Championship title.
> Gene Church wins Battle of the Twins series, Grand Prix class.

Model Year 1984

1984 XR-1000. *Randy Leffingwell*

Main Models

84-XLX-61: 1,000cc Sportster OHV V-twin with four-speed transmission

84-XLH: 1,000cc Sportster OHV V-twin with four-speed transmission

84-XLS Roadster: 1,000cc Sportster OHV V-Twin with four-speed transmission

84-XR-1000: 1,000cc Sportster OHV V-twin with four-speed transmission

84-FXE Super Glide: 80ci Shovelhead OHV V-twin with four-speed transmission

84-FXST Softail: 80ci Evolution OHV V-twin with four-speed transmission

84-FXSB Low Rider: 80ci Shovelhead OHV V-twin with four-speed transmission

84-FXWG Wide Glide: 80ci Shovelhead OHV V-twin with four-speed transmission

84-FXRS Low Glide: 80ci Evolution OHV V-twin with five-speed transmission

84-FXRT Sport Glide: 80ci Evolution OHV V-twin with five-speed transmission

84-FXRP Police: 80ci Evolution OHV V-twin with five-speed transmission

84-FXRDG Disc Glide: 80ci Evolution OHV V-twin with five-speed transmission

84-FLH 80 Electra Glide: 80ci Shovelhead OHV V-twin with four-speed transmission

84-FLHS Electra Glide: 80ci Shovelhead OHV V-twin with four-speed transmission

84-FLHX Electra Glide: 80ci Shovelhead OHV V-twin with four-speed transmission

84-FLTC Classic Tour Glide: 80ci Evolution OHV V-twin with five-speed transmission

84-FLHTC Classic Electra Glide: 80ci Evolution OHV V-twin with five-speed transmission

Sidecar Models

84-LE

Retail Prices

Model FXRS: $7,560
Model FXRDG: $8,199
Model FLHTC: $8,799

Production Totals

Model XLH (alternators): 2,278
Model XLH (331 with alternators): 2,164
Model XLS (alternators): 678
Model XLS (191 with alternators): 457
Model XLX (alternators): 2,165
Model XLX (alternators): 2,119
Model XR 1000 (generators): 759
Model FXE (single tank): 1
Model FXE (single tank): 666
Model FXE (twin tank): 1,076
Model FXE (twin tank): 364
Model FXST: 3,303
Model FXST: 2,110
Model FXB: 942
Model FXB: 1,935
Model FXWG: 2
Model FXWG: 2,225
Model FXRS: 1,079
Model FXRS: 1,731
Model FXRT: 834
Model FXRT: 1,196
Model FXRDG: 853
Model FXRSDG: 3
Model FXRSDG: 7
Model FLH-80: 155
Model FLH-80: 1,828
Model FLHX: 791
Model FLHX: 467
Model FLHS: 499
Model FLTC Classic Tour Glide: 446
Model FLTC: 855
Model FLTC and sidecar: 11
Model FLTC and sidecar: 24
Model FLHTC Classic Electric Glide: 974
Model FLHTC: 1,517
Model FLHTC and sidecar: 14
Model FLHTC and sidecar: 22
Model FLHTP Police: 100
Model FLHTP: 53
Model FLH (belt): 216
Model FLH (belt): 173
Model FLH: 565
Model FLH: 123
Model FXRP: 588
Model FXRP Chips: 189
Model FLHT Shrine: 36
Model FLHT: 19
Model FLH: 5
Model FLH: 10

Paint Colors

Birch White, Vivid Black, Classic Tan, Classic Creme, Indigo Blue, Claret Red, Candy Purple, Rose Metallic, or Slate Gray Metallic

Series XR-1000 Sportster

First/Only Year
  Improved brakes
  Orange and Black H-D racing colors optional

Series XLH Sportster

First Year
  One large front disc brake
  Diaphragm-spring clutch (midyear)
  Alternator (midyear)

Series XLS Sportster Roadster

First Year
  One large front disc brake
  Diaphragm-spring clutch (midyear)
  Alternator (midyear)

Series XLX-61 Sportster

First Year
  One large front disc brake
  Diaphragm-spring clutch (midyear)
  Alternator (midyear)

Series FXRS Low Glide

First Year
  Engine: 80ci Evolution V-twin with 3.50x4.25in bore and stroke (some very early 1984 FXRSs may have been assembled with Shovelhead engines)
  Lowered shocks
  Front forks shortened
  Diaphragm-spring clutch
  Single front disc brake

Series FXRDG Disc Glide with Evolution Engine

First/Only Year
  The FXRDG Disc Glide is a one-year limited-edition model based on the FXRS, with special paint and graphics and a solid rear wheel
  Engine: 80ci Evolution V-twin with 3.50x4.25in bore and stroke
  Rear wheel is solid spun aluminum disc
  Chain final drive
  Wire front wheel
  Tank emblem is "Genuine Harley-Davidson" in ornate script
  Diaphragm spring clutch
  Chrome engine and gearbox cover

Series FXRT Sport Glide

First Year
  Engine: 80ci Evolution V-twin with 3.50x4.25in bore and stroke (some very early 1984 FXRTs may have been assembled with Shovelhead engines)
  Diaphragm-spring clutch

Series FXRP Police

First Year
  The FXRP is a new police model based on the FXRT
  Engine: 80ci Evolution V-twin with 3.50x4.25in bore and stroke
  Diaphragm-spring clutch

Series FXST Softail

First Year
  The FXST Softail is a new model, based on the FXWG Wide Glide, but with a new type of rear suspension that mimics the look of the old "hardtail" frames by hiding the shocks underneath the frame
  Engine: 80ci Evolution V-twin with 3.50x4.25in bore and stroke (some very early 1984 Softails may have been assembled with Shovelhead engines)
  Belt drive
  Four-speed transmission
  Rigid-mounted engine
  Triangulated swingarm
  Wheelbase measures 66.3in
  Weight (with half-tank) is 630lb
  Tank capacity is 5.2gal
  Seat height is 27.5in
  Single 11.5in disc front brake
  Wire-spoked wheels
  Buckhorn-style handlebars
  21in front wheel
  16in rear wheel
  Bobbed rear fender
  Chromed oil tank
  Kickstarter
  Dual gas-charged expansion shock absorbers
  Diaphragm spring clutch (midyear)

Series FXB Low Riders and FXE Super Glides

Last Year
  1984 FXBs and FXEs are thought to have been powered by the Shovelhead engine, but some very late machines may have been assembled with the Evolution engine

Series FXWG Wide Glides

First Year
  Chain primary
  Belt final drive
  (1984 FXWGs are thought to have been powered by the Shovelhead engine, but some very late machines may have been assembled with the Evolution engine)

Series FLH-80, FLHS, and FLHX Electra Glides

First/Only Year
Diaphram-spring clutch (midyear)

Staggered dual exhaust and forward foot controls with pegs instead of footboards (FLHS; late year)

FLHX Last Edition Shovelhead Electra Glide offered in Black or White, with Gold stripes and Red pinstriping, with wire wheels and full touring equipment

Last Year
Shovelhead engine discontinued

Series FLHTC Classic Electra Glide

First Year
Engine: 80ci Evolution V-twin with 3.50x4.25in bore and stroke (some very early 1984 FLHTCs may have been assembled with Shovelhead engines)

Tool kit supplied with motorcycle

Diaphragm-spring clutch

Air shocks

Air forks with antidive system

Sixteen-spoke cast wheels

Starter wiring revised

Enclosed rear chain drive

Series FLTC Classic Tour Glide with Evolution Engine

First Year
Engine: 80ci Evolution V-twin with 3.50x4.25in bore and stroke (some very early 1984 FLTCs may have been assembled with Shovelhead engines)

Tool kit supplied with motorcycle

Final drive is belt

Five-speed transmission

Lock style change on luggage

Starter wiring revised

Clutch features a diaphragm spring

Motor Company Minutes, 1984
The V2 Evolution engine introduced on many Big Twin Models. The new engine is more oil-tight and maintenance-free, lighter in weight, cooler running, and more powerful.

Bill Davidson, Willie G.'s son, joins the company, overseeing the National Demo Ride Program.

Bill Davis, an independent engineer, designed and built the suspension layout for the Model FXST Softail.

H-D wins California Highway Patrol contract; 155 motorcycles ordered.

H-D sells 131 Model FXRP Police Special to California Highway Patrol at $4,393 each.

H-D receives a U.S. Navy contract for production of gun-shell casings.

H-D brand beer is sold.

Racing Notes
Gene Church wins Battle of the Twins series, Grand Prix class.

Will Roeder wins Battle of the Twins/Stock Class.

Model Year 1985

1985 FXR. *Jeff Hackett*

Main Models
85-XLH: 1,000cc Sportster OHV V-twin with four-speed transmission

85-XLX-61: 1,000cc Sportster OHV V-twin with four-speed transmission

85-XLS Roadster: 1,000cc Sportster OHV V-twin with four-speed transmission

85-FXEF Fat Bob: 80ci Evolution OHV V-twin with five-speed transmission

85-FXST Softail: 80ci Evolution OHV V-twin with five-speed transmission

85-FXSB Low Rider: 80ci Evolution OHV V-twin with four-speed transmission

85-FXWG Wide Glide: 80ci Evolution OHV V-twin with four-speed transmission

85-FXRS Low Glide: 80ci Evolution OHV V-twin with five-speed transmission

85-FXRT Sport Glide: 80ci Evolution OHV V-twin with five-speed transmission

85-FXRC: 80ci Evolution OHV V-twin with five-speed transmission

85-FLTC Classic Tour Glide: 80ci Evolution OHV V-twin with five-speed transmission

85-FLHTC Classic Electra-Glide: 80ci Evolution OHV V-twin with five-speed transmission

Sidecar Models
85-LE

Retail Prices
Model XLS Roadster: $5,599

Model XLH 1000: $4,795

Model XLX-61: $4,695

Model FXST Softail: $8,399

Production Totals

Model XLH: 4,074
Model XLS: 616
Model XLX: 1,824
Model FXEF: 2,324
Model FXST: 4,529
Model FXSB: 2,359
Model FXWG: 4,171
Model FXRS: 3,476
Model FXRT: 1,252
Model FLTC: 1,602
Model FLTC (chrome): 205
Model FLTC (plus sidecar): 40
Model FLHTC: 3,409
Model FLHTC (chrome): 598
Model FLHTC (plus sidecar): 51
Model FLH-80: 41
Model FLHX: 80
Model FXRS (high performance): 1,008
Model FXRS (chrome): 299
Model FXRC (Candy and Orange chrome): 1,084
Model FLHTP Police: 216
Model FLH (belt): 296
Model FXRP: 341
Model FXRP Chips: 161
Model FXRP (fairing): 474
Model FLHTC Shrine: 102

Paint Colors

Birch White, Vivid Black, Classic Tan, Classic Creme, Slate Gray Metallic, or Candy Blue

Series FXRS Low Glides

First Year

Belt final drive
Performance suspension package optional

Series FXRC Low Glide Customs

First/Only Year

The FXRC Low Glide Custom is a one-year limited-edition model based on the FXRS
Twelve engine covers chrome-plated
Candy Orange with Root Beer trim
Wheels are wire-spoked
Front fender from Model XR-1000

Series FXRT Sport Glides

First Year

Belt final drive

Series FXEF Fat Bobs and FXSB Low Riders

First/Only Year

Engine: 80ci Evolution V-twin with 3.50x4.25in bore and stroke
Wet multiplate clutch
Final belt drive
(Both models discontinued at the end of the model year)

Series FXWG Wide Glides

First Year

Engine: 80ci Evolution V-twin with 3.50x4.25in bore and stroke
Wet multiplate clutch
Belt final drive

Series FLHTC Electra Glides

First Year

Belt final drive

Series FLHTC Tour Glides

First Year

Belt final drive

Model Year 1986

1986 Wide Glide FXWG. © *Harley-Davidson*

Main Models

86-XLH-883 Sportster: 883cc Evolution Sportster V-twin with four-speed transmission

86-XLH-883 Sportster (upgrade): 883cc Evolution Sportster V-twin with four-speed transmission

86-XLH-1100: 1,100cc Evolution Sportster with four-speed transmission

86-FXR Super Glide: 80ci Evolution V-twin with five-speed transmission

86-FXRS Low Rider: 80ci Evolution V-twin with five-speed transmission

86-FXRT Sport Glide: 80ci Evolution V-twin with five-speed transmission

86-FXRD Sport Glide Grand Touring: 80ci Evolution V-twin with five-speed transmission

86-FXSTC Softail Custom: 80ci Evolution V-twin with five-speed transmission

86-FXST Softail: 80ci Evolution V-twin with five-speed transmission

86-FXWG Softail: 80ci Evolution V-twin with four-speed transmission

86-FLHTC Classic Electra Glide: 80ci Evolution V-twin with five-speed transmission

86-FLTC Classic Tour Glide: 80ci Evolution V-twin with five-speed transmission

86-FLST Heritage Softail (midyear): 80ci Evolution V-twin with five-speed transmission

Specialty Models

86-FLTC Liberty Edition: FLT with Statue of Liberty graphics on tank and front fender and certificate of ownership

86-FLTC Special Anniversary

86-FXRS Low Rider Liberty Edition: FXRS with Statue of Liberty graphics on tank and front fender and certificate of ownership

86-FXRT Liberty Edition: FXRT with Statue of Liberty graphics on tank and front fender and certificate of ownership

86-XLH-1100 Liberty Edition: XLH-1100 with Statue of Liberty graphics on tank and front fender and certificate of ownership

86-FXRS Special Anniversary Edition

86-FLHTC Special Anniversary Edition

86-FLHTC Electra Glide Liberty Edition: FLHTC with Statue of Liberty graphics on tank and front fender and certificate of ownership

Sidecar Models

86-TLE

Retail Prices

Model FLHTC: $10,224

Model FXRD: $ 9,474

Model FLST: $ 9,099

Model XLH-1100: $ 5,199

Model XLH-883 Sportster: $ 3,995

Model FLTC Tour Glide Classic with sidecar: $13,423

Production Totals

Model XLH-883 Sportster: 8,026

Model XLH-883 (upgrade): 2,322

Model XLH-1100 Sportster: 3,077

Model XLH-1100 Liberty: 954

Model FXST: 2,402

Model FXSTC: 3,782

Model FXWG: 573

Model FXWG (California): 626

Model FXR: 2,038

Model FXRS: 1,846

Model FXRS Sport Edition: 1,247

Model FXRS Special Anniversary: 962

Model FXRS Liberty: 744

Model FXRT: 591

Model FXRD: 1,000

Model FLTC Classic Tour Glide: 1,039

Model FLTC Special Anniversary: 202

Model FLTC Liberty: 160

Model FLTC and sidecar: 41

Model FLHTC: 1,879

Model FLHTC Special Anniversary: 536

Model FLHTC Liberty: 810

Model FLHTC and sidecar: 62

Model FLHT: 711

Model FLST: 2,510

Model FLHTP (fairing): 239

Model FLHTP (windshield): 71

Model FXRP (fairing): 252

Model FLTC Shrine: 14

Model FLHTC: 134

Paint Colors

Birch White, Vivid Black, Candy Red, Slate Gray Metallic, Candy Blue, Candy Pearl, or Signal Red

Series XLH-883 Sportsters

First Year

The Model XLH-883 is an updated Sportster with an all-new engine and updated chassis
Engine: 883cc Evolution V-twin with 3x3.81in bore and stroke
Aluminum heads and cylinders
Hydraulic lifters
34mm fixed-venturi Keihin carburetor standard
Redesigned frame for the new engine
Powder-coated frame
Four-speed transmission
Cast-aluminum wheels: 19in front and 16in rear
Solo seat
Low bars
Speedometer only
Single-disc front brake
Peanut tank
Final drive is single-row chain
Turn signals that double as running lights
Seat height is 30in
Wheelbase is 60in
Weight is 478lb
Upgrade package offered with special paint and trim

Series XLH-1100 Sportsters

First Year

The Model XLH-1100 Sportster is a larger-displacement variant of the Evolution XLH-883, with deluxe trim
Engine: 1,100cc Evolution Sportster OHV V-Twin with 85.1x96.8mm bore and stroke
Turn signals that double as running lights

Series FXRT Sport Glides

First Year

Revised turn-signal switch
Turn signals that double as running lights
The Model FXRD Sport Glide Grand Touring trim package offered; includes the following special items:
Rear suspension uses one air shock and one standard coil-spring shock
Rubber-mounted handlebars
Deluxe stereo that adjusts volume to compensate for increases and decreases in background noise
Stereo on/off and scan control placed below turn signal button on handlebar
Full touring luggage including top trunk
Footboards
Two-into-one exhaust system

Series FXR Super Glides

First Year

The Model FXR Super Glide is a new revival of the Super Glide name, attached to a stripped variant based of the FXRS
Revised turn-signal switch
Turn signals that double as running lights

Only Year

Final drive is by chain

Series FXRS Low Riders

First Year

Revised turn-signal switch
Turn signals that double as running lights
The FXRS Sport Edition package is offered; includes the longer suspension and twin front discs that had once been standard on the FXRS

Series FXST Softails

First Year

Five-speed transmission
Revised turn-signal switch
Turn signals that double as running lights
The FXSTC Softail Custom trim package offered; includes 16in solid rear wheel, more chrome, and deluxe paint and graphics

Series FLST Heritage Softails

First Year

The Model FLST Heritage Softail is a new version of the Softail with restyled front forks and 16in wire wheels front and back to imitate the look of the hardtail Hydra-Glide Big Twins of 1949–1957
Horizontally mounted rear shocks underneath engine
Front fork shrouds restyled to resemble those of the Hydra-Glide fork
Wide bars
Five-speed transmission
16in front and rear spoke wheels
Round air cleaner
Belt final drive
Wheelbase measures 62.5in
Seat height is 26.5in
Turn signals that double as running lights
(Mid-year introduction of this model)

Series FLT Tour Glides
First Year

Round air cleaner
Revised turn-signal switch
Turn signals that double as running lights

Series FLHT Electra Glides

First Year

Round air cleaner
Revised turn-signal switch
Turn signals that double as running lights

Motor Company Minutes, 1986

H-D receives Corporate Quality Award from Colorado's American Society of Quality Controls.
December, H-D purchases the Holiday Rambler Corporation, producers of quality motor homes.
June, H-D goes public to refinance and pay-off debts with two million company shares of common stock.

Model Year 1987

1987 Heritage Softail FLST. © *Harley-Davidson*

Main Models

87-XLH-883 Sportster: 883cc Evolution Sportster V-twin with four-speed transmission

87-XLH-883: 883cc Evolution Sportster V-twin with four-speed transmission

87-XLH-883 (upgrade): 883cc Evolution Sportster V-twin with four-speed transmission

87-XLH-1100: 1,100cc Evolution Sportster with four-speed transmission

87-FLHS Electra Glide Sport: 80ci Evolution V-twin with five-speed transmission

87-FLHTC Electra Glide Classic: 80ci Evolution V-twin with five-speed transmission

87-FLHS Electra Glide Sport: 80ci Evolution V-twin with five-speed transmission

87-FLST Heritage Softail: 80ci Evolution V-twin with five-speed transmission

87-FLSTC Heritage Softail Special: 80ci Evolution V-twin with five-speed transmission

87-FXRT Sport Glide: 80ci Evolution V-twin with five-speed transmission

87-FXST Softail: 80ci Evolution V-twin with five-speed transmission

87-FXSTC Softail Custom: 80ci Evolution V-twin with five-speed transmission

87-FLTC Tour Glide: 80ci Evolution V-twin with five-speed transmission

87-FXRS-SP Sport Edition Low Rider: 80ci Evolution V-twin with five-speed transmission

87-FXR Super Glide: 80ci Evolution V-twin with five-speed transmission

87-FXRS Low Rider: 80ci Evolution V-twin with five-speed transmission

87-FXLR Low Rider Custom: 80ci Evolution V-twin with five-speed transmission

Specialty Models

87-FXLR Low Rider Custom Anniversary Edition: 10th Anniversary graphics on both front fender and gas tank

87-FXLR 10th Anniversary Low Rider: gas tank with 10th Anniversary leather center strap

87-XLH-1100 Sportster Anniversary: 30th Anniversary graphics on both the front fender and gas tank

87-FLTC Special Anniversary

87-FLHTC Special Anniversary

Sidecars and Chassis

87-TLE

Retail Prices

Model FLHS: $ 8,545

Model FLHTC Electra Glide Classic: $10,395

Model XL 883: $ 4,495

Model FXLR: $ 9,219

Model FLHTC: $10,545

Model FLHTC Electra Glide Classic: $10,395

Model FXSTC Softail Custom: $ 9,499

Model FXRS Low Rider: $ 8,449

Model FXRS Low Rider Sport: $ 8,649

Production Totals

Model XLH-883 Sportster (low): 2,106

Model XLH-883 Sportster (upgrade): 2,260

Model XLH-883 Sportster: 4,990

Model XLH-1100 Sportster: 4,018

Model XLH-1100 Sportster (Anniversary): 600

Model FXST Softail: 2,024

Model FXST Special: 398

Model FXSTC Softail Custom: 5,264

Model FXR Super Glide: 1,265

Model FXRS Low Rider: 784

Model FXRT Sport Glide: 287

Model FXRS Low Rider Sport Edition: 1,142

Model FXRC Special: 736

Model FXLR Low Rider Custom: 3,221

Model FLHTC Classic Tour Glide: 699

Model FLTC Special/Anniversary: 125

Model FLTC and sidecar: 32

Model FLHTC Classic Electra Glide: 2,858

Model FLHTC Special/Anniversary: 800

Model FLHTC and sidecar: 146

Model FLHT Electra Glide Sport: 87

Model FLHS: 1,054

Model FLST: 2,794

Model FLST Special: 1,545

Model FLHTP (Fairing): 194

Model FLHTP (Windshield): 203

Model FXRP Chips: 171

Model FXRP (Windshield): 149

Model FXRP (Fairing): 245

Model FLTC Shrine: 68

Model FLHTC: 411

Series XLH-883 Sportster Huggers

First Year

Low edition option with shorter suspension and thinner seat

Series FLHS Electra Glide Sport

First Year

The FLHS Electra Glide Sport is an Electra Glide with a detachable windshield in place of the fairing and no top box or sissy bar

Series FXLR Low Rider Customs

First Year

The FXLR Low Rider Custom is a new model, based on the FXRS Low Riders
  21in spoked front wheel
  16in disc rear wheel
  Special tank with one filler and no center console
  Two-piece high handlebars welded with two cross-braces between them
  Speedometer mounted between bars
  Blacked-out cylinders and crankcases with chrome-plated rocker covers, gear-case cover, and primary cover
  Highway pegs
  Final drive is belt
  Single-disc front brake
  Single-disc rear brake

Series FXR Super Glides

First Year

  Final drive is belt
  Smaller front fender

Series FXRS Low Riders

First/Only Year

  Smaller front fender
  Sport Edition suspension is improved

Series FXRT Sport Glides

First Year

  Improved sound system

Series FLST Heritage Softails

First Year

  Series FLSTC Heritage Softail Special package offered; includes the following special accessories: windshield, passing lamps, leather saddlebags, two-piece seat with backrest, studs, and conchos

Motor Company Minutes, 1987

  March, Richard Teerlink named president of the Motorcycle Division.
  H-D exports 1,600 motorcycles to Canada.
  H-D exports 1,200 motorcycles to Western Europe.
  H-D exports 1,300 motorcycles to Japan.
  H-D starts their special "Buy Back Program" for the Model XLH-883 Evolution Sportster. The program offers full trade-in value within two years on either a Model FL or Model FX.
  H-D again wins the California Highway Patrol contract.
  March 17, H-D moves to have five-year motorcycle tariff lifted earlier than planned. This move sent message to Japan that we can compete.
  May 6: The first time a U.S. president ever toured the H-D factory. President Ronald Reagan stays two hours and receives a tour of the H-D Plant in York, Pennsylvania, starts up a 30th Anniversary Sportster, and praises the company's comeback in a speech he delivers.
  July 1, H-D is approved for listing on New York Stock Exchange. Original issue price is $11 per share.
  October 10, H-D buys all design and manufacturing rights from Armstrong Equipment of England, for the Military Model MT-500 Off-road motorcycle. The Model MT-500 features a 500cc single-cylinder four-stroke engine.

1988 Sport Glide FXRT. © *Harley-Davidson*

Main Models

  88-XLH-883 Sportster: 883cc Evolution Sportster V-twin with four-speed transmission
  88-XLH-883 Sportster Hugger: 883cc Evolution Sportster V-twin with four-speed transmission
  88-XLH-883 Sportster Deluxe: 883cc Evolution Sportster V-twin with four-speed transmission
  88-XLH-1200 Sportster: 1,200cc Evolution Sportster V-twin with four-speed transmission
  88-FXR Super Glide: 80ci Evolution V-twin with five-speed transmission
  88-FXRS Low Rider: 80ci Evolution V-twin with five-speed transmission
  88-FXLR Low Rider Custom: 80ci Evolution V-twin with five-speed transmission
  88-FXRS-SP Low Rider Sport Edition: 80ci Evolution V-twin with five-speed transmission
  88-FXST Softail: 80ci Evolution V-twin with five-speed transmission
  88-FXSTC Softail Custom: 80ci Evolution V-twin with five-speed transmission
  88-FXSTS Springer Softail: 80ci Evolution V-twin with five-speed transmission and spring front forks
  88-FLST Heritage Softail: 80ci Evolution V-twin with five-speed transmission
  88-FLSTC Heritage Softail Classic: 80ci Evolution V-twin with five-speed transmission
  88-FXRT Sport Glide: 80ci Evolution V-twin with five-speed transmission
  88-FLHS Electra Glide Sport: 80ci Evolution V-twin with five-speed transmission
  88-FLTC Tour Glide Classic: 80ci Evolution V-twin with five-speed transmission
  88-FLHTC Electra Glide Classic: 80ci Evolution V-twin with five-speed transmission

Specialty Models

  88-FXRS 85th Anniversary
  88-FLTC 85th Anniversary
  88-FLHTC 85th Anniversary
  88-FXSTS Springer Softail 85th Anniversary graphics

Sidecars and Chassis
88-TLE

Retail Prices
Model 883 Sportster: $ 3,995
Model 883 Sportster Deluxe: $ 4,424
Model 883 Hugger: $ 4,199
Model XLH-1200: $ 5,875
Model FXSTS: $10,695
Model FXST: $ 9,375
Model FXLR: $ 9,219
Model FLHTC: $10,545

Production Totals
Model XLH-883 Sportster Hugger: 4,501
Model XLH-883 Sportster Deluxe: 1,893
Model XLH-883 Sportster: 5,387
Model XLH-1200 Sportster: 4,752
Model FXST Softail: 1,467
Model FXSTC Softail Custom: 6,621
Model FLST Heritage Softail: 2,209
Model FLSTC Heritage Softail Classic: 3,755
Model FXSTS Springer Softail: 1,356
Model FXR Super Glide: 1,205
Model FXRS Low Rider: 2,637
Model FXRS Special/Anniversary: 519
Model FXRS-SP Low Rider Sport Edition: 818
Model FXLR Low Rider Custom: 902
Model FXRT Sport Glide: 243
Model FLTC Classic Tour Glide: 745
Model FLTC Special/Anniversary: 50
Model FLTC and sidecar: 44
Model FLHTC Classic Electra Glide: 3,958
Model FLHTC Special/Anniversary: 715
Model FLHTC and sidecar: 207
Model FLHS Electra Glide Sport: 1,677
Model FLHTP Police (fairing): 278
Model FLHTP Police (windshield): 343
Model FXRP (fairing): 348
Model FXRP (windshield): 230
Model FXRP CHIPS: 217
Model FLTC Shrine: 9
Model FLHTC Classic Electra Glide: 136

Paint Colors
Vivid Black, Bright Cobalt Candy Blue, Bright Candy Plum, Candy Brandywine, Brandywine and Crimson, Bright Cobalt Candy Blue and Brilliant Silver, Candy Crimson, Candy Bronze and Creme, Vivid Black and Creme, Metallic Blue and Cadet Blue Metallic, or Creme and Champagne Gold

Series XLH-883 Sportsters

First Year
40mm constant velocity Keihin slide-type carburetor standard
Taller shocks
Longer swingarm
Stiffer 39mm front fork
Solo seat
Cast wheels
XLH-883 Hugger package offered; includes lowered suspension and saddle and buckhorn bars
XLH-883 package offered; includes two-tone paint, buckhorn bars, spoked wheels, dual seat, extra chrome, and tachometer

Series XLH-1200 Sportsters

First Year
The XLH-1200 Sportster replaces the XLH-1100
Engine: 1,200cc Evolution Sportster engine with 3.498x3.812in bore and stroke
39mm front fork
Two-tone paint
Dual seat
Buckhorn bars
Speedometer and tachometer

Series FXR Super Glides

First Year
39mm front fork
Buckhorn handlebars

Series FXRS Low Riders

First Year
39mm front fork

Series FXLR Low Rider Customs

First Year
39mm front fork

Series FXST Softails

First Year
39mm front fork
FXSTS Springer Softail offered; has chrome-plated springer front forks

Series FXRT Sport Glides

First Year
39mm front fork

Motor Company Minutes, 1988
August, Richard F. Teerlink named president and chief operating officer of H-D.
August, James H. Patterson named president and chief operating officer of the Motorcycle Division.
First year of the H-D traveling museum. Pulled by a Peterbilt tractor, the museum displays for the public H-D memorabilia and seven classic motorcycles.
Celebration of 85th Anniversary in Milwaukee in a carnival-type atmosphere.
This year to celebrate 85th Anniversary, H-D organizes a ride for the Muscular Dystrophy Association (MDA). The proceeds total almost $600,000 and are donated for the cause. Over 6,000 riders attend.
H.O.G.'s membership totals over 90,000 riders.

Racing Notes
Chris Carr wins 600cc Championship.
Scott Parker wins the AMA Grand National Championship.

Model Year 1989

1989 FXSTS with owner modifications. *Frank Wilson*

Main Models

89-XLH-883 Sportster: 883cc Evolution Sportster V-twin with four-speed transmission

89-XLH-883 Sportster Hugger: 883cc Evolution Sportster V-twin with four-speed transmission

89-XLH-883 Sportster Deluxe: 883cc Evolution Sportster V-twin with four-speed transmission

89-XLH-1200: 1,200cc Evolution Sportster V-twin with four-speed transmission

89-FXR Super Glide: 80ci Evolution V-twin with five-speed transmission

89-FXRS-CONV Low Rider Convertible: 80ci Evolution V-twin with five-speed transmission

89-FXRS-SP Low Rider Sport Edition: 80ci Evolution V-twin with five-speed transmission

89-FXLR Low Rider Custom: 80ci Evolution V-twin with five-speed transmission

89-FXRT Sport Glide: 80ci Evolution V-twin with five-speed transmission

89-FXSTS Springer Softail: 80ci Evolution V-twin with five-speed transmission

89-FXST Softail: 80ci Evolution V-twin with five-speed transmission

89-FXSTC Softail Custom: 80ci Evolution V-twin with OHV, five-speed transmission

89-FLST Heritage Softail: 80ci Evolution V-twin with five-speed transmission

89-FLSTC Heritage Softail Classic: 80ci Evolution V-twin with five-speed transmission

89-FLHS Electra Glide Sport: 80ci Evolution V-twin with five-speed transmission

89-FLHTC Electra Glide Classic: 80ci Evolution V-twin with five-speed transmission

89-FLHTCU Ultra Classic Electra Glide: 80ci Evolution V-twin with five-speed transmission

89-FLTC Tour Glide Classic: 80ci Evolution V-twin with five-speed transmission

89-FLTCU Ultra Classic Tour Glide: 80ci Evolution V-twin with five-speed transmission

Sidecars and Chassis

89-TLE

Retail Prices

Model FXRS: $ 9,925
Model FXRS Convertible: $ 9,475
Model FXSTS: $10,759

Production Totals

Model XLH-883 Sportster Hugger: 4,467
Model XLH-883 Sportster Deluxe: 1,812
Model XLH-883 Sportster: 6,142
Model XLH-1200 Sportster: 4,546
Model FXSTS Springer Softail: 5,387
Model FXSTC Softail Custom: 6,523
Model FXST Softail: 1,130
Model FXRT Sport Glide: 255
Model FXLR Low Rider Custom: 1,016
Model FXRS-CONV Convertible: 292
Model FXRS-SP Low Rider Sport Edition: 755
Model FXRS Low Rider: 2,096
Model FXR Super Glide: 1,821
Model FLTCU: 530
Model FLTCU and sidecar: 38
Model FLTC: 588
Model FLTC and sidecar: 15
Model FLHTCU: 2,653
Model FLHTCU and sidecar: 237
Model FLHTC: 3,969
Model FLHTC and sidecar: 128
Model FLHS: 2,330
Model FLSTC: 5,210
Model FLST: 1,506
Model FLHTP (fairing): 342
Model FLHTP (windshield): 318
Model FXRP (clear windshield): 214
Model FXRP (fairing): 379
Model FXRP CHIPS: 187
Model FLTC Shrine: 3
Model FLTCU: 11
Model FLHTC Classic Electric Glide: 80
Model FLHTCU: 91

Paint Colors

Vivid Black, Metallic Blue, Candy Brandywine, Brandywine and Crimson, Bright Candy Plum, Metallic Blue and Brilliant Silver, Vivid Black and Creme, Candy Bronze and Creme, Metallic Blue and Cadet Blue Metallic, Creme and Champagne Gold, or Vivid Black and Brilliant Silver

Series XLH-883 and XLH-1200 Sportsters

First Year

Aluminum intake manifold
New air cleaner element
Offset piston pins for pistons
Protective coating added to battery positive cable

Series FXR Super Glides

First Year

32amp alternator
Protective coating added to the battery positive cable
One-piece pinion shaft and right flywheel
New design starter

Series FXRS Low Riders

First Year
    Protective coating added to the battery positive cable
    One-piece pinion shaft and right flywheel
    New design starter
    FXRS-CONV package offered; includes a quick-detachable windshield, quick-detachable leather saddlebags, highway pegs, and sissy bar

Series FXLR Low Rider Customs

First Year
    Protective coating added to the battery positive cable
    One-piece pinion shaft and right flywheel
    New design starter

Series FXRT Sport Glides

First Year
    Protective coating added to the battery positive cable
    One-piece pinion shaft and right flywheel
    New design starter

Series FXST Softails

First Year
    Protective coating added to the battery positive cable
    One-piece pinion shaft and right flywheel
    New design starter

Series FLST Heritage Softails

First Year
    32amp alternator
    One-piece pinion shaft and right flywheel
    Self-canceling turn signals using a microprocessor

Series FLHS Electra Glide Sports

First Year
    32amp alternator
    One-piece pinion shaft and right flywheel
    Self-canceling turn signals using a microprocessor

Series FLHT Electra Glides

First Year
    32amp alternator
    One-piece pinion shaft and right flywheel
    Self-canceling turn signals using a microprocessor
    FLHTCU Ultra Classic Electra Glide package offered; includes cruise control, CB radio, intercom, full front and rear sound systems (rear has its own speakers and separate amplifier), fairing lowers, and special graphics

Series FLST Heritage Softails

First Year
    32amp alternator
    One-piece pinion shaft and right flywheel
    Self-canceling turn signals using a microprocessor

Series FLTC Tour Glides

First Year
    32amp alternator
    One-piece pinion shaft and right flywheel
    Self-canceling turn signals using a microprocessor
    FLTCU Ultra Classic Tour Glide package offered; includes cruise control, CB radio, intercom, full front and rear sound systems (rear has its own speakers and separate amplifier), fairing lowers, and special graphics

Racing Notes
    The H-D 883 Twin Sports Road Racing Series begins. It has full sanction of the AMA.
    Scott Parker wins the AMA Grand National Championship.

CHAPTER 10

1990-1996

Model Year 1990

Main Models

90-XLH-883 Sportster: 883cc Evolution Sportster V-twin with four-speed transmission

90-XLH-883 Sportster Hugger: 883cc Evolution Sportster V-twin with four-speed transmission

90-XLH-883 Sportster Deluxe: 883cc Evolution Sportster V-twin with four-speed transmission

90-XLH-1200: 1,200cc Evolution Sportster V-twin with four-speed transmission

90-FXRS-CONV Low Rider Convertible: 80ci Evolution V-twin with five-speed transmission

90-FXRS-SP Low Rider Sport Edition: 80ci Evolution V-twin with five-speed transmission

90-FXR Super Glide: 80ci Evolution V-twin with five-speed transmission

90-FXLR Low Rider Custom: 80ci Evolution V-twin with five-speed transmission

90-FXRS Low Rider: 80ci Evolution V-twin with five-speed transmission

90-FXRT Sport Glide: 80ci Evolution V-twin with five-speed transmission

90-FLSTF Fat Boy: 80ci Evolution V-twin with five-speed transmission

90-FXST Softail: 80ci Evolution V-twin with five-speed transmission

90-FXSTC Softail Custom: 80ci Evolution V-twin with five-speed transmission

90-FXSTS Springer Softail: 80ci Evolution V-twin with five-speed transmission

90-FLST Heritage Softail: 80ci Evolution V-twin with five-speed transmission

90-FLSTC Heritage Softail Classic: 80ci Evolution V-twin with five-speed transmission

90-FLHS Electra Glide Sport: 80ci Evolution V-twin with five-speed transmission

90-FLHTC Electra Glide Classic: 80ci Evolution V-twin with five-speed transmission

90-FLTC Tour Glide Classic: 80ci Evolution V-twin with five-speed transmission

90-FLHTCU Ultra Classic Electra Glide: 80ci Evolution V-twin with five-speed transmission

90-FLTCU Ultra Classic Tour Glide: 80ci Evolution V-twin with five-speed transmission

Specialty Models

90-FXRP CHIPS (police)
90-FLHTP (police)
90-FLTC Classic Tour Glide (Shrine)

Sidecars and Chassis

90-TLE

Retail Prices

Model XLH-883 Sportster: $ 4,250
Model FLSTF: $10,995
Model FLTCU: $13,345
Model Electra Glide Ultra: $13,695

Production Totals

Model XLH-883 Sportster Hugger: 4,040
Model XLH-883 Sportster: 5,227
Model XLH-883 Sportster Deluxe: 1,298
Model XLH-1200: 4,598
Model FXSTS Springer Softail: 4,252
Model FXSTC: 6,795
Model FXST: 1,601
Model FXRT: 304
Model FXLR: 1,143
Model FXRS-Convertible: 989
Model FXRS-Sp: 762
Model FXRS Low Rider: 2,615
Model FXR: 1,819
Model FXDS: 28
Model FXDB: 10
Model FXDS: 4
Model FXDB: 2
Model FXDS-Convertible: 1
Model FLTCU: 575
Model FLTCU and sidecar: 37
Model FLTC: 476
Model FLTC and sidecar: 9
Model FLHTCU: 3,082
Model FLHTCU and sidecar: 323
Model FLHTC: 3,497
Model FLHTC and sidecar: 100
Model FLHS: 2,410
Model FLSTF: 4,440
Model FLSTC: 5,483
Model FLST: 1,567
Model FLHTP (fairing): 467
Model FLHTP (windshield): 218
Model FXRP (clear windshield): 221
Model FXRP (fairing): 572
Model FXRP Chips: 15
Model FLTC Shrine: 3
Model FLTCU: 8
Model FLHTC: 94
Model FLHTCU: 122

Paint Colors

Vivid Black, Bright Candy Plum, Bright Candy Ruby, Bright Candy Hi-Fi Blue, Bright Candy Hi-Fi Blue and Silver, Bright and Dark Candy Ruby, Fine Silver Metallic, Dark Candy Ruby, Vivid Black and Black Pearl, Vivid Black and Creme, Creme and Champagne Gold, or Bright and Dark Candy Hi-Fi Blue

Series XLH-883 and XLH-1200 Sportsters

First Year

Paper air filter
New paint options
Copper washer for rear fender strut bolts and rear directional nuts
40mm Keihin carburetor; constant velocity-type with an accelerator pump

Series FXRS Low Riders

First Year

40mm Keihin carburetor; constant velocity-type with an accelerator pump
One-piece right hand flywheel
New clutch and redesigned diaphragm spring

Series FXR Super Glides

First Year

40mm Keihin carburetor; constant velocity-type with an accelerator pump
One-piece right-hand flywheel
New clutch and redesigned diaphragm spring

Series FXLR Low Rider Customs

First Year

40mm Keihin carburetor; constant velocity-type with an accelerator pump
One-piece right hand flywheel
New clutch and redesigned diaphragm spring

Series FXRT Sport Glides

First Year

40mm Keihin carburetor; constant velocity-type with an accelerator pump
One-piece right hand flywheel
New clutch and redesigned diaphragm spring

Series FLSTF Fat Boys

First Year

The FLSTF Fat Boy is a new model, based on the FLST Heritage Softail
16in disc wheels front and rear
Restyled front fender
Wide FLH handlebar
Dual shotgun-style exhaust system
Braided leather tank strap
Special silver paint on frame, fenders, and tank
Dark yellow highlights on center section of rocker covers
One-piece right hand flywheel
New clutch featuring eight friction plates, a spring plate and then six steel plates. Also a redesigned diaphragm spring
One-piece clutch adjusting screw
Clutch release ramps

Series FXST Softails

First/Only Year

40mm Keihin carburetor; constant velocity-type with an accelerator pump
One-piece right hand flywheel
New clutch and redesigned diaphragm spring

Series FLST Heritage Softails

First Year

40mm Keihin carburetor; constant velocity-type with an accelerator pump
One-piece right hand flywheel
New clutch and redesigned diaphragm spring

Series FLHS Electra Glide Sports

First Year

40mm Keihin carburetor; constant velocity-type with an accelerator pump
One-piece right hand flywheel
New clutch and redesigned diaphragm spring

Series FLTC Tour Glide Classics

First Year

40mm Keihin carburetor; constant velocity-type with an accelerator pump
One-piece right hand flywheel
One-piece clutch adjusting screw
Clutch release ramps
Improved cruise control and intercom (FLTCU)

Series FLHTC Electra Glide Classics

First Year

40mm Keihin carburetor; constant velocity-type with an accelerator pump
One-piece right hand flywheel
New clutch and redesigned diaphragm spring
Improved cruise control and intercom (FLHTCU)

Motor Company Minutes, 1990

The European parts and accessories warehouse opens.

Racing Notes

Nigel Gale wins the Twin Sports Championship title.
Scott Zampach wins Lightweight Twins Championship.
Scott Parker wins the AMA Grand National Championship.

1991 FXSB. *Doug Mitchel*

Main Models

91-XLH-883 Sportster: 883cc Evolution Sportster V-twin with five-speed transmission

91-XLH-883 Sportster Hugger: 883cc Evolution Sportster V-twin with five-speed transmission

91-XLH-883 Sportster Deluxe: 883cc Evolution Sportster V-twin with five-speed transmission and belt drive

91-XLH-1200: 1,200cc Evolution Sportster V-twin with five-speed transmission and belt drive

91-FXSTC Softail Custom: 80ci Evolution V-twin with five-speed transmission

91-FXSTS Springer Softail: 80ci Evolution V-twin with five-speed transmission

91-FLSTF Fat Boy: 80ci Evolution V-twin with five-speed transmission

91-FLSTC Heritage Softail Classic: 80ci Evolution V-twin with five-speed transmission

91-FXR Super Glide: 80ci Evolution V-twin with five-speed transmission

91-FXRS-SP Low Rider Sport Edition: 80ci Evolution V-twin with five-speed transmission

91-FXRS-CONV Low Rider Convertible: 80ci Evolution V-twin with five-speed transmission

91-FXRS Low Rider: 80ci Evolution V-twin with five-speed transmission

91-FXRT Sport Glide: 80ci Evolution V-twin with five-speed transmission

91-FXLR Low Rider Custom: 80ci Evolution V-twin with five-speed transmission

91-FLHS Electra Glide Sport: 80ci Evolution V-twin with five-speed transmission

91-FLHTC Electra Glide Classic: 80ci Evolution V-twin with five-speed transmission

91-FLHTCU Ultra Classic Electra Glide: 80ci Evolution V-twin with five-speed transmission

91-FLTC Tour Glide Classic: 80ci Evolution V-twin with five-speed transmission

91-FLTCU Ultra Classic Tour Glide: 80ci Evolution V-twin with five-speed transmission

91-FXDB Sturgis: 80ci Evolution V-twin with five-speed transmission

Specialty Models

91-FXRP CHIPS (police)
91-FLHTP (police)
91-FLTC Classic Tour Glide (Shrine)

Sidecars and Chassis

91-TLE: Touring Models
91-RLE: Low Riders, Sport Glides, and Police Models

Retail Prices

Model XLH-883 Sportster: $ 4,359
Model XLH-1200: $ 6,245
Model FXRS Low Rider: $ 9,760
Model FXRS-SP: $ 9,775
Model FXDB: $11,520

Production Totals

Model XLH-883 Sportster Hugger: 3,487
Model XLH-883 Sportster: 4,922
Model XLH-883 Sportster Deluxe: 3,034
Model XLH-1200: 6,282
Model FXSTC Softail Custom: 1
Model FXSTS: 4,265
Model FXSTC Softail Custom: 7,525
Model FXR: 272
Model FXLR: 1,197
Model FXRS-CONV: 1,721
Model FXRS-SP: 683
Model FXRS Low Rider: 2,183
Model FXR Super Glide: 1,742
Model FXDS Dyna: 1
Model FXDB Dyna: 1,546
Model FLTCU: 458
Model FLTCU and sidecar: 41
Model FLTC: 250
Model FLTC and sidecar: 9
Model FLHTCU: 3,204
Model FLHTCU and sidecar: 311
Model FLHTC: 3,117
Model FLHTC and sidecar: 108
Model FLHS: 2,383
Model FLSTF: 5,581
Model FLSTC: 8,950
Model FLHTP (fairing): 509
Model FLHTP (windshield): 263
Model FXRP (fairing): 248
Model FXRP (windshield): 483
Model FXRP Chips: 1
Model FLTC Shrine: 3
Model FLTCU: 26
Model FLHTC: 90
Model FLHTCU: 113

Paint Colors

Vivid Black, Bright Sapphire Metallic, Wineberry Pearl, Vivid Yellow, Bright Candy Ruby, Candy Sapphire Sun-Glo, Bright and Dark Sapphire Metallic, Bright and Dark Candy Ruby, White and Vivid Yellow, White and Turquoise, or White and Yellow

Series XLH-883 Sportsters

First Year
>Five-speed transmission
>Belt drive (XLH-883 Deluxe)
>O-ring chain (XLH-883 and Hugger)
>Automotive-type lifters
>Rider foot pegs rubber-mounted
>Self-canceling turn signals
>Jiffy stand relocated farther back on frame
>Alternator moved to the crankshaft
>Right-side timing hole
>Tappet blocks and rear motor mount integrated with the case
>Oil filter mount integrated to crankcase assembly
>Umbrella-valve breather in rocker boxes
>One-piece pushrod tubes
>Easy removal primary inspection cover
>40oz fluid level for primary/transmission
>New design primary chain adjuster
>5/8in hex Champion spark plug

Series XLH-1200 Sportsters

First Year
>Five-speed transmission
>Belt final drive
>Automotive-type lifters
>Rider foot pegs rubber-mounted
>Self-canceling turn signals
>Jiffy stand relocated further back on frame
>Alternator moved to the crankshaft
>Right-side timing hole
>Tappet blocks and rear motor mount integrated with the case
>Oil filter mount integrated to crankcase assembly
>Umbrella-valve breather in rocker boxes
>One-piece pushrod tubes
>Easy removal primary inspection cover
>40oz fluid level for primary/transmission
>New design primary chain adjuster
>5/8in hex Champion spark plug

Series FXST Softails

First Year
>Kevlar base gaskets
>Graphite head gaskets
>New gas cap gasket
>Self-canceling turn signals
>Black-and-chrome engine (FXSTC)
>Extra hole in transmission access door
>Two dowels on transmission end cover
>Air/oil separator in air-duct tube
>Four-sided fuel inlet valve
>Transmission sprocket lock plate
>Locating dowel pins for both transmission support blocks

Series FLSTF Fat Boys

First Year
>Kevlar base gaskets
>Graphite head gaskets
>New gas cap gasket
>Extra hole in transmission access door
>Two dowels on transmission end cover
>Air/oil separator in air-duct tube
>Four-sided fuel inlet valve
>Transmission sprocket lock plate
>Black-and-chrome engine treatment
>Locating dowel pins for both transmission support blocks
>Improved footboards

Series FLST Heritage Softails

First Year
>Improved footboards
>Kevlar base gaskets
>Graphite head gaskets
>New gas-cap gasket
>Self-canceling turn signals
>Black-and-chrome engine (FLSTC)
>Extra hole in transmission access door
>Two dowels on transmission end cover
>Air/oil separator in air-duct tube
>Four-sided fuel inlet valve
>Transmission sprocket lock plate
>Locating dowel pins for both transmission support blocks

Series FXR Super Glides

First Year
>Alignment hole on both sides of rear fork
>Steering stem nut cover
>Kevlar base gaskets
>Graphite head gaskets
>New gas-cap gasket
>Self-canceling turn signals
>Black-and-chrome engine
>Extra hole in transmission access door
>Two dowels on transmission end cover
>Alignment hole on both sides rear fork
>Air/oil separator in air-duct tube
>Four-sided fuel inlet valve
>Transmission sprocket lock plate
>Locating dowel pins for both transmission support blocks

Series FXRS Low Riders

First Year
>Alignment hole on both sides of rear fork
>Kevlar base gaskets
>Graphite head gaskets
>New gas-cap gasket
>Self-canceling turn signals
>Extra hole in transmission access door
>Two dowels on transmission end cover
>Air/oil separator in air-duct tube
>Four-sided fuel inlet valve
>Transmission sprocket lock plate
>Locating dowel pins for both transmission support blocks
>Beryllium-copper retaining ring in saddlebag attachment kit (FXRS-CONV)

Series FXRT Sport Glides

First Year
>Kevlar base gaskets
>Graphite head gaskets
>New gas-cap gasket
>Self-canceling turn signals
>Extra hole in transmission access door
>Two dowels on transmission end cover
>Alignment hole on both sides rear fork
>Air/oil separator in air-duct tube
>Four-sided fuel inlet valve
>Transmission sprocket lock plate
>Locating dowel pins for both transmission support blocks

Series FXLR Low Rider Customs

First Year
>Kevlar base gaskets
>Graphite head gaskets
>New gas-cap gasket
>Self-canceling turn signals
>Black-and-chrome engine
>Extra hole in transmission access door
>Two dowels on transmission end cover
>Air/oil separator in air-duct tube
>Four-sided fuel inlet valve
>Transmission sprocket lock plate
>Locating dowel pins for both transmission support blocks

Series FXDB Dyna Glide Sturgis

First/Only Year
>The FXDB Dyna Glide Sturgis is a new model powered by the 80ci Big Twin motor
>Dyna-Glide rubber-mounted frame
>Frame backbone redesigned using a large diameter rectangular extrusion, welded to the cast steering head
>New computer-engineered engine mounting system using two less mounting points, new engine tilt and location, and redesigning of mounts
>Integrated fork lock
>Rear shocks mounted farther forward than standard
>Ignition designed near right top shock mount
>New oil tank, located behind engine, on top of the transmission
>FXRS forks and front end
>Single disc front brake
>Two-filler tank with center console; false cap on left gas tank
>Speedometer on center console
>19in front tire
>16in rear tire
>Belt final drive
>Chain primary drive
>All-black engine and transmission
>Black fenders, tank, center console, and handlebars
>Foot pegs
>Kevlar base gaskets
>Graphite head gaskets
>Self-canceling turn signals
>Extra hole in transmission access door
>Two dowels on transmission end cover
>Air/oil separator in air-duct tube
>Four-sided fuel inlet valve
>Transmission sprocket lock plate
>Locating dowel pins for both transmission support blocks

Series FLHS Electra Glide Sports

First Year
>Kevlar base gaskets
>New gas-cap gasket
>Graphite head gaskets
>Extra hole in transmission access door
>Two dowels on transmission end cover
>Air/oil separator in air-duct tube
>Four-sided fuel inlet valve
>Transmission sprocket lock plate
>Locating dowel pins for both transmission support blocks

Series FLHTC Electra Glide Classics

First Year
>Kevlar base gaskets
>Graphite head gaskets
>New gas-cap gasket
>Extra hole in transmission access door
>Two dowels on transmission end cover
>Air/oil separator in air-duct tube
>Four-sided fuel inlet valve
>Transmission sprocket lock plate
>Locating dowel pins for both transmission support blocks
>Circuit that shuts off radio amplifier when CB is used and voice-actuated intercom (FLHTCU)
>Relay installed in brake-lamp electrical circuit

Series FLTC Tour Glide Classics

First Year
>Kevlar base gaskets
>New gas-cap gasket
>Graphite head gaskets
>Extra hole in transmission access door
>Two dowels on transmission end cover
>Lower input impedance on radio mute lead
>Circuit that shuts off radio amplifier when CB is used and voice-actuated intercom (FLTCU)
>Relay circuit installed in brake-lamp electrical circuit
>Air/oil separator in air-duct tube
>Four-sided fuel inlet valve
>Transmission sprocket lock plate
>Locating dowel pins for both transmission support blocks

Motor Company Minutes, 1991

H-D International offices are moved from Connecticut to Milwaukee. This move triples the staff.

Production begins on a new $24 million paint facility.

In June, European H.O.G. Rally held in England.

Bill Davidson named director of operations of H.O.G. and its 135,000 members.

650 H.O.G. Chapters worldwide.

Motorcycle exports are up over 30 percent.

June 1, H-D stock splits two-for-one to almost $56.

H-D earns 62 percent market share of 850cc-and-larger motorcycles.

Celebration of 50th Anniversary Black Hills Motorcycle Classic held in Sturgis, South Dakota. Around 300,000 motorcyclists attend rally, concert of big name performers, and MDA auction. Among items auctioned at Sturgis is Peter Fonda's *Easy Rider* belt buckle. H-D raises over $154,000 at Sturgis for MDA.

An H-D motorcycle sells for over $34,000 at MDA auction, a Willie G. Davidson specially detailed 1991 Sturgis.

H-D sponsors a traveling version of the Vietnam Veterans Memorial, the "Moving Wall."

New assembly line for 883cc and 1,200cc Sportster engines at Capitol Drive Plant results in relief on old line and overall improved quality.

MotorClothes Line outlet store opens in the Bannister Mall in Kansas City. Store features line of clothes, jewelry, collectibles, and accessories.

Racing Notes

Lou Gerencer Jr. wins Grand National Championship.

Scott Zampach wins U.S. Twins Championship.

Scott Zampach wins Twin Sports Series.

Nigel Gale wins third place in the 883 Twins Sport Championship.

Scott Parker wins the AMA Grand National Championship title.

H-D team riders Scott Parker and Chris Carr win between them 11 of 15 races.

Model Year 1992

Main Models

92-XLH-883 Sportster: 883cc Evolution Sportster V-twin with five-speed transmission

92-XLH-883 Sportster Hugger: 883cc Evolution Sportster V-twin with five-speed transmission

92-XLH-883 Sportster Deluxe: 883cc Evolution Sportster V-twin with five-speed transmission

92-XLH-1200: 1,200cc Evolution Sportster V-twin with five-speed transmission

92-FXR Super Glide: 80ci Evolution V-twin with five-speed transmission

92-FXLR Low Rider Custom: 80ci Evolution V-twin with five-speed transmission

92-FXRS-SP Low Rider Sport Edition: 80ci Evolution V-twin with five-speed transmission

92-FXRS CONV Low Rider Convertible: 80ci Evolution V-twin with five-speed transmission

92-FXDB Daytona Dyna-Glide: 80ci Evolution V-twin with five-speed transmission

92-FXDC Dyna Glide Custom: 80ci Evolution V-twin with five-speed transmission

92-FXSTC Softail Custom: 80ci Evolution V-twin with five-speed transmission

92-FXSTS Springer Softail: 80ci Evolution V-twin with five-speed transmission

92-FXRT Sport Glide: 80ci Evolution V-twin with five-speed transmission

92-FLSTF Fat Boy: 80ci Evolution V-twin with five-speed transmission

92-FLSTC Heritage Softail Classic: 80ci Evolution V-twin with five-speed transmission

92-FLHS Electra Glide Sport: 80ci Evolution V-twin with five-speed transmission

92-FLHTC Electra Glide Classic: 80ci Evolution V-twin with five-speed transmission

92-FLHTC Ultra Classic Electra Glide: 80ci Evolution V-twin with five-speed transmission

92-FLTC Tour Glide Classic: 80ci Blockhead V-twin with OHV, five-speed transmission

92-FLTC Ultra Classic Tour Glide: 80ci Evolution V-twin with five-speed transmission

Specialty Models

92-FXRP CHIPS (police)

92-FLHTP (police)

92-FXDB Dyna Glide Daytona: features 50th Anniversary graphics

Sidecars and Chassis

92-TLE: Touring Models

92-RLE: Low Riders, Sport Glides, and Police Models

Retail Prices

Model FLHTC: $15,350

Model FLTC: $15,350

Model FLHS: $11,700

Model FXDB: $12,120

Model XLH-883 Sportster Deluxe: $ 5,559

Model XLH-1200: $ 6,400

Model XLH-883 Sportster: $ 4,499

Model XLH-883 Sportster Hugger: $ 5,075

Paint Colors
Vivid Black, True Pearl, and others

Series XLH-883 Sportsters

First Year
Improved brake pad material
New-style grease fittings
New halogen headlight assembly
Standardized Sportster hand controls
Relocated ignition switch, now preventing scratching of the horn cover
O-ring chains
Continuously vented gas tanks
Harder plunger in neutral switch
New-style horn, featuring more power
Thinner seat and lower suspension (Hugger)

Series XLH-1200 Sportsters

First Year
Improved brake pad material
New-style grease fittings
New halogen headlight assembly
Standardized Sportster hand controls
Relocated ignition switch, now preventing scratching of the horn cover
Continuously vented gas tanks
Harder plunger in neutral switch
New-style horn, featuring more power

Series FXDB Daytona Dyna Glides

First/Only Year
The FXDB Daytona Dyna Glide is a new, limited-edition model based on the FXDB Sturgis Dyna Glide
Limited edition of 1,700
Two-tone Indigo Blue Metallic/Gold Pearlglo paint scheme
Gold colored wheels
Gold colored rear belt-drive sprocket
Dual-disc front brakes
Ignition switch detent
New brake pad material
Continuously vented gas tanks
New belt-drive sprocket retainer
Buckhorn handlebars
Caged needle bearing for camshaft
Harder plunger in neutral switch
New-style grease fittings
New-style horn, featuring more power

Series FXDC Super Glide Dyna Customs

First/Only Year
The FXDC Super Glide Dyna Custom is a new model based on the FXDB Sturgis Dyna Glide
Limited edition
Super Dyna Glide chassis
Dual-disc front brake
Two-tone Silver and Black paint scheme
Frame is silver powder-coated
Unpainted aluminum powertrain having chrome covers
New halogen headlight assembly
Ignition switch detent
New brake-pad material
Continuously vented gas tanks
New belt-drive sprocket retainer
Caged needle bearing for camshaft
Harder plunger in neutral switch
New-style grease fitting
New-style cylinder base gaskets
New-style horn, featuring more power

Series FXST Softails

First Year
New halogen headlight assembly
Caged needle bearing for camshaft
Harder plunger in neutral switch
New-style grease fittings
New-style horn, featuring more power

Series FLST Heritage Softails

First Year
Caged needle bearing for camshaft
Harder plunger in neutral switch
New-style grease fitting
New-style horn, featuring more power

Series FLSTF Fat Boys

First Year
Caged needle bearing for camshaft
Harder plunger in neutral switch
New-style grease fittings
New-style horn, featuring more power

Series FXRS Low Riders

First/Only Year
New halogen headlight assembly
Caged needle bearing for camshaft
Harder plunger in neutral switch
New-style grease fittings
New-style horn, featuring more power

Series FXR Super Glides

First Year
Lower halogen headlight assembly
Caged needle bearing for camshaft
Harder plunger in neutral switch
New-style grease fittings
New-style horn, featuring more power

Series FXRT Sport Glides

First/Only Year
New halogen headlight assembly
Caged needle bearing for camshaft
Harder plunger in neutral switch
New-style grease fittings
New-style horn, featuring more power

Series FXLR Low Rider Customs

First Year
New halogen headlight assembly
Caged needle bearing for camshaft
Harder plunger in neutral switch
New-style grease fittings
New-style horn, featuring more power

Series FLHTC Electra Glide Classics

First Year
Trunk receives a glossy interior finish
Trunk receives an Ultra-style pouch (FLHTC only)
Tape guard system
Improved saddlebag gaskets
Caged needle bearing for camshaft
Harder plunger in neutral switch
New-style grease fitting
New-style horn, featuring more power

Series FLHS Electra Glide Sports

First Year
Lower seat
Improved saddlebag gaskets
Caged needle bearing for camshaft
Greater plunger hardness in neutral switch
New-style grease fitting
New-style horn, featuring more power

Series FLTC Tour Glide Classics

First Year
Trunk receives a glossy interior finish
Trunk receives an Ultra-style pouch (FLTC only)
Tape guard system
Improved saddlebag gaskets
Caged needle bearing for camshaft
Harder plunger in neutral switch
New-style grease fitting
New-style horn, featuring more power

Specialty Notes

First Year
Sidecar Models RLE and TLE have powder-coated frames
Sidecar Model TLE Ultra Classic receives a refined ABS-molded lower and improved carpeting

Motor Company Minutes, 1992
Worldwide licensing of trademarks and logos.
The last year of Japanese-made carbon canister emission filters.
A $23 million robotic painting system set up at the York plant.
H-D stock worth almost seven times original price.
Miss H-D, Krisann Whitley, is crowned at Daytona.

Racing Notes
Scott Parker wins Grand National Championship.
Nigel Gale wins second place at 883 Twins Sport Championship.
Chris Carr wins AMA Camel Pro National Championship.
Randy Snyder on "2001" sets new land speed record at Bonneville Salt Flats with record of 173.809mph.
Randy Snyder on "2001" sets new 1-Mile Standing Start Record of 116mph
Scott "Z-Man" Zampach wins the Twin Sports Championship.
Chris Carr wins the AMA Grand National Championship.

Model Year 1993

1993 Heritage Softail. *Randy Leffingwell*

Main Models

93-XLH-883 Sportster: 883cc Evolution Sportster V-twin with five-speed transmission

93-XLH-883 Sportster Hugger: 883cc Evolution Sportster V-twin with five-speed transmission

93-XLH-883 Sportster Deluxe: 883cc Evolution Sportster V-twin with five-speed transmission

93-XLH-1200: 1,200cc Evolution Sportster V-twin with five-speed transmission

93-FXDL Dyna Low Rider: 80ci Evolution V-twin with five-speed transmission

93-FXDWG Dyna Wide Glide: 80ci Evolution V-twin with five-speed transmission

93-FXSTS Springer Softail: 80ci Evolution V-twin with five-speed transmission

93-FXSTC Softail Custom: 80ci Evolution V-twin with five-speed transmission

93-FXRS CONV Low Rider Convertible: 80ci Evolution V-twin with five-speed transmission

93-FXRS-SP Sport Edition: 80ci Evolution V-twin with five-speed transmission

93-FXLR Low Rider Custom: 80ci Evolution V-twin with five-speed transmission

93-FXR Super Glide: 80ci Evolution V-twin with five-speed transmission

93-FLHTCU Ultra Classic Electra Glide: 80ci Evolution V-twin with five-speed transmission

93-FLSTF Fat Boy: 80ci Evolution V-twin with five-speed transmission

93-FLSTC Heritage Softail Classic: 80ci Evolution V-twin with five-speed transmission

93-FLSTN Heritage Softail Nostalgia: 80ci Evolution V-twin with five-speed transmission

93-FLHTC Electra Glide Classic: 80ci Evolution V-twin with five-speed transmission

93-FLTC Tour Glide Classic: 80ci Evolution V-twin with five-speed transmission

93-FLHTCU Ultra Classic Electra Glide: 80ci Evolution V-twin with five-speed transmission

93-FLTCU Tour Glide Ultra Classic: 80ci Evolution V-twin with five-speed transmission

93-FLHS Electra Glide Sport: 80ci Evolution V-twin with five-speed transmission

Specialty Models

93-XLH-1200 90th Anniversary Limited Edition: Special Silver-and-Charcoal custom paint, serialized nameplates, and 90th Anniversary gas tank emblems

93-FXLR: Low Rider Custom 90th Anniversary Edition: Special Silver-and-Charcoal custom paint, serialized nameplates, and 90th Anniversary gas tank emblems

93-FXDWG Dyna Wide Glide 90th Anniversary Edition: Special Silver-and-Charcoal custom paint, serialized nameplates, and 90th Anniversary gas tank emblems

93-FLHTC: Electra Glide Classic 90th Anniversary Edition: Special Silver-and-Charcoal custom paint, serialized nameplates, and 90th Anniversary gas tank emblems

93-FLHTC Ultra Classic Electra Glide 90th Anniversary Edition: Special Silver-and-Charcoal custom paint, serialized nameplates, and 90th Anniversary gas tank emblems

93-FLTC Ultra Classic Tour Glide 90th Anniversary Limited Edition: Special Silver-and-Charcoal custom paint, serialized nameplates, and 90th Anniversary gas tank emblems

93-FXRP Pursuit Glide (police only)

93-FLHTP (police only)

Sidecars and Chassis

93-TLE: Touring Models

93-RLE: Low Riders, Sport Glides, and Police Models

Retail Prices

Model FLHTCU Ultra Classic Tour Glide 90th Anniversary Edition: $16,100

Model FLHTCU Classic Electra Glide 90th Anniversary Edition: $16,100

Model FLHTC: $13,000

Model FLHS: $11,700

Model FLSTC: $12,800

Model FLSTF: $12,600

Model FLSTN: $13,000

Model FXSTF: $12,600

Model FXSTC: $12,200

Model FXDWG 90th Anniversary Edition: $12,550

Model FXDL: $11,800

Model FXRS: $11,800

Model FXRS-SP: $11,400

Model FXLR: $11,600

Model FXR: $ 9,950

Model XLH-1200: $ 6,800

Model XLH-883 Sportster Hugger: $ 5,420

Model XLH-883 Sportster Deluxe: $ 5,820

Model XLH-883 Sportster: $ 4,775

Paint Colors

Vivid Black, Mandarin Orange, Scarlet Red, Victory Red Sun-Glo, Bright Aqua Sun-Glo, 90th Anniversary, Bright Wineberry Sun-Glo, Two-tone Aqua Sun-Glo and Silver, Two-tone Victory Red Sun-Glo, or Two-tone Black and Scarlet Red

Series XLH-883 Sportsters

First Year
Belt drive
Fingertip "blade" profile brake and clutch levers

Series XLH-1200 Sportsters

First Year
Fingertip "blade" profile brake and clutch levers

Series FXR Super Glides

First Year
Fingertip "blade" profile brake and clutch levers
Horizontal Vehicle Identification Number on left side of engine, above the timing hole

Series FXRS Low Riders

First Year
Fingertip "blade" profile brake and clutch levers
Horizontal Vehicle Identification Number on left side of engine, above the timing hole

Series FXLR Low Rider Customs

First Year
Fingertip "blade" profile brake and clutch levers
Horizontal Vehicle Identification Number on left side of engine, above the timing hole

Series FXDWG Dyna Wide Glides

First Year
The FXDWG Dyna Wide Glide is a new Big Twin model built on the Dyna Glide chassis
Wide-set front forks
21in laced front wheel
16in laced rear wheel
Factory "Ape-hanger" handlebars
One-piece Fat Bob gas tank
Fingertip "blade" profile brake and clutch levers
Bobbed rear fender
Staggered shorty dual exhaust system
Primary drive is double-row chain
Single 11.5in disc front brake
Single 11.5in disc rear brake
Horizontal Vehicle Identification Number on left side of engine, above the timing hole

Series FXDL Dyna Low Riders

First Year
The FXDL Dyna Low Rider is a new Big Twin model built on the Dyna Glide chassis
Removable pillion seat
Dual 11.5in disc front brakes
Single 11.5in disc rear brake
Black-and-chrome powertrain
Staggered shorty dual exhaust system
Primary drive is double-row chain
Wheels are black-painted nine-spoke cast
Standard speedometer with odometer and resettable trip meter
Tachometer
Fingertip "blade" profile brake and clutch levers
Horizontal Vehicle Identification Number on left side of engine, above the timing hole

Series FXST Softails

First Year
Fingertip "blade" profile brake and clutch levers
Horizontal Vehicle Identification Number on left side of engine, above the timing hole
Floating front fender (FXSTS only)
Horizontal Vehicle Identification Number on left side of engine, above the timing hole

Series FLSTF Fat Boys

First Year
Fingertip "blade" profile brake and clutch levers
Horizontal Vehicle Identification Number on left side of engine, above the timing hole

Series FLST Heritage Softails

First Year
Fingertip "blade" profile brake and clutch levers
Horizontal Vehicle Identification Number on left side of engine, above the timing hole
FLSTN Heritage Softail Nostalgia limited edition offered; includes two-tone Birch White and Black paint scheme and small leather saddlebags and seat with hair-on cowhide trim

Series FLHS Electra Glide Sports

First/Only Year
Fingertip "blade" profile brake and clutch levers
Remote oil reservoir mounted under the engine and transmission
Battery placement under the seat
Saddlebags 15 percent larger
Saddlebag lids hinged and attached permanently
Horizontal Vehicle Identification Number on left side of engine, above the timing hole

Series FLHTC Electra Glide Classics

First Year
Fingertip "blade" profile brake and clutch levers
Remote oil reservoir mounted under the engine and transmission
Battery placement under the seat
Saddlebags 15 percent larger
Saddlebag lids hinged and attached permanently
Horizontal Vehicle Identification Number on left side of engine, above the timing hole

Series FLTC Tour Glide Classics

First Year
Fingertip "blade" profile brake and clutch levers
Remote oil reservoir mounted under the engine and transmission
Battery placement under the seat
Saddlebags 15 percent larger in size
Saddlebag lids hinged and attached permanently
Horizontal Vehicle Identification Number on left side of engine, above the timing hole

Motor Company Minutes, 1993
Use of an American carbon canister emission filter manufactured by Miniature Precision Components of Delavan, Wisconsin.

H-D buys into the Buell Motorcycle Company, expanding its capacity to further research and development.

New Buell/H-D model on the drawing board, the Thunderbolt.

In June, the celebration of the company's 90th Anniversary.

June 12, first time an interstate highway was ever closed down specifically for H-D motorcycle riders, all 100,000 of them, for the 90th Year Reunion.

June 12, Willie G. Davidson leads a group of motorcyclists, 15,000 strong, 35 miles north from the airport in Kenosha to the 90th Year Reunion, held at Milwaukee's Summerfest grounds.

Racing Notes
Scott "Z-Man" Zampach wins the Twin Sports Championship.

1994 Sportster. *Jeff Hackett*

Main Models
94-XLH-883 Sportster: 883cc Evolution Sportster V-twin with five-speed transmission

94-XLH-883 Sportster Hugger: 883cc Evolution Sportster V-twin with five-speed transmission

94-XLH-883 Sportster Deluxe: 883cc Evolution Sportster V-twin with five-speed transmission

94-XLH-1200: 1,200cc Evolution Sportster V-twin with five-speed transmission

94-FXR Super Glide: 80ci Evolution V-twin with five-speed transmission

94-FXLR Low Rider Custom: 80ci Evolution V-twin with five-speed transmission

94-FXDS-CONV Low Rider Convertible: 80ci Evolution V-twin with five-speed transmission

94-FXDWG Dyna Wide Glide: 80ci Evolution V-twin with five-speed transmission

94-FXDL Dyna Low Rider: 80ci Evolution V-twin with five-speed transmission

94-FXSTC Softail Custom: 80ci Evolution V-twin with five-speed transmission

94-FXSTS Springer Softail: 80ci Evolution V-twin with five-speed transmission

94-FLSTF Fat Boy: 80ci Evolution V-twin with five-speed transmission

94-FLSTC Heritage Softail Classic: 80ci Evolution V-twin with five-speed transmission

94-FLSTN Heritage Softail Special: 80ci Evolution V-twin with five-speed transmission

94-FLHR Electra Glide Road King: 80ci Evolution V-twin with five-speed transmission

94-FLHTC Electra Glide Classic: 80ci Evolution V-twin with five-speed transmission

94-FLHTCU Ultra Classic Electra Glide: 80ci Evolution V-twin with five-speed transmission

94-FLTC Tour Glide Classic: 80ci Evolution V-twin with five-speed transmission

94-FLTCU Ultra Classic Tour Glide: 80ci Evolution V-twin with five-speed transmission

Specialty Models
94-FXRP Chip (police only)
94-FLHTP (police only)

Sidecars and Chassis
94-TLE:
94-RLE: Low Riders, Sport Glides, and Police Models

Paint Colors
Vivid Black, Aqua Pearl, Victory Red Sun-Glo, Two-tone Aqua Pearl and Silver, or Two-tone Victory Red Sun-Glo

Series XLH-883 Sportsters

First Year
Interference-fit carburetor float-pin pedestal

Series XLH-1200 Sportsters

First Year
Interference-fit carburetor float-pin pedestal

Series FXR Super Glides

First/Only Year
Interference-fit carburetor float-pin pedestal
Larger engine sprocket
Smaller sprocket on clutch basket

Series FXLR Low Rider Customs

First/Only Year
Interference-fit carburetor float-pin pedestal on all Models
Larger engine sprocket
Smaller sprocket on clutch basket

Series FXDS-CONV Low Rider Convertibles

First/Only Year
The FXDS-CONV is a new Dyna Low Rider model with quick-detachable saddlebags and windshield
Interference-fit carburetor float-pin pedestal

Series FXDWG Dyna Wide Glides

First Year
Interference-fit carburetor float-pin pedestal
Larger engine sprocket
Smaller sprocket on clutch basket

Series FXDL Dyna Low Riders

First Year
Interference-fit carburetor float-pin pedestal
Larger engine sprocket
Smaller sprocket on clutch basket

Series FXSTC Softail Customs

First Year
Interference-fit carburetor float-pin pedestal
Larger engine sprocket
Smaller sprocket on clutch basket

Series FXSTS Springer Softails

First Year
Interference-fit carburetor float-pin pedestal
Larger engine sprocket
Smaller sprocket on clutch basket

Series FLSTF Fat Boys

First Year
Interference-fit carburetor float-pin pedestal
Larger engine sprocket
Smaller sprocket on clutch basket

Series FLSTC Heritage Softail Classics

First Year
Interference-fit carburetor float-pin pedestal
Larger engine sprocket
Smaller sprocket on clutch basket

Series FLSTN Heritage Softail Specials

First Year
The FLSTN Heritage Softail Special is an update of the FLSTN Heritage Softail Nostalgia, with different colors and trim

Only Year
Two-tone Birch and Silver paint scheme

Series FLHR Electra Glide Road Kings

First/Only Year
The FLHR Electra Glide Road King is a new model based on the FLHTS, minus the fairing
Quick-detach windshield
Quick-detach passenger seat
Air-adjustable suspension
Chrome-and-wrinkle-black engine scheme
Huge headlight and nacelle
Interference-fit carburetor float-pin pedestal
Larger engine sprocket
Smaller sprocket on clutch basket
Dual exhaust system
Primary drive is double-row chain
Dual 11.5in disc front brakes
Single 11.5in disc rear brake
16in front tire
16in rear tire
Wheels are 10-spoke cast
Speedometer with odometer and resettable tripmeter

Series FLHTC Electra Glide Classics

First Year
Interference-fit carburetor float-pin pedestal
Larger engine sprocket
Smaller sprocket on clutch basket
Sealed cruise "set/resume" switch (FLHTCU only)

Series FLTC Tour Glide Classics

First Year
Interference-fit carburetor float-pin pedestal
Larger engine sprocket
Smaller sprocket on clutch basket
Sealed cruise "set/resume" switch (FLTCU only)

Motor Company Minutes, 1994
The Las Vegas Metro Police motorcycle unit now totals eight H-Ds in their fleet.
June 1, the Michigan State Police officially return to riding H-D motorcycles for freeway patrol.

Model Year 1995

1995 XLH-883. *Dara Longhenry*

Main Models

95-XLH-883 Sportster: 883cc Evolution Sportster V-twin with five-speed transmission

95-XLH-883 Sportster Deluxe: 883cc Evolution Sportster V-twin with five-speed transmission

95-XLH-883 Sportster Hugger: 883cc Evolution Sportster V-twin with five-speed transmission

95-XLH-1200: 1,200cc Evolution Sportster V-twin with five-speed transmission

95-FXD Dyna Super Glide: 80ci Evolution V-twin with five-speed transmission

95-FXDS-CONV Dyna Convertible: 80ci Evolution V-twin with five-speed transmission

95-FXDWG Dyna Wide Glide: 80ci Evolution V-twin with five-speed transmission

95-FXDL Dyna Low Rider: 80ci Evolution V-twin with five-speed transmission

95-FXSTC Softail Custom: 80ci Evolution V-twin with five-speed transmission

95-FXSTS Springer Softail: 80ci Evolution V-twin with five-speed transmission

95-FXSTSB Bad Boy: 80ci Evolution V-twin with five-speed transmission

95-FLSTF Fat Boy: 80ci Evolution V-twin with five-speed transmission

95-FLSTC Heritage Softail Classic: 80ci Evolution V-twin with five-speed transmission

95-FLSTN Heritage Softail Special: 80ci Evolution V-twin with five-speed transmission

95-FLHT Electra Glide Standard: 80ci Evolution V-twin with five-speed transmission

95-FLHR Road King: 80ci Evolution V-twin with five-speed transmission

95-FLHTC Electra Glide Classic: 80ci Evolution V-twin with five-speed transmission

95-FLHTCU Ultra Classic Electra Glide: 80ci Evolution V-twin with five-speed transmission

95-FLHTCUI Ultra Classic Electra Glide 30th Anniversary Edition: 80ci Evolution V-twin with five-speed transmission and sequential-port fuel injection

95-FLTCU Ultra Classic Tour Glide: 80ci Evolution V-twin with five-speed transmission

Specialty Models

95-FLHTP Electra Glide (police only)

Sidecars and Chassis

95-TLE: Touring Models

95-RLE: Low Riders, Sport Glides, and Police Models

Retail Prices

Model XLH-883: $ 4,995

Model XLH-883 Deluxe: $ 6,120

Model XLH-883 Hugger: $ 5,700

Model XLH-1200: $ 7,200

Model FXDWG: $13,425

Model FXDL: $12,475

Model FXDS-CONV: $12,725

Model FXD: $ 9,995

Model FXSTSB: $13,850

Model FXSTC: $13,125

Model FXSTS: $13,375

Model FLSTC: $13,875

Model FLSTN: $13,650

Model FLSTF: $13,425

Model FLHTC 1: $17,500

Model FLHR: $13,475

Model FLHTC: $13,850

Model FLHTCU: $16,050

Model FLTCU: $16,050

Model FLHT: $11,995

Paint Colors

Vivid Black, Aqua Pearl, Victory Red Sun-Glo, Two-tone Aqua Pearl and Silver, Two-tone Nugget Yellow and Birch White, two-tone Victory Red Sun-Glo, Two-tone Charcoal Satinbrite and Vivid Black, Two-tone Vivid Black and Silver, Two-tone Birch White and Gold, Two-tone Burgundy Pearl and Scarlet Red, or Two-tone Vivid Black and Burgundy Pearl with 30th Anniversary graphics

Series XLH-883 Sportsters

First Year

Electronic speedometer with odometer and resettable trip-meter

Series XLH-1200 Sportsters

First Year

Electronic speedometer with odometer and resettable trip-meter

Series FXD Dyna Super Glides

First Year

The FXD Dyna Super Glide is the new base-model Super Glide, based on the Dyna Glide chassis

Staggered shorty dual exhaust system

Wheels are nine-spoke cast

Electronic speedometer with odometer and resettable trip-meter

Fuel gauge

Series FXDS-CONV Dyna Convertibles

First Year
Electronic speedometer with odometer and resettable trip-meter

Series FXDWG Dyna Wide Glides

First Year
Electronic speedometer with odometer and resettable tripmeter

Series FXDL Dyna Low Riders

First Year
Electronic speedometer with odometer and resettable trip meter

Series FXSTSB Bad Boys

First Year
The FXSTSB Bad Boy is a new model based on the FXSTS Springer Softail
Blacked-out steel Springer forks
Staggered shorty dual exhaust system
Primary drive is double-row chain
Belt final drive
Front wheel is laced
Rear wheel is slotted disc
Floating disc brakes
Scallop graphics
Hidden gas-charged shocks

Only Year
Standard speedometer with odometer and resettable trip meter

Series FLSTN Heritage Softail Specials

Only Year
Two-tone Charcoal Satinbrite and Vivid Black paint scheme

Series FLHT Electra Glide Standards

First Year
The FLHT Electra Glide Standard is the new base-model of the FLHTC Electra Glide Classic
Wheels are 10-spoke cast
Speedometer with odometer and resettable tripmeter
Tach standard
Fuel gauge standard
Voltmeter standard
Oil-pressure gauge standard
Air-adjustable suspension
Fork-mounted fairing
Saddlebags featuring barrel-type locks
Luggage rack
Accessory plug

Series FLHR Road Kings

First Year
The FLHR Road King is a new model based on the FLHTC Electra Glide Classic, minus the fairing
Quick-detach windshield
Saddlebags but no top trunk
Special two-tone paint and graphics

Series FLHTC Electra Glide Classics

First/Only Year
Sequential port fuel injection (FLHTCUI 30th Anniversary)
30th Anniversary graphics (FLHTCUI 30th Anniversary)

Motor Company Minutes, 1995
October 1, H-D announces plans to double production to 200,000 motorcycles annually by the year 2003, the company's 100th Anniversary. H-D announces the probability of building a new plant to accommodate the proposed increase in production.

Model Year 1996

1996 Road King FLHR. *Tom Wien*

Main Models

96-XLH-883 Sportster: 883cc Evolution Sportster V-twin with five-speed transmission

96-XLH-883 Sportster Hugger: 883cc Evolution Sportster V-twin with five-speed transmission

96-XLH-1200: 1,200cc Evolution Sportster V-twin with five-speed transmission

96-XL 1200C Custom: 1,200cc Evolution Sportster V-twin with five-speed transmission

96-XL 1200S Sport: 1,200cc Evolution Sportster V-twin with OHV, five-speed transmission

96-FXD Dyna Super Glide: 80ci Evolution V-twin with five-speed transmission

96-FXDS-CONV Dyna Convertible: 80ci Evolution V-twin with five-speed transmission

96-FXDWG Dyna Wide Glide: 80ci Evolution V-twin with five-speed transmission

96-FXDL Dyna Low Rider: 80ci Evolution V-twin with five-speed transmission

96-FXSTC Softail Custom: 80ci Evolution V-twin with five-speed transmission

96-FXSTS Springer Softail: 80ci Evolution V-twin with five-speed transmission

96-FXSTSB Bad Boy: 80ci Evolution V-twin with five-speed transmission

96-FLSTF Fat Boy: 80ci Evolution V-twin with five-speed transmission

96-FLSTC Heritage Softail Classic: 80ci Evolution V-twin with five-speed transmission

96-FLSTN Heritage Softail Special: 80ci Evolution V-twin with five-speed transmission

96-FLHT Electra Glide Standard: 80ci Evolution V-twin with five-speed transmission

96-FLHR Road King: 80ci Evolution V-twin with five-speed transmission

96-FLHRI Road King: 80ci Evolution V-twin with five-speed transmission and sequential-port fuel injection

96-FLHTC Electra Glide Classic: 80ci Evolution V-twin with five-speed transmission

96-FLHTCI Electra Glide Classic: 80ci Evolution V-twin with five-speed transmission

96-FLHTCU Ultra Classic Electra Glide: 80ci Evolution V-twin with five-speed transmission

96-FLHTCUI Ultra Classic Electra Glide: 80ci Evolution V-twin with five-speed transmission and sequential-port fuel injection

96-FLTCUI Ultra Classic Tour Glide: 80ci Evolution V-twin with five-speed transmission and sequential-port fuel injection

Sidecars and Chassis

96-TLE

96-RLE: Low Riders, Sport Glides and Police motorcycles

Retail Prices

XLH Sportster 883: $ 5,095

XLH Sportster 883 Hugger: $ 5,760

XLH Sportster 1200: $ 7,360

XL-1200S: $ 7,910

XL-1200C: $ 8,360

FXD: $10,195

FXDL: $13,030

FXDS-CONV: $13,330

FXDWG: $14,030

FXSTC Softail Custom: $13,630

FXSTS: $14,030

FXSTSB: $14,425

FLSTN: $14,655

FLSTF: $13,930

FLSTC: $14,435

FLHT: $12,235

FLHR: $14,035

FLHRI: $14,035

FLHTC: $14,410

FLHTCI: $14,410

FLHTCU: $16,610

FLHTCUI: $16,610

FLTCUI: $17,410

Paint Colors

Vivid Black, Patriot Red Pearl, States Blue Pearl, Platinum Silver, Mystique Green Metallic, Violet Pearl, Two-tone Victory Sun Glo and Platinum, Two-tone Violet and Red Pearl, Two-tone Platinum Silver and Black, or Two-tone Mystique Green and Black

FXSTSB: Vivid Black with Yellow graphics, Vivid Black with Purple graphics, or Vivid Black with Turquoise graphics

Series XLH-883 Sportsters

First Year

Tank capacity of 3.3gal

Series XLH-1200 Sportsters

First Year

Tank capacity of 3.3gal

Series XL-1200S Sports

First Year

The XL-1200S Sport is a new Sportster model based on the XLH-1200

Adjustable-damping front forks

Adjustable rear shocks

Tank capacity of 3.3gal

Series XL-1200C Customs

First Year
    The XL-1200C Custom is a new Sportster model based on the XLH-1200
        Staggered shorty dual exhaust system
        Front wheel is laced
        Rear wheel is disc

Series FXSTC Softail Customs

First Year
    Electronic speedometer with odometer and resettable tripmeter

Series FXSTS Springer Softails

First Year
    Electronic speedometer with odometer and resettable tripmeter

Series FXSTSB Bad Boys

First Year
    Electronic speedometer with odometer and resettable tripmeter

Series FLSTN Heritage Softail Specials

First Year
    Electronic speedometer with odometer and resettable tripmeter

Series FLSTF Fat Boys

First Year
    Electronic speedometer with odometer and resettable tripmeter

Series FLSTC Heritage Softail Classics

First Year
    Electronic speedometer with odometer and resettable tripmeter

Series FLHRI Road Kings

First Year
    The FLHRI Road King is a fuel-injected version of the Road King

Series FLHTCI Electra Glide Classics

First Year
    The FLHTCI Electra Glide Classic is a fuel-injected version of the FLHTC

Series FLHTCUI Ultra Classic Electra Glides
First Year
    The FLHTCUI Electra Glide Classic is a fuel-injected version of the FLHTCU

Series FLTCUI 80ci Evolution Big Twins

First Year
    The FLTCI Electra Glide Classic is a fuel-injected version of the FLTC

Motor Company Minutes, 1996

    January 22, sale of the Holiday Rambler Recreational Vehicle Division to the Monaco Coach Corp, of Coburg, Oregon, for a price of about $50 million.

    January 28, announcement is made that the site of the proposed new plant has been trimmed from 10 possible sites, still including the Milwaukee and York locations.

    February 5, announcement of the initial attempt to make the sound that the H-D motorcycle makes a registered soundmark/trademark. Company spokesman Steve Piehl states, "We don't want the sound of our motorcycles to become the generic sound of motorcycles."

    February 29, announcement of a new 250,000sq-ft warehouse and distribution center, a $16.5 million project that replaces the Milwaukee Center and will be built in the Franklin Business Park of suburban Milwaukee.

    August 24, Harley-Davidson breaks ground for a new production plant in Kansas City, Missouri.

INDEX